Children Beware!

Children Beware!

Childhood, Horror and the PG-13 Rating

FILIPA ANTUNES

McFarland & Company, Inc., Publishers
Jefferson, North Carolina

This book has undergone peer review.

LIBRARY OF CONGRESS CATALOGUING-IN-PUBLICATION DATA

Names: Antunes, Filipa, 1987– author.
Title: Children beware! : childhood, horror and the PG-13 rating / Filipa Antunes.
Description: Jefferson : McFarland & Company, Inc., Publishers, 2020. | Includes bibliographical references and index.
Identifiers: LCCN 2019053895 | ISBN 9781476671338 (paperback) ∞ ISBN 9781476638959 (ebook)
Subjects: LCSH: Children's films—United States—History and criticism. | Motion pictures and children. | Horror films—United States—History and criticism. | Motion pictures—Ratings—United States.
Classification: LCC PN1995.9.C45 A55 2020 | DDC 791.43/6523—dc23
LC record available at https://lccn.loc.gov/2019053895

BRITISH LIBRARY CATALOGUING DATA ARE AVAILABLE

**ISBN (print) 978-1-4766-7133-8
ISBN (ebook) 978-1-4766-3895-9**

© 2020 Filipa Antunes. All rights reserved

No part of this book may be reproduced or transmitted in any form or by any means, electronic or mechanical, including photocopying or recording, or by any information storage and retrieval system, without permission in writing from the publisher.

Front cover images © 2020 Shutterstock

Printed in the United States of America

*McFarland & Company, Inc., Publishers
  Box 611, Jefferson, North Carolina 28640
    www.mcfarlandpub.com*

For Alec, Luísa, and Susana

Acknowledgments

My parents, who indulged my childhood love of *Goosebumps* and taught me how to think critically, and my brother, who watched children's horror with me. You planted the seed first.

The film critics and reviewers, who have been my partners in crime for this project and whose work deepened my appreciation for good film criticism.

The students, colleagues, and peers, who discussed these ideas with me and asked tough questions. Special recognition to Mark Jancovich, Alec Plowman, Lincoln Geraghty, Tim Snelson, and the two anonymous peer reviewers, who commented thoroughly on this manuscript.

The team at McFarland, who made this book a reality.

My family, who came on this journey with me. I couldn't have finished this book without your support and endless patience—thank you.

Table of Contents

Acknowledgments vi
Introduction. Read If You Dare: The Problem of Children and Horror 1
- Pre-Adolescence, a Millennial "Discovery" 3
- Horror and the Childhood/Adulthood Frontier 7
- PG-13: A Critical Milestone 12
- Eye of the Storm: The Children's Horror Trend 14
- A Map for the Road Ahead 21

PART I: RUPTURE 23

1. "This could be our *Exorcist!*" Disney, Horror and the New Rules of Childhood 25
   - Learning New Rules: Ron Miller's Disney, 1978–1983 27
   - A Ghastly Landmark: *The Watcher in the Woods* 31
   - Conclusion: Miller's Last Effort 42

2. Parents Strongly Cautioned: PG-13, a Cultural Turning Point 44
   - Discussing Classification: A History of Not Asking All the Questions 45
   - The *Poltergeist* Before the Storm 50
   - *Temple of Doom*: The Children Will Scream with Delighted Horror! 52
   - *Gremlins* Against America 55
   - Conclusion 62

3. Horror vs. Children: Confronting Young Audiences After PG-13 65
   - Establishing an Identity: PG-13 from 1984 to 1989 67

- Quintessential Children's Horror: *The Gate*   72
- Whose Genre Is It? *The Gate, The Lost Boys, The Monster Squad*   77
- Conclusion   82

PART II: NEGOTIATION   85

4. Backlash: The R-Rated 1990s   87
- Restoring Horror's Maturity: Back to the 1970s?   88
- So What of Children's Horror?   99
- Conclusion: The End of a Film Cycle, the Start of a New Era   106

5. The Final Conflict: Children's Horror Meets Family Entertainment   109
- Family Values: A New Hollywood for New Cultural Attitudes   111
- A Short-Lived Truce: *The Witches*   115
- Closing the Cycle: *Casper*   121
- Conclusion   126

6. "Viewer beware … you're in for a scare": The Horror of Puberty, Televised and Serialized   128
- Meanwhile, in Other Media: The Children's Market Welcomes Horror   129
- Building an Empire: The *Goosebumps* Franchise   133
- Monstrous Puberty or, When Is a Formula Something Else?   141
- Conclusion   145

Conclusion: Sometimes It Comes Back: Children's Horror Today   149
- Summary: The Insights of Children's Horror   150
- The (Il)Legitimacy of Children in Horror   158
- PG-13 and the End of Children's Cinema?   161
- The Millennial Twist (or, the Generation Who Came of Age Twice)   165

Appendix: A Selection of Children's Horror   169
- A. Before the Trend: Early Wave   169
- B. The Children's Horror Film Cycle, 1980–1995   169
- C. The Children's Horror Trend, 1980–1997   171
- D. After the Trend: Children's Horror Today   172

Chapter Notes   175
Works Cited   189
Index   199

Introduction.
Read If You Dare:
The Problem of Children and Horror

This is a book about childhood, horror, and what happens when the two ideas meet. At first glance, perhaps this seems a tired topic. As any participant, indeed any observer, of American culture can point out, there are numerous instances where childhood and horror have crossed paths with no outstanding consequence, from nursery rhymes and fairy tales to the iconic demon children of horror fiction and film. Yet we need only dig a little deeper to see that, despite its frequency, the combination of childhood and horror often works in paradoxical ways. Fairy tales and nursery rhymes, gruesome and cruel as they sometimes are, are seldom thought of as being part of the horror genre, and the horror films which so proudly feature children in the main roles, such as *The Innocents* (1961), *The Omen* (1976), or *It* (2017), are rarely considered entertainment for children. What is more, should a fairy tale be too scary, or a horror film too child-like, the culture quickly excises it—whether from the canon of children's fiction or from the horror genre—for being inappropriate.

There is a rule, then, that guides encounters between childhood and horror, and it is one so commonsensical that it often (but not always) goes unspoken: childhood and horror are concepts antagonistic to each other. If they meet they struggle, and in the end one always dominates and the other always submits. Children are rarely welcome in the horror genre, unless they are transformed to fit the genre's expectations (whether as marginalized audiences or as othered subjects), and the horror genre is rarely entirely welcome in children's culture, unless it does the same (usually by giving up its horror affiliation entirely).

But what happens when this rule is broken? What happens when neither horror nor childhood relinquish its dominance over the meaning of a text?

These exceptional intersections between childhood and horror are my concern in this book. More precisely, my focus is a very specific pop culture moment in the 1980s and 1990s, what I call here the children's horror trend.[1] This included a small niche of horror texts made for children, in a variety of media—films like *Gremlins* (1984), *The Gate* (1987), and *The Nightmare Before Christmas* (1993), television shows like *Are You Afraid of the Dark?* (1990–1996) and popular fiction series like *Goosebumps* (1992–1997), among others. Some of these titles were very popular and some, not many, have remained openly influential. These bigger titles often feature in Millennial nostalgia, but the children's horror trend is rarely talked about as a thing of cultural importance; indeed, it is not often recognized as a collective at all.

This situation is somewhat baffling when we consider the strangeness of this trend: a cluster of texts which openly and deliberately broke the rule of antagonism between childhood and horror, positioning themselves not as a subversion of mainstream values but a legitimate part of children's culture—and which were rewarded for it with commercial (if not always critical) success. Children's horror was, moreover, an all-consuming trend while it lasted, particularly in the mid–1990s when children's culture was positively saturated with horror stories and motifs. Contemporary nostalgia for the 1980s and 1990s is indicative of the impact these themes and aesthetics had on their first audience, as illustrated in titles like *Scouts Guide to the Zombie Apocalypse* (2015), *Stranger Things* (2016–), or the *Goosebumps* film adaptations (2015, 2018). These suggestions of cultural value are enough to make children's horror worth studying, but the case is even more compelling when we note the way controversy was interwoven with its success, particularly in relation to its theatrical offerings.

Children's horror films in the 1980s generated heated controversies, both within the horror genre and the mainstream, and these debates are directly linked to pivotal moments in film history, such as the reinvention of the Disney brand and the introduction of the PG-13 classification to the film ratings system. These were not isolated moments of cultural relevance. Rather, when we plot them together, we see a very clear continuum of debate around the notions of childhood and horror throughout the children's horror trend, with defined phases of challenge, rebuttal, and synthesis. This map in turn matches up with significant moments of transformation in American attitudes, of which things like the PG-13 rating are a symptom. In other words, the children's horror trend was not just a pop culture fashion, but a vehicle for a sustained and important cultural conversation about the limits of childhood and horror.

In this book, therefore, I present the children's horror trend as a document of tremendous sociocultural change. My argument is that the concepts of childhood and horror were fundamentally ruptured and reconstructed during the 1980s and the 1990s, as the new social category of pre-adolescence emerged and became established in American culture. Film ratings and other cultural characteristics of the media are especially important markers to trace these changes, which are not just sociocultural but industrial, and long-lasting.

In this introduction, my aim is to set the scene for this argument and its development. I begin by addressing the three main strands of this study and clarifying how they connect in theme as well as time period: horror and its conflicted relationship with childhood and in particular the problem of acknowledging child audiences; ratings, specifically the PG-13 rating and its challenging liminality; and the emergence of the pre-teen as a distinct social group in American culture. After this discussion, I directly address the children's horror trend and its privileged position at the heart of these conflicts, providing a working definition for the ambiguous label of children's horror as well as a word on methodology. I then close with a brief preview of the next chapters.

Pre-Adolescence, a Millennial "Discovery"

One of the central premises of this book is that the advent of pre-adolescence is a Millennial event. By this I mean that the idea of pre-adolescence did not exist before the 1980s but was "discovered" and became culturally established with the generation of people born between 1982 and 2000, commonly known as Millennials. My use of the word discovery is meant to evoke Philippe Ariès's famous claim that childhood has not always existed but was "discovered" in the seventeenth century. He writes:

> This preoccupation [with children today] was unknown to medieval civilization, because there was no problem for the Middle Ages: as soon as he had been weaned,

or soon after, the child became the natural companion of the adult.... Medieval civilization failed to perceive this difference [between children and adults] and therefore lacked this concept of transition. The great event [leading to the "discovery" of childhood as a concept] was therefore the revival, at the beginning of modern times, of an interest in education.[2]

Beyond education, Ariès also highlights other cultural and social changes that made childhood possible only at this time and not before, such as a decreased rate of child mortality and changes in the value of the nuclear family. His key point is that the notion of childhood is not mainly biological but cultural: its genesis, like any of its subsequent transformations, comes out of cultural agreements and their enactment in our social structures.[3] This argument has been emphasized by other authors, including Neil Postman who, in his influential book *The Disappearance of Childhood*, defines childhood by its socially-agreed limits of knowledge: "Children are a group of people who do *not* know certain things that adults know."[4] These limits, he argues, are directly shaped by a society's preferred forms of communication:

> [T]he school curriculum itself has always been the most stringent and persistent expression of adult-imposed censorship. The books that are read in the fourth grade or seventh grade or ninth are chosen not only because their vocabulary and syntax are judged to be suitable for a given age but also because their content is considered to contain fourth-, seventh- or ninth-grade information, ideas, and experience. The assumption is that a fourth grader does not yet know about seventh-grade experience, nor a seventh grader about ninth-grade experience.... But with television, the basis of this information hierarchy collapses.[5]

Postman raises a critical point: "electric media find it impossible to withhold any secrets. Without secrets, of course, there can be no such thing as childhood."[6] Postman's concern is specifically with the ways television changes the way societies enforce the boundaries of childhood—thus making the concept "disappear." Postman's conclusion was perhaps needlessly alarming (even if many critics today would apply his thoughts anew to the internet), but his main point still stands: childhood is a concept explicitly constructed through its boundaries. We know childhood because we know its limits.

These limits and their disruptions are important to my argument in this book. When I talk about the history of pre-adolescence I position it as a "discovery" of new boundaries and the establishing of new cultural standards for what sort of knowledge or "secrets" should be beyond the reach of children. As I suggest, the limits of childhood changed dramatically in the 1980s in order to allow for the idea of pre-adolescence to emerge and remained contested and uncertain until the 1990s, when they solidified again.

What does the Millennial generation have to do with this? My claim is that this is the cohort who carried these struggles and first lived this new idea of childhood. There is, in fact, a very neat correlation between the years of the children's horror trend (1980–1997) and the years of the Millennial cohort (1982–2000), the point being that the debates around childhood prompted by children's horror had a direct connection to not just actual Millennial child audiences (especially in the 1990s, when the trend peaked) but were also driven by sociocultural questions directly prompted by this cohort of children and their parents.

The relation between Millennials and a new idea of childhood has been made by other authors, notably the optimistic Neil Howe and Bill Strauss. In their book *Millennials Rising: The Next Great Generation*, the authors track the origins of the Millennial cohort to a period of intense change in American society, culture and attitudes as a result of a "rediscovery" of the values of childhood and family in the early 1980s.[7] This shift led to what is known as the echo boom: a sharp increase in America's birth rate caused by a large number of Baby Boomers starting their families, and which led to the first wave of Millennial children.

Throughout the 1980s and more explicitly even in the 1990s, when fertility rates peaked, children suddenly became a significant portion of America's population, and family concerns rose to the top of the culture's priorities. This is clear across the board. In politics, for instance, Ronald Reagan and Bill Clinton used notions of family and childhood in fairly similar ways, despite their opposing party affiliations. For Reagan, an emphasis on family values and ideals of childhood innocence were natural parts of a conservative ethic (as was the championing of self-reliance and independence, which the notion of pre-adolescence also embodied), but Clinton often used the concept of family in service of liberal ideals, as in his 1993 Memphis speech in favor of restoring family values in black communities or, more obviously still, in Hillary Clinton's speeches and campaigns as First Lady, including her book *It Takes a Village: And Other Lessons Children Teach Us*.[8] Note this excerpt from a 1996 speech, for example:

> I want to talk about what matters most in our lives and in our nation, children and families. I wish we could be sitting around a kitchen table, just us, talking about our hopes and fears about our children's futures. For Bill and me, family has been the center of our lives. But we also know that our family like your family is part of a larger community that can help or hurt our best efforts to raise our child.[9]

The Clintons' emphasis on family values became especially pronounced after the Lewinski scandal, when the First Lady's support and the preservation of their marriage became a vital part of sustaining the president's public image. Generally, however, the rhetoric of family values used by both Reagan and Clinton was less the result of specific political concerns and more a response to changes in American attitudes. The centrality of family and childhood elsewhere in American culture is evidence of this. Parenting advice abandoned the parent-centric doctrines of the 1970s and refocused the family on the child, while parenting gurus like Dr. Sears, who preached childhood innocence and parental attachment, hit celebrity status. Children's entertainment proliferated, especially on television, and was the object of much stricter notions of quality. Children and families also became highly valued consumer groups. Dedicated children's networks like Nickelodeon were incredibly profitable, and pop culture was filled with child- and family-friendly acts, such as Hanson or Will Smith, appreciated by children and adults alike. In academia, too, children's culture emerged as a topic to be taken seriously in the 1990s.[10]

This newfound interest in the value of childhood created a schism in the social agreements over the term. On the one hand, childhood was still understood as a moment of transformation into independence, agency, and fewer of the "secrets" that had been championed by the culture of the 1970s and early 1980s, as noted by Postman. On the other hand, however, this new romantic view of childhood and family, led by the values of innocence and attachment theory, was quickly gaining ground. The concept of pre-adolescence emerges from the repeated clash of these two perspectives and transforms the concept of childhood by splitting it in two: an earlier moment for younger children, and a later one for older children, now called pre-teens.

This segmentation also implies, somewhat awkwardly, an extension to the notion of childhood more generally. Pre-adolescence is, in fact, an add-on to childhood: a liminal space in which young people are still defined in terms of their vulnerability while also being allowed a foot in the world of maturity. Crucially, maturity is not understood as adulthood in this instance. What the pre-teen is allowed to know, adolescence, is still full of "secrets" because it is still part of the domain of youth and immaturity.

We see, then, the tremendous implications of "discovering" a concept like this. Not only does pre-adolescence transform one of the foundational pillars of American culture, that is the notion of childhood and family, it also revises cultural perceptions of the entire life cycle. Indeed, pre-adolescence implies both a delay and an anticipation of maturity, hereby triggering two common fears about youth: that they grow too old too fast, and that they may never grow up at all. The Millennial generation, as is well known, has often been on the receiving end of both of these critiques. But there are other, perhaps subtler implications to this shift in attitudes, and it is in their examination that the horror genre comes in especially handy.

Horror and the Childhood/Adulthood Frontier

It may come as no surprise that pre-adolescence disrupted the horror genre as soon as it came into being. This is, after all, a genre almost entirely defined by the distinctions it enforces between children and adults, and the change in those cultural parameters had discernible lasting consequences on the genre's shape.

To understand the centrality of the childhood/adulthood border in horror, we need only look at its history, and particularly the kind of criticism the genre itself has generated. A great deal of literature on horror, popular as well as scholarly, is concerned primarily with establishing whether horror is or is not for children, even if the wording of the question might take a subtler form. The debates tend to follow two strands: moral panic, in which the nefarious effects of horror are discussed; or preoccupations with the cultural legitimacy of horror, where its artistic, philosophical, and political merits are established. In either strand, horror is often distanced from child audiences with the suggestion that they cannot comprehend it—or, alternatively, proposed as a genre so infantile it could never truly appeal to any other audience.

This question of whether horror is or is not for children is not new, by any stretch of the imagination, and it involves every media expression of horror. However, horror on film seems to have prompted especially passionate responses, affecting the genre's reputation more dramatically than in its other media expressions. It is also in film history and criticism that we find an especially persistent string of negotiations about the boundaries of horror and its audience.

The most immediate piece of evidence of the centrality of these questions is, of course, the existence of the rating system and its influence in the horror genre. Before it was instituted in America, films adhered to a production code, also known as the Hays Code, which controlled all content through its list of "Don'ts" and "Be carefuls." The goal was that all films produced were suitable and edifying to even the most vulnerable audiences, often personified as children. In this context, all genres, including horror, were suitable for children as there were no distinctions between young and mature audiences. In the 1960s, however, the foundations of the Code became at odds with America's new liberal attitudes. In the words of Jack Valenti, who would go on to devise the ratings system, the "stern, forbidding catalogue [of the Code had] the odious smell of censorship."[11]

Instead of determining what could and could not be shown, the ratings aimed to simply label the content and divide it into levels of suitability, which viewers could then use as guidelines. Arguably the most important feature of this system is that it provides a clear boundary between children and adults—the R rating—which allowed filmmakers to express their creative visions without being bound to suitability concerns (at least in theory). Thus horror was liberated from the imposition of universal suitability. It could now be as violent or as challenging as filmmakers willed it—or, in a more realistic context of distribution, as far as the scope of the ratings allowed it.

In any case, the possibility to oppose mainstream values and push the limits of what had been acceptable was transformative for horror, and the 1970s were marked by a very different kind of horror film. As Kim Newman puts it in his chronicle of the genre, "horror changed radically in 1968."[12] Newman does not mention the ratings as the reason for this change, but it is clear that the qualities he appreciates in horror of the 1970s are those made possible by the existence of the R rating and the subsequent association between horror and adult audiences. Indeed, when Newman laments the "static, even stagnant" condition of 1980s horror, his criticism is that horror has simply lost its edge,[13] a problem attributed in great part to the genre's pandering to young audiences:

> *House 2: The Second Story* (1987), [tries hard] to be a kiddie comedy rather than a horror movie, despite its impressive 9ft-tall cowboy zombie. These movies—along with such big-budget, major studio films as *Fright Night* [1985] and *The Lost Boys* [1987], and cheapies such as *Trick or Treat* [1986] and *The Gate*—reduce the genre to the level of *Scooby-Doo, Where Are You?* With children, adolescents or childish young men in the leads, and with one scene of knockabout looning for every dose of effect-dripping monstrousness, the films provide the MTV generation with something to watch every three minutes but are unable to get seriously scary, or even seriously funny. All they prove is nobody needs a safe horror picture.[14]

Newman's reasoning may seem curiously flawed, but his reproach of a children's film for targeting children (*The Gate*) and a horror-comedy for being funny (*House* and its sequel) comes out of a very specific definition of horror, in which the genre is so "edgy" it becomes incompatible with the "safety" of youth or humor. Newman's views on this subject seem to have only intensified with time. "Perhaps reflecting the dubious state of youth culture," he later writes, "90s teens are an infantilising rather than edgy horror influence: *Teenage Exorcist* (1990) and the *Elm Street* sequels are emblematic, as perhaps is the boom in young adult horror fiction."[15]

What makes Newman's opinions especially interesting is not the intensity of his dislike for young audiences, but the obvious struggle for legitimacy that this dismissal represents. As Mark Jancovich points out, there can often be "violent disagreements among the consumers of a specific genre over their respective constructions of the field [as] each group distinguishes between the 'real' and 'authentic' examples of a genre and its 'inauthentic' appropriation. On occasion, this distinction becomes a matter of exclusion from the category."[16] As Newman would summarize it, horror made for children is simply not horror at all.

It should be noted here that, if young audiences were a sign of inauthenticity for Newman and a vast number of critics like him, they were a sign of authenticity for others as well. James B. Twitchell, for example, reads the genre as strictly teenage fare, "fables of sexual identity" meant to prepare the teenager for the anxieties of reproduction.[17] Though he wrote in the 1980s, Twitchell's analysis is not restricted to this decade; nevertheless, his conclusions were likely influenced by horror's tone in the 1980s, when the genre was dominated by slasher franchises, all of which are notoriously set in teenageland, full of proms, summer camps, babysitting jobs and, as Twitchell points out, sexual anxiety.

As Jancovich also notes, "genre distinctions operate not to designate or describe a fixed class of texts, but as terms that [negotiate] questions of cultural value, privilege and the authority to determine cultural legitimacy through the act of genre definition."[18] In this light, Newman's critiques of "childish" horror and Twitchell's dismissal of all horror as juvenile are two sides of the same coin: both authors use horror's perceived connection with children to determine the genre's cultural status.

This conversation continues to exist but the 1980s stand out as a point of crisis, a moment in which the shape of horror changed as dramatically as it had in 1968. Further evidence of this crisis is the way 1990s Hollywood responded to the accusations that horror was, as Robin Wood suggests, only children's film in disguise[19]—not by returning to "edgy" content but through a labored, and often expensive, association with adult tastes. Teenagers remained popular casting choices but, as the hit franchise generated with *Scream* (1996) exemplifies, they were now wittier, wiser and far more mature than all the babysitters of the 1980s combined, a situation more appealing to young adults (especially those old enough to get all the references) than young teens. More often than not, however, filmmakers simply rejected the idea of young people as the audience for their films, producing a more serious kind of horror, played between adults, busy with adult preoccupations. *Wolf* (1994) is a striking example, which removed lycanthropy's strong associations with adolescence by setting its drama in the business world. The 2000s and beyond continued to change the shape of horror, of course, but this sort of dramatic shift in the position of young audiences has not been seen again, nor has the issue been as contested.

Outside of film, the relationship between horror and young audiences has been far more ambiguous. In literature and popular fiction, especially, the assumption of educational (or at least edifying) material has been strongly influential in how horror content is interpreted. As Jacqueline Rose suggests, children's literature is based on adult notions of the idyllic child with the purpose of shaping child readers to meet this ideal.[20] Horror, therefore, is usually read as cautionary, just as Jack Zipes notes in relation to the German children's literature classic of 1845, *Der Struwwelpeter*: "The explicit drastic punishments that the children experience in the stories were to be held before the eyes of children (and adults) as warnings of what awaited them if they were to make the same mistake."[21]

There is nothing wrong with these readings, but they carry connotations: if horror is above all a moralizing educator, its audience must be a vulnerable mass in need of education. And while this is something often accepted in relation to children it becomes problematic when applied to adults. This is, after all, why Twitchell's views are unpopular with horror fans and why Newman reacts so strongly to the idea of "safe" horror. In their view, horror is a challenging site of reflection, free from dominant ideology and its moralizing, infantilizing influence.

This distinction is fundamental to explain why, even in cases when young people are accepted as legitimate audiences for (non-educational) horror, a line is still drawn between children and teenagers. A good example of this distinction in action can be found in *Frightening Fiction*, one of the first academic studies of youth-oriented horror fiction. In the introduction to that book, Kimberley Reynolds observes how horror "spectacularly dominated children's publishing"[22] in the 1990s and expresses a desire to explore what is effectively a new genre of fiction. So far so good; Reynolds's goal seems to be that of tackling one important part of the children's horror trend. But as Reynolds goes on to explain her selection of texts it quickly becomes apparent that this is not the case. The *Goosebumps* series, for instance, is swiftly rejected as an object of study because of its young target audience (seven- to eleven-year-olds)—even though it is the absolute pioneer in horror fiction for children and a record-breaking commercial success. Reynolds clarifies the decision as such: horror is based on "the drive to leave readers feeling uneasy and fearful in the face of uncertainty," whereas "the fiction now sold as horror and written with a juvenile audience in mind is notable for the sense of security it ultimately engenders"—comments which echo Newman's accusations of "safe horror." Indeed, for Reynolds, *Goosebumps* is not horror but only "what [young people] refer to as 'horror.'"[23]

I am not convinced of the value of ascribing a different genre to these texts when children—and often, the texts' creators themselves—have already declared them to be horror. Why should they be wrong? But the "correction" exercise taken up by Reynolds, Newman and others is still significant, not just for what it says about cultural power but also because it suggests that the acceptance of child audiences in horror might be actually quite far from "safe."

A useful comparison can be made at this point between horror for children and horror for women. In her work on Gothic literature, Kate Ellis writes:

> The debate about the nature and purpose of female education that proliferated in print during the second half of the eighteenth century made it clear that women's reading was a matter of public concern, not just of private choice. Thus the mass-produced novel was both a product of the construction of separate spheres for men and women and, insofar as it gave women examples to follow, a medium through which that construction of gender relations could be elaborated. But it could also subvert that construction, and I will argue that the Gothic novel does this, creating, in a segment of culture directed toward women, a resistance to an ideology that imprisons them even as it posits a sphere of safety for them.[24]

Like the Gothic novel, horror made for children carries with it an uncomfortable disruption of the status quo. On the one hand, it asserts the social and cultural construction of separate spheres for adults and children by presenting a view of life curated especially for children—keeping those "secrets" Postman wrote about. On the other hand, however, it also has the power to subvert these structures by giving children a glimpse into the world of adults—the world of horror—and consequently blurring the boundaries between them.

To dismiss children's horror as "not horror" is to protect this separation. To police the limits of horror is to police the limits of childhood. And if the idea of horror for children seems abhorrent to horror aficionados like Newman, that is because the limits of childhood are also the limits of adulthood. A shift in these boundaries, and therefore in the shape of horror, then creates something like a shared identity crisis, which, as I argue in this book, is exactly what happened in the 1980s.

PG-13: A Critical Milestone

This idea of a radical transformation in horror and childhood might seem abstract but it does have a tangible cultural signpost: the PG-13 rating. If the PG and R classifications established a clear separation between childhood and adulthood, PG-13 not only blurred the boundaries between them, it also constructed a whole new demographic in between by separating young children from young teenagers and ascribing special meaning to this distinction. Just as the R rating was the frontier of adulthood, PG-13 became the frontier of adolescence.

It is my argument that the introduction of PG-13 in 1984 was a cultural moment as critical as the inception of film regulation in 1968, and that it moreover remains the most important change made to the system. That this is not the accepted view of PG-13 today is indicative of how we approach questions of content regulation. All too often these debates become fixated on the protection of children or are entirely overshadowed by concerns over censorship, much like the horror debates mentioned previously. As a result, PG-13 is virtually invisible in ratings history, never addressed as an historical milestone, a symptom of cultural shifts, or a problematic classification—all of which it is.

The most popular academic discourse about PG-13 is the "ratings creep" hypothesis, which refers to the gradual ways in which the system has supposedly become more lenient toward intense content.[25] This theory is ultimately a moral argument, suggesting that violence has "crept" out of the R rating and into PG-13, where it is unethically made available to children. But the problem with this hypothesis is that it is divorced from all historical context and therefore does not contribute meaningful insight about the ratings, the industry they regulate, or the society which produces both. The "creep" is only persuasive if we believe ratings to be static and the meaning of films to be set in stone, two patently false premises. More importantly, however, the "ratings creep" hypothesis shifts attention away from the real questions posed by PG-13, in the same way that quibbles over horror and authenticity do, because it circumvents the possibility that the meaning of childhood has changed, and in doing so refuses to see how and why its boundaries have transformed.

The resistance to this notion is strong, sometimes verging on moral panic. Consider, for instance, the following accusation by critic Michael Medved in 2001, well after the rating's introduction: "[PG-13 is] the Trojan horse in the movie-rating system—allowing wildly unsuitable material to smuggle its way past walls erected by even the most protective parents."[26] Medved went on to suggest PG-13 be replaced with R-13, a restricted rather than advisory classification.[27] This suggestion is revealing: the real worry is that PG-13 evades control, and therefore actively disrupts the meaning of the R rating and, more importantly, the distinction between children and adults. It may be impossible to completely separate critiques of PG-13 from contemporary values, whether in Medved's case or in that of other critics, but it is nevertheless always a weakness to disregard the rating's history and obscure the important struggles that gave rise to its existence.

The interesting question to me is not how we may best preserve this wall between children and adults but why it is so important that it exists at all. I do not mean to imply here that policy, regulation, and child protection are not important subjects—far from it. My point is that we start and end the conversation there and this self-imposed limit is why we still do not understand the origins of cultural meanings of the PG-13 rating, or even of the ratings system more generally.

The current literature illustrates this perfectly.[28] When the introduction of PG-13 is mentioned, it is viewed as a response to the increased levels of violence found in films like *Indiana Jones and the Temple of Doom* (1984), a reading which dismisses two important points. First, it views the system as a means of regulation only, disregarding that it is also, and perhaps primarily, a manifestation of American attitudes toward childhood. As such, any significant change to it must be considered in terms much bigger than just Hollywood aesthetics and market preferences. Second, it does not contextualize the nature of this increased violence. *Temple of Doom* and the other films associated with PG-13, such as *Poltergeist* and *Gremlins*, were not isolated instances of child-oriented violence, nor were they simply influential instances of boundary-pushing filmmaking. These films were part of a larger trend—children's horror—and were implicated in a wider cultural shift that destroyed and rebuilt the limits of childhood, making room for the notion of pre-adolescence.

The approach I suggest here is therefore to look back and zoom out: ratings are not just restrictions, they are cultural artifacts and as such need to be read in their wider contexts, beyond the film industry. From this perspective PG-13 becomes both the result and the symptom of intense debate around childhood and quickly-changing notions of suitability in 1980s' America.

Eye of the Storm:
The Children's Horror Trend

Together all three of these issues—pre-adolescence, horror authenticity, and ratings—make up the children's horror trend. I have already suggested a definition for the ambiguous term children's horror; quite simply, it is horror made for children. And I have likewise already proposed that this was a popular and proliferous form of popular culture in the 1980s and 1990s; however, the first problem we encounter when seeking to study children's horror is that it has rarely been acknowledged in critical literature. With rare exceptions (mainly in relation to children's fiction),[29] children's horror is only occasionally mentioned, and even then, usually in passing and often only in order to dismiss the subject, as seen earlier in this introduction.

This situation is as fascinating as children's horror itself. This silent space is in fact the eye of the storm, quiet only because it is surrounded by enormous forces. Children's horror itself may not have been the focus of much attention, particularly in film, but the issues it raises have certainly long been at the heart of heated debates and prolonged interrogations, both historically and in the present day: questions about the meaning of childhood, the boundaries of adulthood, and the power to censor and regulate. Its radical disregard for nearly all established assumptions about children, horror, and their relationship is precisely why it has not been addressed; the extent of its significance is why it has been circumvented, and the depth of its challenge is why it has been neutralized.

Take Newman or Reynolds as an example again: to admit that children's horror is horror is to drive a spear through these authors' every assumption about the genre. And the very same thing has happened with authors who emphasized the childhood side of children's horror. Timothy Morris's work on the *Goosebumps* book series, for instance, bypasses an analysis of the series' most central theme, namely the presentation of puberty as a horrific moment (which Morris very briefly acknowledges), in order to pursue a more conventional argument about children's entertainment and consumerism: "the dynamic of reading and collecting may ultimately be of more cultural importance than anything in the 'content' of these series. The way we buy and save these books may effectively be their content."[30]

Morris's position, like Reynolds' and Newman's, is strongly articulated and supported, and it is even persuasive within its context. But arguments like this are limited by their dismissal of what is evidently the key feature in *Goosebumps* and other children's horror texts, namely that children consumed them unironically as horror, and that this is also how producers and distributors framed the content. There is a clear parallel here between these critics and proponents of the "ratings creep," in that both seem to disregard the contextual nature of all classification, be it ratings or genre labels.

Even so, I admit the concept can be challenging. Unlike with "horror," there is no immediate clear association for "children's horror," partly because of cultural expectations about the antagonism of childhood and horror as detailed earlier, but also because, despite having a long history now, horror for children has not necessarily had a consistent form, nor have critics established a "canon" for it. On the contrary, the force with which children's horror has been neutralized has made it quite impossible to recognize any sort of unity or thread between these texts: stories like *Hansel and Gretel* are not children's horror, they are fairy tales; films like *Gremlins* are not children's horror, they are horror comedies (and those like *The Gate* are adventures, and those like *Nightmare Before Christmas* are animation); books like *Goosebumps* are not children's horror, they are "what young readers call 'horror'"; and so on and so forth.

Another problem of not having a set association for children's horror is that it becomes tempting to take existing definitions of adult-oriented horror and stretch them to fit children's horror. Here the issue is not that children's horror is erased out of existence but that the category could potentially include everything, therefore becoming meaningless. Films like *Snow White and the Seven Dwarves* (1937) or *Sleeping Beauty* (1959) include frightening sequences, but are they really horror films? What about texts which happened to scare a particular child, even if that response was not intended by the creators? Or horror films which include children as characters but do not address themselves toward child audiences, such as *Child's Play* (1988)?

This level of ambiguity is inevitably problematic, even when critics start by accepting as valid the premise of horror made for children. The edited collection *Reading in the Dark*, for instance, aims to "examine a variety of texts that engage, both overtly and subtly, with constructs of gothic horror in order to begin to demonstrate the pervasiveness of and the appeal of horror in children's and young adult literature, film, and television"—but the editor, Jessica McCort, also stresses the volume's concern with "the appropriation and application of motifs, characters, themes, and tropes from horror texts designed for adults in children's and young adult texts." The word appropriation is key, as it implies an understanding of horror as a genre primarily for adults and of its presence in children's media as a breach of expectations rather than just a different way of doing horror. Indeed, as McCort clarifies, "some of the texts considered are not, in fact, easily classifiable as horror, per the traditional definition of the term."[31] As a result, *Reading in the Dark* is, like other works which have addressed horror in children's culture, focused primarily on the textual and emotional uses of horror rather than the idea of children's horror as a distinct category with its own boundaries and motifs (and, it follows, its own set of intellectual questions and insights).

Catherine Lester has tackled the problem of defining children's horror more explicitly than most. As she argues, "the children's horror subgenre largely adopts narrative and formal strategies of horror films for adults [but can also] successfully mediate content that might be considered 'unsuitable' for children."[32] Although Lester also begins from the assumption that children's horror appears to be a strange combination of terms, her use of the label subgenre suggests that children's horror has a significant historical presence in film, which is unified by a specific way of handling fear and intensity, as shown in *ParaNorman* (2012) and *Frankenweenie* (2012).

These are significant conclusions, which I also support in this book. Nevertheless, Lester's approach continues the tradition of restricting children's horror to debates of suitability and generic purity. Even though she reaches a different conclusion than critics like Reynolds and Newman, Lester's discussion follows the same format of applying pre-established definitions of horror and suitability to a text, and is, as a result, limited by the same disregard of context. Categories like horror, suitability, and even children's horror, are not fixed but fundamentally dependent on their cultural, historical, and industrial contexts.[33]

This downplaying of context is critical because it inadvertently obscures some of the most interesting questions posed by children's horror. For example, the use of the word subgenre is helpful in establishing the legitimacy and significance of these texts, especially as Lester's article also claims to chart "the development of the children's horror subgenre in Hollywood,"[34] but it implies that children's horror has had a stable, continuous presence in film, which is not the case. In Hollywood, horror for children has had two clear peaks, the 1980s and the 2010s, separated (and preceded) by a period of almost complete absence from cinema's landscape. As authors like McCort suggest, this patchy presence is a feature of other media, too. What explains this ebb and flow? And why does the popularity of children's horror in a given media seem to parallel moments of radical industrial change, such as the introduction of PG-13 in the 1980s, the explosion of children's entertainment (television and popular fiction especially but not cinema) in the 1990s, and the trend for nostalgia in the 2010s?

Similarly, while Lester's analysis demonstrates some of the ways horror for children negotiates its intensity within the text, contemporary films like *ParaNorman* are not comparable to those of other periods, in particular the 1980s, when children's horror was surrounded by intense controversy. Films like *Gremlins* and *The Gate* negotiated suitability and the boundaries of the horror genre not just within their textual choices but also their often-conflicted promotional frameworks and, notoriously, their heated critical reception. Why was children's horror so contentious in the 1980s but not in the 2010s?

These questions are worth asking because they are what makes children's horror more than a textual form. The temptation to reduce children's horror to questions of genre and textual meanings, or to match it against a supposedly universal notion of suitability, is understandable given the cultural importance of issues like childhood and children's well-being, but it is also exactly why the topic has not been fully explored in current literature. For the discussion to be taken further, children's horror must be understood as a cultural artifact, fundamentally inseparable from its sociocultural, historical, and industrial contexts.

My aim in this study, therefore, is to address children's horror as a pop culture trend tied to a specific cultural moment in the 1980s and 1990s.[35] During this period, children's horror is clearly a legitimate participant in both the children's and horror genres, but it is also an explicit part of much broader and significant cultural debates and a significant marker of industrial transformation. It is only when these texts are contextualized and protected from overbearing pre-existing debates that we can begin to see the perfectly clear way in which they articulated, and often struggled to negotiate, America's changing ideas of childhood and of the horror genre.

Three Steps to Children's Horror

One of the aims of this book is to provide a working map of the children's horror trend, to counter the instances in which it has been dismembered, diluted, or avoided. So let us start with a definition. The children's horror trend (1980–1997) is an historical cluster of horror texts made for children in a variety of media, which articulated new understandings of childhood and of horror, particularly in relation to the emergence of pre-adolescence. It has two important moments: a film cycle (1980–1995), during which most of the cultural struggles happened, and a more general period (1990–1997) that encompassed other media, notably popular fiction and television, during which the trend was less controversial and peaked in popularity.

There is children's horror before and after this timeline.[36] However, these instances are different in two important ways. The first is that children's horror outside of the trend tends to not be attached to cultural debates or conflicts over the limits of childhood, or over the definition of horror. The reasons for this are thoroughly explained in the following chapters but, briefly, it is because newer (and older) children's horror operates in relation to a more stable cultural understanding of the boundaries between children and horror. If the texts in the trend were read as ambiguous, that is because they were created at a time when those boundaries were themselves ambiguous.

The second reason children's horror within the trend is different comes as a result of the first: because the trend was part of the rearrangement of these boundaries, its texts do not have a cohesive form. As more recent children's horror shows, there is a clear "template" for the combination of childhood and horror today—but it was only generated as a result of the trend's trial and error.

These specificities are, as I hope to show in this book, part of what makes the children's horror trend so interesting: its changes in content, tone, and preferred media come as direct responses to sociocultural shifts. But this fluidity also poses a problem, in that it can make it hard to identify exactly which texts are part of the trend. An appendix at the end of this book includes the most significant titles, and each chapter that follows is structured around specific case studies, which should give readers a clear idea of the flow of this trend. Nevertheless, it is useful to say a bit more about my selection criteria and about the way I define children's horror during this period.

Titles in the children's horror trend meet three important criteria, all of which relate to the central issue of changing childhood:

> 1. *Children's horror texts were perceived at their time of release by their creators and their audiences to have a connection (positive or negative) to both the horror genre and young audiences.*

This is a key defining element. Not only does it highlight the cultural challenge posed by these texts, it also suggests the contextual nature of children's horror. The precise definition of children's horror can and does change historically because it is inherently connected to dominant ideas of what is and is not suitable children's entertainment. Frequently, the texts in this trend contain surprising levels of intensity or, conversely, unexpected humor, depending on the set of assumptions with which each individual reader approaches them. Children's horror is therefore not identified by the meaning a viewer or reader today might give it, but by the meaning ascribed to it by its contemporaneous culture.

As an example, consider *Gremlins*, which recently has enjoyed a resurgence of popularity. Today's context, as well as the nostalgia which surrounds it, has effected some significant changes in how *Gremlins* is perceived. The first film and its sequel have become one in collective memory ("the *Gremlins* franchise"), with the result that the first film's humor is much highlighted by its sequel and its horror much downplayed by today's advanced technology and expectations of the genre. The franchise's prestige is evident in its current merchandise line, which is popular even though the last film release was over two decades ago. This line targets adult collectors with large, elaborate and expensive action figures meant for the display cabinet rather than the playroom, board games and "Collector's Edition" card games, as well as fashionable vintage-inspired t-shirts and other memorabilia based on all the main gremlins—a vast difference from the original merchandise lines of the 1980s, aimed at children and almost exclusively based on Gizmo. Furthermore, the original objections to violence which surrounded the first film (and the rating debates that followed them) are almost entirely irrelevant for contemporary consumers of this franchise.

Similarly, *Goosebumps* today holds a much different cultural status than it did in the 1990s. Although it is still published and R.L. Stine is still a popular author, *Goosebumps* is no longer a children's culture phenomenon and has not been in the children's bestselling list for many years. Unlike *Gremlins*, and despite its recent film adaptations, *Goosebumps* does not hold much prestige with adult collectors today, even if it was an undeniably significant brand in the 1990s. As the physical texts of either franchise have not changed since their original release dates, the only explanation for these radical shifts in cultural perception must be found in their different historical contexts.

Additionally, a children's horror text is always intended as children's horror by its creators, as this book shows. Therefore, children's horror is not simply horror that children happen to like, and it is not horror that adults find "childish," sub-standard or otherwise "mild." These instances may constitute "accidental" children's horror, so to speak, but they are not like the texts I highlight here, which were made with the specific goal of appealing to children (either in addition to or instead of adult audiences). Equally, children's horror does not simply place children in threatening situations which may or may not be perceived as scary, as this may happen in any genre (especially adventure, a staple in children's culture), but does so using specific horror motifs, which it prominently signals to its audience.

As a result, the children's horror trend includes all texts identified as cross-over objects between horror and children's culture at the time of their production, regardless of their individual specificities and whether they articulated horror with humor (*The Monster Squad*), without it (*The Gate*), or with a mixed approach (*Gremlins*). It also includes texts which are playful in their use of horror motifs and tropes so long as these elements have a significant impact in the text's aesthetics (*The Nightmare Before Christmas*) and narrative (*The Witches*), and particularly if these elements were singled out for major use in advertising campaigns (*Casper*).

> 2. *Children's horror adopts the perspective of a child or a childlike character (be it monster, animal or adult in its appearance) and usually explores childhood anxieties, particularly the on-set of puberty.*

This deliberate association with a child's perspective is one of the main ways in which children's horror establishes its sense of "belonging" in children's culture. It rejects any form of othering of children or childhood, and does not use children as horrific motifs—there are no Terrible Children in children's horror. Because this characteristic refers to content, it is a more fluid identifier than the first criteria. In the cinema especially, children's horror sometimes crossed over into the family film, resulting in narratives told from a mixed perspective of adults and children. In these cases, however, the narrative tends to remain focused on questions of childhood, childhood boundaries and parenting anxieties related to the on-set of puberty, as in *Gremlins* and *Casper*.

> 3. *Children's horror is not associated with notions of education or quality.*

This is a crucial point. It anchors children's horror in children's culture in a way that implies subversion: children's horror is circulated and made popular within children's culture primarily by children, their word of mouth and independent play, rather than being handed down, suggested, or otherwise pre-approved by parents and educators. For this reason, ratings are of no consideration when identifying a children's horror film or television show, even if these ratings might have a lot to say about how the text was received by adults. Consequently, children's horror in the cinema is usually rated PG or PG-13, but can also be found under the R rating. In popular fiction, it will usually be found under the young adult label, but might exist elsewhere too. And in the few instances where a connection can be established between children's horror and educational campaigns (as in Scholastic's slogan "reading is a scream" attached to the *Goosebumps* series), it is not significant to its consumption or reception. Children's horror does not educate or edify, and it does not provide cautionary tales, at least not primarily. What it does is open a window into the "secret" world of maturity.

* * *

These three criteria suggest in children's horror a fundamental breach of assumptions about the combination of childhood and horror. Indeed, this might be a simpler way of defining it: children's horror during the trend period is the outcome of—and the chart to—a radical overhaul in America's boundaries of childhood, adulthood, and the horror genre.

A Map for the Road Ahead

By this point it is clear what this book wants to accomplish; what is left are the more practical questions about how it does so. Each chapter makes use of one or more case study, chosen to illustrate both the progression of the trend and a point of cultural tension. My approach is contextual, so my claims are based primarily on the contemporary voices found in critical reception, marketing campaigns, and interviews, though I have complemented this material throughout with critical readings of children's horror narratives, particularly their representations of childhood. The book is organized chronologically and split into two parts of three chapters each. A brief description of the main arguments and their progression follows.

Part I charts the emergence of pre-adolescence in American culture, its disruption of the concepts of childhood and horror, and its effects on the film industry. Chapter 1 focuses on Disney's first horror experiments to outline a rupture in the concept of childhood and, by proxy, notions of suitability. Chapters 2 and 3 both focus on the PG-13 rating and its association with the establishment of pre-adolescence as a concept in

American culture. Chapter 2 examines the rating's creation and proposes it as a major turning point in cultural and industrial history. Chapter 3 then explores the aftermath of PG-13, particularly the consequences it had in the cultural position of the horror genre.

Part II chronicles the cultural responses to the rupture caused by pre-adolescence and examines the subsequent reconstruction of the concepts of childhood and horror, as well as of the cultural meaning of the cinema as a medium. Chapter 4 addresses horror's response to the legitimization of pre-teen audiences and notes how the genre reconstructed its identity in the cinema to exclude this demographic. Chapter 5 focuses on Hollywood's response to the rise of the family audience and to the cultural dominance of attachment parenting philosophies, noting how its narratives and representations returned pre-adolescence to the ideals of childhood innocence. Together, these chapters explain the end of the children's horror film cycle and stress the impact of the PG-13 rating in the film industry's business model. Chapter 6 explores children's horror after the film cycle, noting how its embracing of children's culture and its expectations contributed to its success—as well as to a renewed cultural opposition between the concepts of childhood and horror.

The book's conclusion points out the ongoing conflict between the ideals of childhood and horror, particularly when brought together in the cinema, and reflects on the specific implications of this book's arguments. The reader will also find an Appendix at the end, which includes a selection of children's horror titles in film and other media.

Part I

Rupture

THE NEXT THREE CHAPTERS map the first decade of the children's horror film cycle and trace the establishment of pre-adolescence as a concept in American culture. One of my key arguments here concerns the cultural and social significance of the film ratings system, which I present as a tangible manifestation of America's definition of childhood. The biggest change to the system, and thus to childhood, was the introduction of the PG-13 classification in 1984, which I present here both as the outcome of children's horror's challenges and as the milestone of pre-adolescence's acceptance into American culture.

The chapters in this part also problematize horror's relationship with children. As PG-13 becomes a symbol of a changed childhood, it also becomes a symbol of anxiety and threat to horror's established order—not to mention its legitimacy and subcultural capital. This part culminates in a head-to-head between horror champions and child audiences, foreshadowing the unraveling of children's horror in Part II.

Chapter 1 explores Disney's early attempts at children's horror and argues that these productions reveal not just an initial awareness of pre-teens as a separate social group but also the rating system's view of childhood as an emerging point of cultural tension. In light of these claims, this chapter also argues for the need to reappraise Ron Miller's leadership of the Disney studio.

Chapter 2 examines the escalation of suitability conflicts with the creation of the PG-13 rating, suggesting it as a key industrial and cultural milestone—a rewrite to America's idea of childhood, in which pre-adolescence is acknowledged and explicitly included.

Chapter 3 addresses the immediate consequences of PG-13's introduction, noting how pre-teens quickly became a more distinct audience but also how PG-13's identity became very similar to that of the PG rating, causing dissonance within the horror genre's character.

Together, the three chapters in this part paint a picture of the children's horror cycle during its strongest point, illustrating a move from tentative and disparate narratives toward cohesive form in the late decade. The films used as case studies here serve primarily as illustrations of the hot spots in the historic timeline of pre-adolescence, but readers interested in the details of form in the children's horror cycle can refer to the comprehensive list in this book's Appendix.

CHAPTER 1

"This could be our *Exorcist*!" Disney, Horror and the New Rules of Childhood

This story of children's horror begins, rather appropriately, in the "dark era" of the Disney studio: those uncertain years between Walt Disney's death in 1966 and the renaissance that came with Michael Eisner's leadership in 1984. The studio's despair came out of a struggle to redefine the Disney brand after losing Walt's vision and was well noted by the critics of the time, who saw creative paralysis and lethargy in the post–Walt efforts. This problem peaked during Ron Miller's leadership (late 1970s and early 1980s) and was especially bad in the film division, particularly where live-action releases were concerned. The unbroken string of commercial flops and lukewarm receptions brought the studios dangerously close to dissolution, progressively hurting the Disney brand name as well as its finances. As Disney historian Janet Wasko puts it, "by the mid–1980s, most analysts agreed that the company's management was basically 'sitting on its assets,' trying to 'do what Walt would have done' and not doing a very good job of it."[1]

The light at the end of this tunnel was children's horror. Or at least that seems to have been the thinking behind Disney's sudden enthusiasm for the genre in the early 1980s, beginning with a ghost story pitched by Tom Leetch to Ron Miller in the most unlikely terms: "This could be our *Exorcist*!"[2] Miller greenlight it with a generous budget, giving the world one of the most notorious Disney disaster stories, *The Watcher in the Woods*

(1980). *The Watcher* was certainly not a success, but it did not quell Miller's belief that horror was a good bet for Disney—and other features soon followed, namely *Something Wicked This Way Comes* (1983) and *The Black Cauldron* (1985).

These films may have been commercial and critical disappointments, but they collectively pose the first striking question about children's horror: What could have driven a studio like Disney, so closely associated with family values and wholesomeness, to produce and so emphatically bet on all-out horror stories? Why do it when no one else had? And, moreover, why do it again (and again), after each attempt proved a box-office failure?

In answering these questions, this chapter frames Disney's experimental horror films as the first clear marker of change in America's notions of childhood and the trigger point for the children's horror film cycle. My claim is that the narratives in these films, and more explicitly their turbulent productions and conflicted reception, are a window into the contested notions of childhood and suitability in America in the late 1970s and early 1980s. In revealing the challenges of pursuing an emerging but as yet undefined audience—pre-teens—the first children's horror films highlight the incompatibility between emergent notions of a segmented childhood and the cultural myth of childhood innocence.

My argument in this chapter thus goes beyond the simple charting of a trend's beginnings. My aim is not to position these experimental films as coincidental trend-setters, nor to frame children's horror as a random outcome of Disney's moment of identity crisis. Rather, I see *The Watcher in the Woods* and Disney's other titles as evidence of impressive awareness and vision—frustrated vision, but vision nevertheless. It is no coincidence that children's horror only started in earnest with Disney, a business built on American childhood, just as it is no coincidence that these efforts were failures in the commercial landscape of the early 1980s. I suggest, then, that Disney was ahead of the curve in sensing a change toward the pre-teen as a separate audience, but it was up against two powerful forces: its own reputation, built on an extended and deliberate cultivation of wholesomeness, and the influence of the ratings system in the American film market.

In this sense, this analysis of the early days of "making" pre-adolescence contains a second intervention, concerned with the historical relationship between Disney and the ratings system. If the most popular histories and analyses of Disney are to be believed, this relationship is either non-existent or insignificant, for the topic is never mentioned. But

I contend that the progression of Disney's "dark times," and even the very existence of this low point, was fundamentally dictated by the ratings system. To be more precise, what I propose is that the problematic business decisions made by Ron Miller during his time in power were attempts to negotiate the growing gap between public perceptions of child audiences and the rigid categories imposed by the ratings system before the creation of PG-13. One of the most obvious and immediate implications of this claim is that Miller's leadership is in dire need of reconsideration by film historians, so that is where this analysis starts.

Learning New Rules: Ron Miller's Disney, 1978–1983

It is strange to talk of "Ron Miller's Disney" because it is so rarely done by others. Miller is remembered as a limp leader, accused of having "no guts or vision,"[3] and whose management added very little to the Disney company. In nearly every current history of Disney, the Miller period is reduced to a (brief) critique of his investment choices, a (brief) note of his failed attempts at rejuvenating the film division or, more often than not, simply omitted altogether. Douglas Gomery's account of Disney history, for example, places the entire period between Walt's death and Michael Eisner's hiring under the same umbrella: simply "Looking for a Successor, 1966–1984." When Gomery comments on Miller specifically, it is only to say how his Disney "seemed to have lost touch with making money-making movies."[4]

As this "money-making" emphasis suggests, Gomery sees Disney as a corporation and reads the company's leaders in light of their business dexterity. His observations consistently highlight how most Disney executives (but not Ron Miller) successfully dealt with "real business conditions," such as technical change, the business cycle, and war. Gomery is very clear about the sort of things he believes made Disney a success: "the skilful use of new technologies," specifically sound and color in the 1930s (with Walt) and home video and cable TV in the 1980s (with Eisner). This sort of contextualized business approach is useful because it firmly places Disney in the context of American society. But Gomery misses one important "business condition," one that challenged Ron Miller almost exclusively: the introduction of the MPAA's film rating system.

Just like the introduction of sound and color, or the home video and cable TV markets, the rating system revolutionized the way films were made and sold in America—and, in so doing, fundamentally changed Disney's place in the market. It should not be forgotten that Disney in the 1960s was different from every other studio in America: its product was incredibly specialized, overtly anchored on family values, and therefore impossible to dissociate from family entertainment. This position had been comfortably aligned with the ideology of Hollywood in the days of the Hays Code, when *all* film was family entertainment, but it proved a difficult adjustment after the ratings.

Because of its moral foundations, the Code allowed only for the subtlest maturity and only the most covert challenges to mainstream morality—things like violence, sexuality or other risqué themes were either not included or presented as cautionary tales. Under the Code, film was obliged to provide a sort of public service, or at the very least an edifying experience to all of its audiences, including the most vulnerable. These restrictions, too close to censorship for the changing mindsets of the 1960s, were what ultimately led to the replacement of the Code with the ratings system. Since then, we have argued and will continue to argue about the authority and ideological forces behind certain classifications, namely R and X (now NC-17), because we can easily see how these ratings have shaped cinema's landscape (production, form, and consumption included).

But we must apply this thinking to children's cinema and child audiences, too, because here the effect was just as radical and just as immediate, if not more so. Even if we were to leave aside the issue of content, we simply cannot ignore the consequences of segmenting audiences based on their age: children went from being automatically part of mainstream audiences to being automatically *excluded* from them. I don't mean here to say that under the Code all films were made with children in mind as the primary target; however, the structures of the industry, determined by the Code and its restrictions, meant that no mainstream film could be released that did not at least acknowledge the possibility of children watching it. With the ratings system this assumption is entirely reversed: films suitable for family viewing were deliberately made this way, clearly labeled as such, and constituted only a fraction of all output.

If we accept, as I propose here, that this was a fundamental change in the rules of the filmmaking game—and one that affected Disney more so than other studios because of its specialization in family entertainment—Gomery's umbrella terms and dates tell a very different story. Disney was not "looking for a successor" between the year of Walt's death and the year Michael Eisner was hired; it was learning the rules of a completely different game, played in a smaller market by a radically-transformed industry.

That is to say, Disney's point of crisis was not primarily prompted by the death of a charismatic leader or the choice of an incompetent new head but was the result of an inevitable period of adaptation to the film industry's new rules. This adaptation took place gradually, in the years between the introduction of the ratings system (1968) and the introduction of PG-13 (1984), but clearly reached its peak conflicts in the years immediately before the introduction of PG-13—the Ron Miller period.

As I argue in this book, the late 1970s and especially the early 1980s were troublesome because of their increasing cultural and social uncertainty around childhood—it was at that time that "pre-adolescence" emerged. And Disney's moves during this time support as much: not only did the company's film efforts grow more experimental, its commercial appeal also dropped steeply.[5] Reading these developments in context is key to fruitful readings of Ron Miller's Disney, whether they are informed by cultural concerns, "great man" views, or business-focused analyses.

To return to Gomery's success stories: Miller can only be compared to Walt or Eisner if the terms of comparison are fair. Walt might have had the savvy to use sound and color to his advantage, but he never had to deal with a fundamental shift in the rules of the filmmaking game—his challenges were technical. And likewise, Michael Eisner might have had the business smarts to diversify Disney's assets, but he did not have to do it during a time of intense cultural change—his challenges were corporate. Ron Miller, on the other hand, was forced to juggle technological advancements and diversification tactics while also navigating the uncertainty of a segmented market and the restrictions of the ratings.

I point this out not to champion Ron Miller or dampen the accomplishments of other Disney leaders, but to make clear just how important the cultural context is to this issue. This point can be labored further by noting how this growing gap between the scope of the ratings and the expectations of the American public was not a mystery to critics, or even some Disney historians, despite these authors not having seen great significance in the matter. As Disney historian Ron Grover notes, the problem of this troubled period was that "America's viewing public had changed, but Disney hadn't."[6] Or, put differently by Bart Mills, youngsters "seemed to be growing up faster, demanding more sophistication in their movies,"[7] a development Disney had been unable to respond to.

Note how another critic, Ed Blank, assessed Disney's situation in 1982:

> Every scene is staged with an artifice unique to Disney movies. It's phenomenal how every director who works for the company makes movies that look and feel like every other live-action adventure or comedy produced by the studio since Walt Disney's death 25 years ago.
>
> How do they do it? And why do they bother? The company has failed with almost every non-animated release since the early '60s. They can't get the adults or teens they're after, and children instinctively and rightly turn off to condescension.[8]

While Blank notes Disney's lack of an original vision, his comments here do not echo the common accusation of creative lethargy but speak of a different sort of stagnated understanding of Disney's audience and brand. Only these tensions were not a mystery to Ron Miller: "Sure, I'm a hypocrite," he once said in interview. "I let my children see everything—R's, PG's, the lot. But I have a responsibility to this company. One racy picture could do incredible damage to a name built up over 55 years."[9] Miller's statements reflect an understanding of the market and of the new American reality far greater than what is popularly attributed to his leadership and moreover go straight to the point: the issue with the ratings was that they came with a set of expectations, and this was hard to merge with the heavy weight of Disney's wholesome reputation, established under very different circumstances.

As Miller assessed, it was difficult to strike a balance between the kind of film that was expected from Disney as bastion of childhood innocence (G rated) and the sort that would draw a large audience (not G-rated). "I would love to have been able to do it," Miller continued in the same interview, "but I couldn't. The people ... who have supported Disney for years, wouldn't stand for it.... They'll have to blindfold and gag me before I'll let them do anything more than a soft PG."[10]

Other Disney figures of the time were equally open about the disconnection between the ethos of the Disney films made before the ratings and the reality of post-ratings audiences. "It's time to start taking risks," said Tom Wilhite, head of film production, in a 1980 interview about Disney's lack of success. "We have to talk to kids about things that are concerning them in their real lives."[11] In a different interview, Wilhite also went on to acknowledge the "tremendous change in the movie audience in the last ten to fifteen years" and state his belief that Disney's response should be "to broaden the audience, not divorce ourselves from the Disney image."[12]

The trouble, therefore, was not what to do after Walt but how to go about doing it without losing the public's favor. This is the conflict that makes Miller's period fascinating, and it is the core of the children's horror question.

A Ghastly Landmark: *The Watcher in the Woods*

With this background of conflict in place, it is easier to understand the significance of *The Watcher in the Woods*, Disney's first PG live-action film and the first high-profile children's horror film. It is, to borrow J.P. Telotte's term, an important part of Miller's attempts at "course correction" for the Disney brand. Telotte's observations come from an analysis of two of Miller's other frustrated high-budget high-hopes features, *The Black Hole* (1979) and *Tron* (1982). Though he does not make a broader point about Miller's leadership, Telotte reads these titles as Disney's attempt to update itself and engage with new popular discourses (i.e., technology) by poaching cues from the period's trends (i.e., science-fiction).

A similar logic is at play in Miller's horror ventures—only with more cultural anxiety mixed in. *The Watcher in the Woods* is the perfect illustration: not only is it one of Disney's most turbulent productions, its problems stemmed entirely from the difficulties of mediating the Disney brand and America's changing attitudes. This first section will outline the film's conflicted history, in order to prepare the way for the arguments about childhood, ideology, and the horror genre that follow.

Like other children's horror productions, *The Watcher* started out in optimism. Miller and Leetch produced it together and began by taking the *Exorcist* pitch to the letter: the film was populated with horror actors (David McCallum, Kyle Richards, and Bette Davis), a horror director (John Hough) and horror locations (the mansion was one shared with horror classic *The Haunting* [1963]) and was moreover hyped as such. "We're going to scare the hell out of them this summer with a sort of horror story," Miller declared proudly to the press.[13]

But this initial excitement soon degenerated into conflict over the production. Though both Leetch and Miller were committed to the vision of a horror film, they could not agree on the film's intensity level. This prompted a number of rewrites and changes to the original script, even after shooting had began. The production's atmosphere was suitably tenuous—"an irritable Bette Davis, nervous executives and an embattled director"[14]—and it all affected the film's tone and narrative coherence, both of which fluctuate wildly. This issue was further aggravated when Disney decided to tie the film's release to Bette Davis's career anniversary, a marketing move which underestimated how far away the film's special effects were from completion. Instead of waiting for the finished product, Disney decided to simply cut the scenes with unfinished effects.

Unsurprisingly, the premiere was a disaster. The deleted scenes were crucial to the film's narrative, and the released film both confused and insulted the critics who previewed it. According to Scott Michael Bosco, who was present at the first screening, critics seemed to be enjoying the film up until the final act. In his report, Bosco described how the audience "leaned forward with expectation" and "lurched back into their seats, with a gasp" at the Watcher's reveal, applauding. "I had not experienced a preview response like that since *Alien*, when the creature broke out from John Hurt's chest," Bosco wrote.

The problem, he continued, was that when the film ended "no one had understood exactly what had transpired." The situation worsened during the Q&A that followed the screening, in which main actress Lynn-Holly Johnson was asked "what was it they had just seen." The actress responded with a summary of the dropped scenes (known as The Other World Sequence), until "a press agent quickly covered the mic, pulled Lynn-Holly away, and whispered something to her. Returning to the mic, Lynn-Holly responded with a slight giggle, 'But you didn't see that.' A murmur of disbelief expelled from the audience."[15]

The film's production team tells a different version of the events, attributing the disaster of the premiere to the unfished special effects that remained in the shown cut, not to narrative incoherence. According to director John Hough, "the public's and critics' reaction to the look of the alien was so horrendous—everybody started laughing practically. And so Disney ... re-shot the ending without any special effects, without the alien." Hough continued, "Everybody flew back the next morning to Los Angeles to lick their wounds and to rethink on what to do with the film.... [Disney] had a lot at stake and full marks in and they were willing to spend the money and keep their belief in the project going."[16]

The immediate decision was to withdraw it from circulation; then, a series of edits, cuts, and reshoots, particularly in relation to the film's ending. *The Watcher in the Woods* was re-released a year later, to marginally improved reception. Vincent Canby's review in the *New York Times*, often quoted by other critics, contains the following sharp remarks: "I challenge even the most indulgent fan to give a coherent translation of what passes for an explanation at the end. The movie's metaphysics, bogus anyway, are not helped by the appearance of a creature that looks as if it had been stolen from a Chinese New Year's parade."[17]

A VHS of the film was eventually released, but that was the end of Disney's investment on the film. It was simply not talked about again. And, following Disney's lead, critics soon forgot about *The Watcher,* too. In 1982, for example, only a year after the film's re-release, *American Film* magazine published an in-depth retrospective commentary on Disney in which *The Watcher* is not only omitted but actually erased from Disney history: the writer describes *Something Wicked This Way Comes*, released two years after *The Watcher in the Woods*, as having "the kind of phantasmagorical menace often suggested in Disney cartoons, but so far never before included in its live-action product."[18]

More recently, however, *The Watcher* has become something of a cult object. As *Sight and Sound* magazine put it, *The Watcher* is a "curio" surrounded by a "dense thicket of rumour and myth."[19] Part of this image comes from the outreach efforts of journalist Scott Bosco, a friend of Tom Leetch and *The Watcher*'s biggest champion. Bosco's tell-all online account of the film's production is full of intrigue and accusations against Disney, whom he claims is still withholding the film's darker scenes by claiming them lost instead of archived. Bosco's contributions were also the foundation of the film's Special DVD Edition (2002), released not by Disney (whose home media efforts for the film were very limited) but by Anchor Bay, who specialized at the time in obscure horror and cult releases.

Like the film itself, this DVD release had a turbulent production process. The original plan was to release a director's cut of the film, which would include the darker scenes previously vetoed by Miller, but this decision met strong opposition from Disney. The director's cut was scrapped, but the Anchor Bay special edition DVD went ahead as a prestige release, presenting *The Watcher in the Woods* as a mysterious and unfairly forgotten gem in Disney (and film) history. From the tagline on its cover ("The most legendary monster of all time can now be seen for the first time") to its selection of extras (interviews, trailers and TV spots, alternate endings, commentaries with the director), this special edition provides a map to the events of its production history, highlighting not just the controversies around the making of the film but also its "what ifs." This Special Edition is now out of print, replaced in the market by Disney's own release (2004), which contains some of the same material but (perhaps strategically) leaves out the more revealing extras, such as John Hough's commentary which exposed *The Watcher*'s production trouble and goes into detail about the fateful premiere.

The cultural presence of *The Watcher in the Woods* is nothing short of curious, and while I relate its story here also for its intrigue, its bigger insights about Disney and childhood are yet to come. Though history has marked it as such, the tug-o-war between Leetch and Miller (and later, between Disney and Scott Bosco) was not about grudges or the desire to cover up an unsuccessful endeavor. I propose it here as the acting out of a careful process of dual discovery: a new audience of children, and Disney's relationship to them.

Ratings and the Illusive Pre-Teen Audience

The promotional campaigns for *The Watcher in the Woods* were anchored on the film's biggest selling point, its intensity. This was also the film's biggest challenge, given the Disney brand and its traditional audience, so the promotion material also engaged in some explicit signposting. The trailer, for example, sets it all up as an eerie ghost story, and ends with a clarification from the narrator: "*The Watcher in the Woods*, from Walt Disney Pictures. It is not a fairy tale." These words, also included in the film's poster, were then followed by a further warning: "As proud as we are of *The Watcher in the Woods*, Walt Disney Productions strongly recommends that parents pre-screen this film for pre-teens. It is not for small children!" In addition to these precautions, *The Watcher* was also Disney's first PG film, signaling an important move away from the all-audience G which had so far been the studio's brand. As clear as this marketing framework may seem, down to its explicit rejection of very young audiences, audiences were nevertheless baffled by *The Watcher*'s address. In the words of one critic, echoed by many more, "I'm not sure at which market this film is intended."[20]

The reason for this confusion is that Disney was playing with a different set of rules, unaware of—or unable to comply with—the structural constraints of the industry (its rating system) and of American culture (its understanding of childhood). In the limited world of Disney films, the difference between a G and a PG may be clear enough, and the notion of "pre-teens" might make perfect sense, but the same was not true in the wider context of American culture in this period.

Rating trends alone illustrate Disney's alienation from mainstream film. By 1980, PG was firmly established as Hollywood's "default" classification, by far more profitable than either the G or R ratings—of the twenty highest-grossing films of the 1970s, fourteen were rated PG, with the remaining six falling under the R rating. Indeed, many of the decade's most popular titles were rated PG: *Star Wars* (1977), *Superman* (1978) and *Superman II* (1980), as well as *The Poseidon Adventure* (1972), *Young Frankenstein* (1974), *Jaws* (1975), and *Close Encounters of the Third Kind* (1977).

Though the PG rating was fundamental to these films' success, this was not because it signaled an intended audience of pre-teens—on the contrary, these films resonated because their appeal was more universal than a specific group of children. The PG connotation, therefore, was not "young teenager," as Disney seemed to think, but simply "everyone."

The G rating, on the other hand, still had strong associations with a particular audience. In the top fifty highest-grossing films of the 1970s only six were rated G—of these, three featured animals, families and puppets, and were ideologically positioned with the more traditional family-friendly features of Disney's golden age: *Benji* (1974), *The Adventures of the Wilderness Family* (1975), and *The Muppet Movie* (1979). The G market was therefore not only a much smaller slice of the pie, but one that imposed considerable restrictions in content and tone—a predicament Disney was actively trying to escape at this time.

In this context, it's easy to see why *The Watcher*'s PG did very little to signpost the film's intensity and target audience. To its contemporary audience, the choice of a PG instead of G must have seemed less like a radical departure and more like a belated adoption of the industry's standard.

This suggestion is confirmed in *The Watcher*'s reception, as critics repeatedly deny awareness of Disney's subtle distinction between audiences. "It's too complicated for young kids and probably too mild for teenagers used to more spectacular cinematic thrills,"[21] wrote one reviewer, while another felt it was "too unconvincing for adults and too scary for youngsters."[22] Critics seemed to agree that this was "the latest, half-hearted attempt by Walt Disney Productions to improve its film-industry image by aiming toward a wider, more adult-oriented audience,"[23] but their reviews never connect this effort with pre-teens—nor do they indicate that this audience even exists outside of Disney's market research department.

What these critical opinions do reveal is a strong cultural agreement over the make-up of film audiences at the start of the 1980s: small children to one side (G), teenagers and adults to the other (PG and, less often, R). This blunt separation between "obvious" children and "obvious" adults is significant. As the contemporary discussion around *The Watcher* also make clear, there is a distinct lack of cultural precision in this period about what constitutes a child, and of where the transition to maturity takes place.

One of the film's main stars, eleven year-old Kyle Richards, is referred to as both "child"[24] (or "innocent little child"[25]) and "adolescent,"[26] while the teenager characters, who in the film are all around the age of seventeen, are called "children" by director John Hough.[27] The teenagers' occultist ceremony is moreover described by reviewers as "a children's game"[28] and "a strange childhood initiation ritual."[29] Here we see the strange interchangeability of the terms child and adolescent, used apparently at random. Their precise distinction is irrelevant because both describe the same thing: not-adulthood.

This is where Disney's insistence on "pre-teens" fails to resonate. By segmenting childhood into such precise groups (young children, pre-teens, and teens), Disney clashed head-on with the dominant concept of childhood, which encompassed all minors more or less indistinctly. This—not a move toward PG ratings—was a radical departure. So radical, in fact, even Disney refused to play along, as the next section will discuss.

Representing Childhood Innocence

Miller and Leetch might have been aware that, economically, the pre-teen market was up-and-coming, but this realization did not translate into a different form of address or representation, creating a confusing rift between what the marketing told the audience (childhood has changed) and what the film then says in its narrative (childhood is the same). Some of this was practical risk-managing on Miller's part, no doubt. But it was also the result of a clash between "rulebooks" or cultural frameworks: that of Disney before the ratings, in which childhood and innocence always went together, and that of the wider culture, where this association was becoming increasingly complex.

The bridge between these two frameworks is the horror genre. Though it had a clear association with mature audiences,[30] this was often balanced with an equally clear reliance on notions of childhood innocence. This second association (as well as ideas of the family as sacred unit) is, in fact, the starting point for many of the biggest hits of the 1960s and 1970s, including *Village of the Damned* (1960), *The Innocents*, *Night of the Living Dead* (1968), *The Exorcist* (1973), *The Omen* and *The Brood* (1979). *The Watcher in the Woods* obviously follows in the footsteps of these titles—an understandably conservative approach for an inexperienced studio, but not without consequence. Contemporary critics were quick to note the aesthetic implications: "In short, every trite ghost-story routine is pulled out of mothballs in an attempt to cash in on the horror craze."[31] But there were some significant ideological ramifications, too.

The most important is the perpetuation of a link between childhood and otherness. The young people in *The Watcher* are an amalgamation of the child stereotypes seen in previous horror, namely the possessed and the malevolent child, which has been widely read as a motif of otherness. According to Robin Wood, "Otherness represents that which bourgeois ideology cannot recognize or accept but must deal with ... either by rejecting and if possible annihilating it, or by rendering it safe and assimilating it, converting it as far as possible into a replica of itself." Wood's perspective is psychoanalytical, and so he theorizes otherness as repression which "makes impossible ... the full recognition and acceptance of the Other's autonomy and right to exist."[32] Unsurprisingly, children usually end up dead in these horror narratives, or, if possession had been their trouble, restored to their more acceptable state of incorrupt innocence.

One can see how the concept of childhood lends itself to associations with otherness, particularly from the perspective of an adult, but the problem with the dominance of the evil child motif is that it does not allow for different associations to be established within the genre. This then extends otherness to children themselves—both because their representation is limited to this stereotype, and because they are seldom addressed by the horror text as its legitimate audience (and therefore not-other).

In children's film, children are rarely othered because they are the legitimate "self" at the center of the story—both as narrative agents and as legitimately addressed audiences. The problem with combining horror's approach of othering children with the children's film need to *not* other them is obvious, and the clash is visible in *The Watcher*'s representations, particularly in its two main characters, sisters Ellie and Jan.

The younger sister, Ellie, is horror's stereotypical possessed child—so innocent and pure she is almost other-worldly—combined with some comedy relief, as per Disney's tradition. When she is not used as the target of mean jokes, Ellie is the conduit for most of the film's horror, with no suggestion that she is meant as a point of identification for the viewer. She hears voices who "tell her to do things" and is often possessed by spirits who make her spell words backwards (in a Disneyfied "Redrum" scene), speak in different voices, and shout out (mild) abuse. Despite being a main character, Ellie is positioned as a dangerous other: not only does she allow in trespassing spirits, she is also utterly incapable of controlling them, or even of providing much help in understanding them. Her innocence is portrayed as an almost negative force—a thought we find in several horror films, where innocence appears as an ideal that simply cannot be sustained.

The older sister, Jan, serves as the main character and main point of viewer identification—although she, too, exists as other in *The Watcher*'s narrative. Her quest in the film is to find Karen, the lost girl from many decades ago, whom the story frames as a metaphor for purity. Effectively, the film is anchored on a progressive emptying of Jan's self so that Karen can take over. Note, for example, the funfair sequence in which Jan finds herself in the house of mirrors. Her reflection appears as a distorted image, but when she reaches a mirror which reflects accurate but repeated images, her image is replaced (not for the first time in the film) by Karen's. The mirror's "truth" is clear: Jan's identity is "wrong," Karen's is (over and over) "right." Or note the film's climax, when Jan reprises the secret ceremony which took Karen away and shouts loud and clear: "I'm Karen now!" Jan's only defining features are what she lacks (agency, power, identity) and what she is not (Karen, that is, innocent).

Again, this situation is borrowed from horror of the 1960s and 1970s, in which children figure prominently but are never the main concern. These films other childhood in order to use it as a means to explore adult concerns, such as fears of responsibility, of change and the unknown, and adult anxieties about the family and current social values. In *The Watcher*, the same is true: the narrative is not about Jan and Ellie solving a mystery but rather about broader cultural struggles over children and innocence.

This concern would not necessarily be out of place in a Disney film, had it not been for the choice to articulate it through such a negative view of childhood. The foundation of the Disney brand is that children are naturally good and that innocence is always constructive—precisely the views denied by Jan and Ellie in *The Watcher*.[33] To reconcile these issues, Miller and Leetch would have had to engage much more closely with Disney's past and with the horror genre in general—and perhaps, as the next section will show, that is where the real problem lie.

An Anti-Horror Exercise

So far I have argued that Disney's horror efforts were an attempt to bridge its brand of wholesomeness and America's rapidly changing culture. This use of horror brought some ideological difficulties of its own, but the obvious point I haven't yet touched on is that of suitability: horror's connotation with maturity may have meant it could reach a culture less focused on child-like innocence, but how could this use of horror be reconciled with audience expectations of intensity for a children's film? The struggle was mentioned by a few reviewers and summarized neatly in Bill Marshall's review: "It is not surprising, given the contradictory notion of a

Disney horror movie, to find that, for all its atmospheric shots ... *The Watcher in the Woods* is really an anti-horror exercise."[34] Indeed, despite Disney's vigorous investment in the idea of a horror film, the film's production was dominated by efforts to tone it down, even to distance the production from the horror genre entirely.

This push and pull between horror and anti-horror was personified in *The Watcher*'s two producers: Tom Leetch, who wanted it to be "our *Exorcist*," and Ron Miller, who wanted to guard the Disney brand. Most, though not all, of the issues with this production come down to the clashes between their visions of childhood, horror, and suitability.

According to Scott Michael Bosco, Miller "constantly interfered with the filming of scenes, afraid of their intensity ... Leetch would come head to head with Miller fighting for his vision while director John Hough would step aside.... Since Miller was head of the studio, he won his way."[35] Director John Hough has never spoken much of these clashes on set, but he has commented on the pre-production disagreements over the first script, written by Brian Clemens, which was "considered too dark and too threatening and black, as [Disney] called it." As a result of these clashes, another writer, Rosemary Anne Sisson, was brought in "to really lighten the script" and take out "a lot of the most sinister things that Brian had put in."[36]

Actress Kyle Richards has also talked about the frequent clashes between Miller and Leetch. She recounted an especially problematic scene, in which the mother was meant to slap her daughter—"Oh boy did they have a debate about that!"[37] In the end, it was decided that the slap would be replaced with a shoulder shake to tone the scene down. Similar conflicts, leading to last-minute changes, were made at every level of production: script, filming, and editing. The film's opening, for example, was completely changed after the film's first cut was completed. This original sequence is now claimed lost by Disney, but it has been described by Bosco:

> A small girl is seen in the woods playing with a doll. The Watcher's presence (a roving camera POV) sneaks up to the girl from behind. She suddenly turns to the camera and screams, dropping her doll and running off. The camera changes its view from the running girl to the doll. There is a growl, the doll floats upward, becoming air borne, and is swiftly launched against a tree where it is struck by a blue beam of light igniting it. The main titles are played over the burning doll face which melts as the credits continue accompanied by a striking "psycho-like" musical strings.[38]

This striking opening was replaced with a montage of daytime shots of the woods set over quiet instrumental music, which then cuts to a scene with the main characters and their family. There is a clear change in tone here—where the first sequence evoked successful horror films like *What Ever Happened to Baby Jane?* (1962) and *Psycho* (1960), the one that ended up in the final cut primes audience for a far mellower family film instead. Bosco has strongly criticized this decision, judging it hypocritical:

> It would seem Disney would rather have newly animated characters talk with the lingo of crack dealers than showing a doll burning. I suppose it was better to hear an African helicopter pilot say "I'd whip the bitch!," as in the film *Baby: Secret of the Lost Legend* [1985] or for that matter have winged harpies, boldly nude, exposing their pink nipples in close-up as in *Fantasia* [1940].³⁹

Like Tom Leetch, Bosco was a champion of *The Watcher*'s horror angle and saw the potential of pressing on with it. But what he does not consider here is that a burning doll has much more severe ideological connotations than bad language and nudity. Dolls are so closely associated with childhood that to show the extended and explicit destruction of one could raise uncomfortable associations with the destruction of childhood and children's innocence or even, less metaphorically, with child abuse. This interpretation could be extremely damaging to Disney's public image.

And, ultimately, that was *The Watcher*'s biggest obstacle. With no existing reference point for what a suitable children's horror film could look like, the existing Disney brand was a strong limiting factor. When talking about how high the stakes were for this production, John Hough makes this point, too: "Their market was children and a young audience, so they were caught between how scary and sinister the film could be and how frightening…. This was a constant source of discussion, what level we should pitch the film at. I think they did have trepidation at the time."⁴⁰ Nowhere is this trepidation more visible than in the film's ending—or rather, its lack of one. For one reviewer, *The Watcher* contained "one of the most baffling denouements ever."⁴¹ For another the final sequence "looks hopelessly tacked on" with "virtually nothing to do with the character relationships built up in the earlier going."⁴² An insightful comment comes from critic Ed Blank:

> During the [scene], something resembling a crab in seaweed bobbed into view briefly. We knew to expect something macabre, but the film—essentially a ghost story—had introduced at the 11th hour a creature appropriate to a horror flick. In doing so, it broke faith with the audience by violating inner logic.⁴³

Blank's comments get at the root of *The Watcher*'s problem: not simply that Disney couldn't decide how intense the film should be, but that it never fully committed to the film's genre in the first place. Despite the horror framing in the marketing and the production's original idea, Miller's many changes variously took *The Watcher* in different directions—ghost story, mystery adventure, science fiction, and monster movie—without settling on any of them. This conflict of themes and expectations culminated in the final scenes, making the ending unsatisfactory for just about every reviewer, particularly those at the film's first screening.

After that disastrous reception, Disney withdrew the film and hired Harrison Ellenshaw, who had previously worked on *The Black Hole*, to rework the ending for *The Watcher*'s second release. Speaking in interview about this experience, Ellenshaw has revealed that he was handed "roughly 152" ideas for new endings—and "they were all awful." The problem for him was that, in the first version, "[the Watcher] came across too much as a monster. I thought making it more of a 'ghost' film with a Watcher that was less concrete added to [it], even though that's still science fiction."[44] Again, Ellenshaw's goal seems to have been to create distance between *The Watcher* and horror, in order to avoid issues with tone, intensity, and suitability.

Leetch has confirmed that this move was intentional: "We dealt with [the film's last sequence] on a much more basic level as we toned down the film each time." The progressively reduced intensity was done in order to leave no doubts that "there was nothing bad about it" and that "it had not been a bad experience for the young girl." Leetch continued, "[We kept] trying to figure out a way to shoot it pictorially to get it across to the audience that she wasn't harmed. The ending was meant to be an uplifting happy one."

In this same interview, Leetch also suggested the extent of his fights with Miller on the subject: "We had, I must admit, a difficulty in coming to an agreement with the powers that were involved as to what was correct and wasn't.... Our backs were up against a wall and we had to make choices."[45] The sense of disappointment in Leetch's words is echoed by Hough, who still claims that "circumstance" worked against him in *The Watcher*, particularly where the ending was concerned (he was never consulted about the changes made for the second release).[46] "I still feel now if I could get that footage of the alien [claimed lost by Disney] I could still make this alien work," he says wishfully in his DVD commentary. "It took me quite a while to get over this."[47]

By all accounts, *The Watcher in the Woods* was a frustrating production. But it also produced some pioneering work, foreshadowing the struggles with ratings, audiences, representation, and intensity that were to accompany the rest of the children's horror film cycle.

Conclusion: Miller's Last Effort

Despite the *Watcher* debacle, Ron Miller persisted in his belief that children's horror could help Disney's recovery. His motivation led to *Something Wicked This Way Comes*, for which he subtracted "more than ten million dollars from the company's bottom line,"[48] and *The Black Cauldron* after that, a production whose goal was to become an astonishing, generation-defining release but became known as one of Disney's biggest disasters. In many ways, the woes behind *The Black Cauldron* echo and reinforce my points in this chapter.

Like *The Watcher*, *Cauldron* was the focus of great hopes. Not only was it the studio's first PG-rated animation, it was also the first film since *Sleeping Beauty* (1959) to be filmed in 70mm widescreen, using 6-track Dolby sound, and including significant computer animation. Had technology been more advanced at the time, this would also have been the first Disney animation to include full holographic sequences. As with *The Watcher*, the biggest selling point of *Black Cauldron* was its horror angle, which the studio predicted would give it "a broader appeal than any of our animated films for years.... It's scary enough so that people will be hiding under their seats. Our villain, the Horned King, has all the worst qualities of Hitler and Genghis Khan. Most of Disney's animated villains in the past have been fairly comic but this guy is bad through and through."[49]

Instead of reviving Disney's animation, *Cauldron* was the film that nearly killed it.[50] The details of *Cauldron*'s production tribulations have been revealed by Michael Peraza, one of the animators, who recounts the first audience reactions to the film's horror with a mix of resignation and delight: "I knew that the 'un-dead' section would most likely be revolting to some in the audience who would not expect to see a bunch of rotted corpses slowly fermenting and in full glorious, I mean *glorious* color in a Disney animated feature." Tickled by this breach of contract, Peraza goes on to describe how he and his fellow animators sneaked into a test screening to watch the audience reactions when "zombie hour" arrived:

> Right on cue, the doors opened and a mom was angrily leaving with her two wailing children in tow. She was followed by another, and soon there was a sizable exodus of crying kids and upset parents fleeing from the theater. You couldn't hear what they were saying but I doubt it was along the lines of, "If only they could have held longer on the decayed flesh dripping off that cute zombie's face. I can't wait to go out and buy some happy meals of those incredibly entertaining undead fellows."[51]

Amusing as they might have been, these reactions suggest that the conflict

which had plagued *The Watcher in the Woods* still prevailed. And just had it had been then, Disney's response to the upset caused by *Cauldron* was to panic: the film suffered radical cuts right before its release, with direct consequences on the film's narrative coherence. Unsurprisingly, *Cauldron* flunked at the box-office.

All things considered, maybe these flops were a small price to pay to finally be rid of the problem of children's horror. Although Disney's relationship with horror continued,[52] *The Black Cauldron* really was the straw that broke the camel's back, definitively ending Ron Miller's children's horror trial. Shortly after, Michael Eisner took over Disney, and his business style meant that very little of Miller's legacy survived, with one important exception: Touchstone Pictures.

Touchstone had been created in 1984 as a subsidiary of Disney, and it quickly became one of the most instrumental pieces in Disney's diversification plan. The strategy was brilliant in its simplicity: the Disney company and the Disney brand needed to become separate entities. While Touchstone released profitable, more intense films such as the R-rated *Ruthless People* (1986), the Disney studio could focus on rebuilding its image not with the aim of challenging audience expectations (as Miller had done) but strengthening them. The triumph of films like *The Little Mermaid* (1989) and *Beauty and the Beast* (1991), the films known today for kick-starting the Disney renaissance, was not due to their ability to prove Disney could be more than a family brand but rather their capacity to reinforce that it was absolutely, wholeheartedly, a family brand.

The secret to Eisner's success (and to Miller's failure) was the realization that diversification can only exist behind the scenes. When out in the open, Disney must conform to the agreed cultural separations between child and adult audiences and respect the values culturally attached to childhood and family.

The conclusion here is not that change is impossible. Far from it: as this book argues, pre-adolescence was eventually "made," and this disruption was eventually assimilated into cultural norms and social expectations. This early in the game, however, the process of acknowledging and legitimizing a new concept of childhood was not a job for Disney, burdened as it was with the reputation of being a beacon of childhood innocence. As the next chapter will show, change was precipitated by other big players in the Hollywood game, those whose ties to childhood were a bit more flexible, such as Steven Spielberg and Joe Dante.

CHAPTER 2

Parents Strongly Cautioned: PG-13, a Cultural Turning Point

After Disney's kick-off, children's horror began to appear elsewhere in the mainstream. For the most part these were cautious films, intense but not terrifying, dark but not horrific, often not even keen to stake a claim to the horror label at all. *The Dark Crystal* (1982), for instance, was darker than anything else Jim Henson made but still not overtly a horror film. And *The Neverending Story* (1984), while violent and often emotionally intense, was still received as a conventional children's fantasy. But not all titles were this contained. In the case of *Gremlins* and *Indiana Jones and the Temple of Doom*, the use of violence, horror, and gore was strongly contested, especially as these were blockbuster PG-rated family films attached to the brand name of Steven Spielberg. The controversy eventually exploded into one of the most significant events in recent film history: the introduction of the PG-13 classification to the film rating system in 1984.

Not only an industrial milestone, the creation of PG-13 is also critical evidence of the transformation of childhood in America and it embodies the questions at the very heart of the children's horror trend: childhood and its limits, horror and its audience. This is because the ratings themselves exist in culture as an articulation of the social agreements about childhood, its meanings and its boundaries. As such, the shape of the system, not just its individual classification criteria, must always be—or become—aligned with its culture's attitudes. In the early 1980s, when the children's horror cycle started and the only rating options for child-friendly features were G or PG, this relationship was in crisis.

In this chapter I am mostly interested in how PG-13 came to be, and how those debates articulated emerging ideas of childhood and horror. My key aim is to present a different framework by which to understand the history of PG-13 and the ratings system and to firmly anchor this system in the concept of childhood. To do so, I will first review current understandings of the ratings, and then explore the three critical moments in the road to PG-13's creation, represented by *Poltergeist*, *Temple of Doom*, and *Gremlins*. As the content and critical reception of these films clearly demonstrates, the early 1980s saw a quick escalation of tension around the idea of pre-adolescence, with debates often explicitly focused on the problem of associating children with horror. I will also discuss how the PG-13 controversy challenged commonly-held links between specific ratings and the genres of horror and family film, and begin my argument for ratings as a central pillar in horror's genre identity—a point I develop further in chapters 4 and 5.

Discussing Classification: A History of Not Asking All the Questions

The American film rating system was implemented by the Motion Picture Association of America (MPAA) in 1968 as a voluntary industrial agreement to replace the Hays Code. The Code had been in place since the 1930s, and prescribed a list of moral rules about what could and could not be included in film. The ratings system, however, had a more liberal foundation. By using classifications to suggest a film's contents, the system allowed filmmakers to do what they wanted while also letting audiences make their own viewing decisions. This simplified description of the ratings' origins will be familiar to most readers, as the history of the MPAA is relatively well documented. The ratings system itself, however, remains poorly understood—despite its constant presence in popular debate and cultural critique—because ratings debates (in and out of the academy) have been more concerned with challenging the MPAA and its system rather than with understanding its place in contemporary culture.

Usually, the conversation follows one of two angles. The first is censorship. Here, scholars detail the problems surrounding the X and NC-17 ratings, often in relation to distribution and the enforcement of moral rules. One common argument is that the MPAA uses its ratings despotically in order to promote or oppress certain views.[1] The second angle is child protection. Here, critics mainly discuss the scope and competence of the ratings (usually focusing on the lower end of the spectrum, PG and PG-13), sometimes defending a change from age-based ratings to detailed content descriptions. A common argument here is that the MPAA's criteria of suitability is not universal, and therefore the system is both confusing and illegitimate.[2]

These two strands of debate rarely acknowledge one another despite raising very similar concerns. Both are troubled by the MPAA's claim to moral authority, and both are committed to the examination of its considerable power in the film industry. But in spite of the validity of their challenges, these conversations are inevitably unsatisfactory because they sidestep the most important question: what cultural role does a system like this play in American society? Why is it needed, or even wanted?

In truth, participants in ratings debates very seldom question the idea of a ratings system or even the cultural foundations of the MPAA's continued existence. These things are taken for granted, as an intrinsic part of society. And, indeed, those who make these arguments often implicitly agree that ratings are a good thing to have. What gives this attitude away is the lack of conversation around the R rating. The restriction it enforces—no person under 17 allowed without an adult guardian—is not only tolerated but almost universally demanded. Both strands of these ratings debates stem from the same, unacknowledged problem: a perceived dilution of the boundary set by the R rating, that is, of the distinction between what is suitable for children and what is intended for adults only.

Each debate understands this dilution, or corruption, in different ways. For those worried about censorship, the existence of another frontier of maturity above the R rating, such as that imposed by the X or NC-17 classification, is infantilizing. Because this new frontier restricts the distribution of certain films without the excuse of it being for the protection of young children, it is seen as imposing an illegitimate restriction on adults who can make their own decisions. Proponents of this argument do not challenge the necessity of the R rating or take issue with its power to "censure," what they argue is that these restrictions should only ever apply to children.[3]

For those worried about the protection of children, on the other hand, the problem is that the R rating now has less power to impose this distinction. As they correctly point out, the PG-13 rating has allowed young viewers to be exposed to previously-restricted images, themes, and situations—a turn of events which has complicated the segregation between children and adults.[4]

In other words, the main problem with X, NC-17, and PG-13 is that they have questioned the meaning of the R rating. They are problematic because they undermine the notion of an unmistakable and straightforward distinction between children and adults—and the need for this separation is so common-sensical that it is simply never even brought up. In the same way, complicating factors such as the existence of teen audiences tend to be sidestepped: child protection advocates do not see teens as their subject and so don't address them, and those worried about censorship similarly avoid real audiences and focus on more abstract ideas, such as the concept of freedom.

Both the censorship and the child protection debates are important, and worth continuing—but ideally with the awareness that their cornerstone assumption about maturity is unstable. Can we argue clearly about child protection or censorship if our central tenet—that children and adults can be easily distinguished—is a muddy concept? The perils of attempting this move are illustrated by the current preoccupation with the "ratings creep."[5] Supporters of this "creep" hypothesis focus on the PG-13 rating, inevitably concluding that films rated this way are not suitable for children. Their evidence seems strong: the content that now passes under PG-13, particularly violent images, was rated R in previous decades. But their conclusion that the system has therefore become too lenient rests on two erroneous assumptions: first, that the concept of suitability is universal and unchanging; and second, that classifications have a clear and static definition.

The reality of the ratings system, as its critics often note, is that it has never had any tangible criteria. It has always been bound to external factors, such as sociocultural climate, the economy, the film industry's trends, and, naturally, the particular biases of the ratings committee. Far from being denied, this situation is readily acknowledged by the Classification and Rating Association, which describes the aim of the ratings as being to "reflect the current sentiment of parents" and "mirror contemporary concern."[6]

Put simply, ratings cannot have definitive criteria because what they classify is always contextual. Even if the focus is clear—the protection of children—the elements of this goal must remain phrased as questions: What is a child? From what should we protect them?

The flaws in the "ratings creep" hypothesis demonstrate the impossibility of having a single unchanging answer to these questions. Even the hypothesis' very existence is evidence of the desire to avoid these questions and to assume their answers are obvious, universal, unchanging—something which the other debates outlined here also suggest. But pose the questions we must, because without them the ratings system makes no sense.

Taking PG-13 Seriously

Let us ask the big questions, then: what is a child, and from what should we protect them? Even if we understand the ratings system as a flawed instrument, it presents us with an invaluable source to gauge how America has understood these questions. The system itself is the answer. And when seen this way, its significance is hard to understate, as every change suffered by the ratings system becomes an important cultural milestone.

Of these milestones, the most significant is without question the introduction of PG-13 in 1984. Unlike the other changes to the system, this was not a mere tweak. The modifications of 1971 and 1972, for instance, may have changed the name of the PG rating (from GP) and added some clarification to its description, but the category itself remained very much the same. Likewise, the introduction of NC-17 in 1990 aimed not to add a new category but to rebrand a problematic one, the X rating. PG-13, on the other hand, was a change to the very foundation of the system.

In spite of this unique characteristic, PG-13 is the classification we least understand. Take Stephen Vaughn's fantastic history of the ratings, *Freedom and Entertainment*. It is a thorough and insightful volume on every count—except in relation to PG-13. Its creation is mentioned almost in passing, limited to a note about how some Spielberg films had caused controversy and prompted discussion about the distinction "between teenagers and preteens."[7] This comment holds tremendous insight, and yet Vaughn never develops it any further. Like so many other authors, he frames PG-13 as a minor event with no great consequence or meaning because he does not consider the idea of childhood an important part of the ratings conversation.

This oversight does not detract from the overall value of Vaughn's work, but it is a missed opportunity nevertheless. To understand the full extent of the rating system's cultural work, we must acknowledge that childhood is its cornerstone—even if that means dealing with resulting thorny issues, like revising ratings history or adjusting academic understandings of the industry and of certain genres (namely horror) to accommodate the central role played in them by childhood, its definitions, and its boundaries.

In popular discourse, PG-13 is already sometimes acknowledged in this way, especially by those within the film industry. Note how Steven Spielberg recounts the saga of PG-13's introduction:

> The story of that was, I had come under criticism, personal criticism, for both *Temple of Doom* and, you know, *Gremlins*, in the same year. I remember calling Jack Valenti [then the president of the MPAA] and suggesting to him that we need a rating between R and PG, because so many films were falling into a netherworld, you know, of unfairness. Unfair that certain kids were exposed to *Jaws* [rated PG], but also unfair that certain films were restricted, that kids who were 13, 14, 15 should be allowed to see. I suggested, "Let's call it PG-13 or PG-14, depending on how you want to design the slide rule," and Jack came back to me and said, "We've determined that PG-13 would be the right age for that temperature of movie." So I've always been very proud that I had something to do with that rating.[8]

This comment, given in an interview almost as an aside, is extraordinarily significant. Spielberg not only signals PG-13 as an important event in film history but he also explains it as a correction to the system. Specifically, he describes PG-13 as a way to match the system with a new understanding of childhood, to update it so that it could recognize the difference between children and teenagers and delineate a transitional demographic between the two. Not only does Spielberg highlight the connection between ratings and childhood, he also stresses its links with audience expectations of film genres, suggesting that PG-13 was not, as it is usually claimed by scholars and historians, "a direct response to charges that the MPAA was soft on violence."[9]

But even Spielberg's comment carefully circumvents discussion of the finer points and implications of this update. This is clear in his choice of illustration: *Jaws*, a film never involved in significant suitability debates and also almost a decade old by the time the MPAA began to consider introducing a new rating. To frame PG-13 around *Jaws* is to explain the controversies around *Gremlins* and *Temple of Doom* as debates about horror slipping through the system's gaps—in other words, as rating mistakes. This changes the PG-13 debate into a confirmation of what is already agreed (i.e., horror is generally unsuitable for children), and avoids confronting the struggles of adapting to new conceptions of childhood and changed expectations of genre.

As I argue here, the problem with the MPAA in the early 1980s was not the way it attributed ratings or even the criteria for each classification. It was the scope of the ratings system itself: with no way to signal suitability for different kinds of children (that is, young children and pre-teens separately), the system no longer described childhood as most Americans saw it. PG-13 was not a way to make the system more efficient; it was a rewrite of America's answer to the question, what is a child?

The *Poltergeist* Before the Storm

The road to PG-13 starts with *Poltergeist* and its uncontroversial PG rating. Technically, there was a "controversy" behind the film (it was initially rated R for intense sound effects and successfully appealed for a PG) but the event is remembered more as an instance of film trivia than as an important moment, in great part because it had no bearing on the film's marketing, reception, or success. If people noticed this was a PG-rated horror film they certainly did not mind; there was no upheaval, no debate, and, most puzzlingly given the wide recognition of *Poltergeist* as a horror film, no reservations about its effect on young viewers. The contrast with *The Watcher in the Woods* is remarkable. What was different about *Poltergeist*, and how was it related to shifting notions of childhood and horror?

The best place to begin is Dave Kehr's succinct retrospective review:

> This Steven Spielberg–produced horror film (1982) neatly inverts the antifamily themes of shockers that were being made during the same period (including those of its nominal director, Tobe Hooper—*The Texas Chainsaw Massacre* and *The Funhouse*), presenting a squad of spooks who help a giggly, dope-smoking young couple mature into the responsible parents they ought to be by kidnapping their daughter. Though the shocks are well conveyed, it's the sweetness that lingers, making this the first cute and cuddly entry in the genre.[10]

Kehr's review was written with the benefit of hindsight and the knowledge of how *Poltergeist* would be remembered in film history, but his summary is nevertheless telling of the way this film has been interpreted. Even if Kehr does not downplay *Poltergeist*'s relationship with the horror genre (and even legitimizes it by positioning *Poltergeist* as a response to the genre trends of its period), he also effectively describes it as a family drama and, moreover, one closely associated with Spielberg's well-known affinity for sentimental morality.

What is intriguing about this juxtaposition is that it does not seem to faze Kehr in the slightest—and the nonchalance is not simply retrospective. Kim Newman, a contemporary critic not usually effusive about child-friendly horror, called *Poltergeist* "the horror equivalent of the exuberant, harmless, greatest show on Earth genre blockbusters [such as] *Star Wars, Raiders of the Lost Ark* [and] *E.T.: The Extra-Terrestrial*"—a description intended not as a backhanded compliment but as genuine praise. A recognition of *Poltergeist*'s links to the world of childhood pervades Newman's commentary on the film, and yet he never once dismisses its claim to the horror genre. On the contrary, he affirms it as "the only successful, non-spoof horror film in which nobody gets killed."[11]

Together with the lack of public controversy, what these reviews suggest is a very efficient framing process at work within *Poltergeist*. Some of this comes from the narrative: although there are child characters in prominent places and the film generally deals with child-friendly sensibilities, the heroes of the story are the parents, and they provide a constant point of identification for adult viewers. But the bigger reason why *Poltergeist* successfully conveyed the possibility of family-friendly horror was that it spoke a language its audience already understood.

Even if *Poltergeist* suggests something quite different from the norm to horror (and family) audiences, it is nevertheless entirely framed in pre-existing discourses to which the names Spielberg and Hooper serve as shorthand. In this sense, it is not insignificant that Hooper directed and Spielberg produced. In the director's role, Hooper's brand gives audiences the main framework to understand *Poltergeist*. As Hooper had never directed a family film and was best known for *The Texas Chainsaw Massacre* (1974), this framework would have been, unquestionably, the horror genre—and this is the conviction we see in the critical reception.

Spielberg's brand also provides a framework to reading *Poltergeist*, but because he appears in the role of producer, usually less associated with creative direction, the family-friendly matrix receives only secondary importance. If Hooper's brand served as pre-interpretation, Spielberg's acts more as a forewarning: you are about to watch a horror film, but it won't be the most intense you've ever seen. The subordination of the family genre to the horror genre is where we see most clearly the contrast with *The Watcher in the Woods*. Where varying degrees of intensity within horror is something already established in horror discourse and accepted by fans, horror content in a children's film, Disney's default framework, was uncommon.

The ready-made interpretation suggested by the interplay of brand names explains how *Poltergeist* was able to introduce the idea of younger audiences as an acceptable part of the horror genre, but it does not directly address questions of childhood or even suitability. For clarification on this point, we should turn to Vincent Canby's review. Like other critics, Canby spends some time decoding *Poltergeist*'s hybridity, and confirms that it is "much closer in spirit and sensibility" to Spielberg than to Hooper, particularly in relation to Spielberg's ability to "preserve the wonderment of childhood."[12] But unlike most other reviewers, Canby takes this observation to its logical conclusion and reads *Poltergeist* as a children's horror film. He writes:

> [*Poltergeist* is] a marvellously spooky ghost story that may possibly scare the wits out of very small children and offend those parents who believe that kids should be protected from their own, sometimes savage imaginations. I suspect, however, that there's a vast audience of teen-agers and others who'll love this film. Indeed, *Poltergeist* often sounds as if it had been dictated by an exuberant twelve-year-old.[13]

In this short paragraph, Canby demonstrates clear awareness of the bigger questions held in *Poltergeist*'s hybridity. Not only does he understand the problem of children's horror, namely that it will offend people with a particular view of childhood, he also points to a problem in the ratings system's inability to differentiate between "very small children" and that "exuberant twelve-year-old." This view of childhood is one Canby had already suggested, if less assertively, in his review of *The Watcher in the Woods*,[14] and in both instances he was virtually the only critic to raise this point. The lack of agreement from other critics stresses that this view of childhood was not yet the majority (and suggests Canby's remarkable perception), but it is also evidence of *Poltergeist*'s successful framework.

The reason *Poltergeist* could plant new ideas without alienating audiences as *The Watcher* had done was that its respect of established norms masked most of its ambiguity. By meeting expectations first and innovating second, *Poltergeist* seduced young audiences without openly targeting them, challenged horror's tropes without destroying them, and subverted the ratings system without breaking its rules. Successful as this strategy was for *Poltergeist*, rapidly increasing ambiguity around childhood quickly rendered it impossible to use, as my discussion of the next two films will show.

Temple of Doom: The Children Will Scream with Delighted Horror!

The first actual controversy in the PG-13 timeline comes with *Indiana Jones and the Temple of Doom*, a family adventure from Spielberg and George Lucas which shocked its audience with surprising levels of violence, gore and frightening scenes. The controversy it provoked is well-known, and its memory lies behind today's understanding that this particular film was "instrumental in motivating ... the PG-13 rating"[15] and that the new classification was a response to violence.[16] It is true that *Temple of Doom* features unprecedented intensity for a PG-rated adventure but its critical reception suggests something different was the cause of public outrage, something already foreshadowed by discussions of *Poltergeist*: the PG rating was no longer an effective signal of suitability because it failed to differentiate small children from pre-adolescents.

The first important point to note is that concerns about the violence in *Temple of Doom* were not perceived to be a major issue by most critics of the time. Roger Ebert, for example, who has never been shy about voicing moral concerns,[17] wrote a glowing review for *Temple of Doom*, without a single mention of the film's violence or its surrounding controversy. Similarly, the main point of contention for Todd McCarthy of *Variety* was not the gore but Spielberg's move "away from nifty stories in favor of one big effect after another." On the specific topic of children and violence, McCarthy had only this to say:

> Kids 10–12 upwards will eat it all up, of course, but many of the images, particularly those involving a gruesome feast of live snakes, fried beetles, eyeball soup and monkey brains, and those in the sacrificial ceremony, might prove extraordinarily frightening to younger children who, indeed, are being catered to in this film by the presence of the adorable 12-year-old Ke Huy Quan.[18]

Although this paragraph suggests some concern over the film's address to young people, what is most striking is that McCarthy does not perceive young children as the target audience, and therefore frames these worries as peripheral. This same nuanced understanding of film audiences (and of *Temple of Doom* audiences in particular) is also found in Vincent Canby's review and is similarly used to justify a lack of commitment to a critique of the film's violence. Note the way Canby opens his review:

> If you've ever been a child or, barring that, if you've ever been around children, ages 7 to about 11, you may remember the sort of game in which each child attempts to come up with the vilest ... meal he can think of.... The children squeal with delighted horror as each new dish is described, finding it all delicious fun, though any adults in the vicinity will probably feel sick.
> This may well be the public's reaction to Steven Spielberg's exuberantly tasteless and entertaining "Indiana Jones and the Temple of Doom," which ... already is causing a ruckus because of its PG rating.[19]

It's difficult not to establish a parallel here with *Poltergeist* and "those parents who believe that kids should be protected from their own, sometimes savage imaginations."[20] Indeed, the "ruckus" around *Temple of Doom* is an escalation of what Canby had already predicted for *Poltergeist*, and, as before, he does not seem to personally support it. Even though Canby addresses these concerns and explicitly warns parents that *Temple of Doom* "contains a lot of explicit violence," his warning is at odds with the way he then describes the film's use of this violence. The following passage, for instance, reads not as a critique but as a defense of Spielberg's choices:

> There's no doubt about it—the movie, in addition to being endearingly disgusting, is violent in ways that may scare the wits out of some small patrons. The kidnapped Indian children, when finally found, are seen being flogged as they slave away deep in the maharajah's mines, though the flogging is so exaggerated that it seems less real than cartoon-like.
>
> There's a vivid sequence in which a man, being offered to Kali, is slowly lowered into a fiery pit, but not before a priest has removed the victim's heart with his bare fingers. This, however, is not only a film-making trick but a trick within the film itself, something that older children may understand more readily than their adult guardians. Nevertheless, it's something to give parents pause.

As in his opening paragraph, Canby stresses the differences between child and adult interpretations of *Temple of Doom*. Moreover—as he had done for *Poltergeist*, and echoing McCarthy's review—Canby distinguishes between different kinds of child audiences: while *Temple of Doom* has strong affinity with the play of children aged seven to eleven,[21] it could frighten "some small patrons." Once again, Canby's position is not that violence is inappropriate in children's film but that it may be inappropriate for *children below a certain age.*

And this was the majority's view on the matter. The trend in critical reception was not to challenge *Temple of Doom* as a film unreasonably violent but rather to praise it as good entertainment for *some* children, namely those in the pre-teen age range. The critics who prioritized this audience as the film's main target (Canby, McCarthy, Kael, and others) consistently used their reviews to deflect the idea that the film was unsuitable for all children by noting that young children are not the film's primary audience. This explicit distinction between older and younger child audiences does not express a worry about children's films becoming more violent or about the MPAA's standards of ratings. Instead, the fact that most critics felt the need to identify *Temple of Doom*'s target audience suggests a desire to clarify the PG rating and correct a weakness not in the rating process but in the system itself.

This recognition of a flaw in the system is the main insight in *Temple of Doom*'s reception. This was a film which respected the rules of the family adventure genre, but failed to comply with the limits of the rating expected for that genre. This was a film, in other words, that spoke the language of children's entertainment (and, given its success, the language of its contemporary culture)—but not that of the ratings system.

This communication obstacle was eventually recognized by the film's studio. In a move reminiscent of Disney's efforts with *The Watcher*, Paramount inserted a last-minute warning into its *Temple of Doom* campaigns: "This film may be too intense for younger children." Spielberg was also moved to do some damage control in the public eye, repeatedly clarifying that he would not let a ten-year-old child see the film's most violent sequences.[22] These clarifications, in addition to those already provided by reviewers, may or may not have been effective in soothing parental reactions, but they are certainly evidence of pre-adolescence as a growing cultural issue, and they prepare the way for the climax of this struggle later in the year, when *Gremlins* attacked American cinemas.

Gremlins Against America

Because of its high-profile controversy, *Temple of Doom* has often been called "the last straw ... that broke the back of support for the single PG rating."[23] But, as I have argued, the complaints around the film were limited to specific population groups. As I move toward the last PG-13 instigator, my goal now is to present *Gremlins* as the culmination of this process and to suggest that the real last straw was not violence or intensity, but the explicit association of children with horror.

Unlike *Poltergeist* and *Temple of Doom*, *Gremlins* is an extremely conflicted text, so I need to split my analysis into two sections. In the first, I will look at its promotion campaigns to note how they tried to avoid the issues of presenting *Gremlins* as a PG family feature. In the second part, I will take a close look at the critical reception to further explain why *Gremlins* posed an ultimatum to the ratings system. As this analysis will show, *Gremlins* represents a radical turning point in understandings of the children's film. *Gremlins* was not a benevolent kind of horror, nor was it simply an envelope-pushing adventure story, but a moral conundrum: at best, a film which expanded the horizons of child-oriented entertainment; at worst, a film intent on violating the very concept of childhood and, through it, of America itself.

Horror? Don't Mention It

As with *Temple of Doom*, the controversy around *Gremlins* started with worried parents. As Joe Dante explained in an interview, "I think people were upset [to have taken] a 4-year-old to see *Gremlins*, thinking it's going to be a cuddly, funny animal movie and then seeing that it turns into a horror picture."[24] Indeed, although the filmmakers attempted a balance between horror and family entertainment in the pre-production process, the marketing campaigns avoided the notion of genre hybridism altogether: all horror elements were disregarded, and *Gremlins* was presented entirely in accordance to the expectations of a PG-rated family film.

A commonly mentioned bit of *Gremlins* trivia is that Chris Columbus's original script told a darker story, one with a much higher kill count (including Mrs. Peltzer, Billy's girlfriend, the young boy next door, and the dog), and no friendly Gizmo to give audiences respite. Columbus's imagined film followed a much more traditional horror blueprint, both in relation to its intensity but also its connection between evil and children, represented by the gremlins. It was, in many ways, a Terrible Child story in monster-movie clothes.

When Spielberg and Dante took on the project, many of their changes were concerned with toning down this aspect of the film. For example, in one of the few death scenes that was kept, the script called for the science teacher to be stabbed in the face with several needles. This was changed to a single needle on the buttocks, dramatically altering the tone of the moment.[25] The most important change, however, was Gizmo. In the original script, the mogwai quickly turned into the leader of the gremlins pack, but Spielberg wanted to keep him an ally all the way through. His character was thus split into two: Gizmo, the good mogwai, and Stripe, the evil gremlin. Joe Dante credits this decision with making the film "much more accessible"[26]—quite possibly because it distanced *Gremlins* from the Terrible Child films of the 1970s, which pitted children against adults and often climaxed in infanticide. Keeping Gizmo cuddly brought the film's message more in line with that of *E.T.: The Extra-Terrestrial* (1982) and similar family narratives.

As is obvious from the end result (and its reception), these changes did not sever *Gremlins*'s ties to the horror genre. This is important because it shows that the filmmakers' intention had never been to take a horror script and make it into a family film. Rather, the goal was to find a balance between the film's horror and family elements, by softening the harder motifs and highlighting the softer ones. In other words, their aim and their challenge was to find an appropriate children's horror sensibility.

This balance between children and horror could have been the starting point for the film's marketing. As *Poltergeist* illustrated, existing discourses could be used to illustrate the character and intensity of a film. But if such attempts were made for *Gremlins*, they must have quickly been abandoned as there are no traces left in the promotional material.

The trailers and television advertisements, for example, flipped *Poltergeist*'s discursive strategy on its head by not allowing Dante's name (associated with horror) and creative position (director) to provide the framework for the film. On the contrary, the trailers opened with the words "Steven Spielberg presents," deliberately evoked the style of *E.T.*'s promotion,[27] and moreover highlighted all the things audiences would expect from a Spielberg film in the early 1980s, such as comedy, romance, adventure, and a cuddly alien friend. Not only were all the threatening scenes omitted or presented humorously, Dante's only mention came at the very end, when audiences would have already formed an understanding of the kind of film *Gremlins* would be. Thus, while the ads were not necessarily misleading about this being a family film, they hardly left any room for audiences to realize that this was *also* a horror film.

The merchandise used the same approach and was dominated by Gizmo's figure. He featured on the box of *Gremlins* breakfast cereal, jigsaw puzzles, stationery, apparel, stickers and transfers, and he was sold as a stuffed animal, action figure, singing doll, in wind-up cars, and in an array of bendable figurines, water hatchers, and other assorted toys. Fast food chain Hardee's sold five *Gremlins* story books and records, described in the style of children's books as "stories about Gizmo and his friends," despite being straight adaptations of the film's narrative. Further testament to the mogwai's enduring popularity was the Gizmo Furby, an interactive electronic pet released in 1999 by Tiger Electronics.

But this Gizmomania was selective. According to the merchandise, Gizmo is a gentle and cheerful cooing little creature; yet in the film, Gizmo spends most of his time weeping, screaming, and trembling in distress. Contrary to his merchandise persona, film–Gizmo has little time for singing or looking cute as he is always in situations of extreme danger (like being pinned to a darts board and used as a target), in a state of overwhelming anxiety (caused by the "bright light!" and the concerning development of the other creatures), or in the process of killing one of his "children," Stripe. All of this was left out of the merchandising, just as it had been left out of the trailer.

Images of the other gremlins underwent a similar process of selection. As Pauline Kael describes them, film-gremlins are "aggressively vulgar … children of the night"[28]—but merchandise-gremlins are simply fun, at worst a bit immature. In obviously secondary place to Gizmo, the gremlins feature mostly in stationery and party items, such as those produced by Hallmark Ambassador, or funny action figures, like those made by LJN— and in every instance the film's drunk and murderous vandals are depicted as harmless clowns.

This domestication was extended even to the film's villain, Stripe.

Though he is still portrayed as the opponent in many of the toys and action figures, he is also frequently relegated to the background (as in an action figure set by LJN that lists him as a nameless "gremlin"), or he appears as a thrill-seeking prankster instead of an evil monster—"Where's the party?" he asks in an Hallmark card invitation. The disparity between film–Stripe and merchandise–Stripe is so strong that one of the advertisements even points it out: "If you've seen the new movie *Gremlins* ... you know how troublesome the gremlins can be. But at Hallmark, our gremlins are as tame as Gizmo."

Again, these depictions are not entirely misleading. Gizmo is indeed fairly cute, and the gremlins are indeed funny. But, as in the trailer, this laser focus on family-friendliness left very little space for audiences to recognize and accept *Gremlins*'s identity as a horror film. These decisions of course made sense in the context of the market, where cuddly toys still sold better than scary figurines. But they also reveal the difficulty of imagining and communicating the idea of a children's horror film in the mid-1980s.

A striking example of this difficulty is the extent to which marketing relied on Christmas themes. Taking advantage of the film's winter setting, the main lines of merchandise were released for the holiday season, replete with images of Gizmo dressed as Santa Claus and of the caroling gremlins. Certainly there is nothing unusual about a desire to capitalize on Christmas sales, but this marketing decision was at odds with the film's box office tactic: *Gremlins* was released in the summer because the filmmakers wished to avoid the Christmas film label.[29] There was, moreover, another popular holiday much closer to the film's release date—Halloween. And yet, despite the many horror elements in the film, no scary toys were ever made nor were there plans for a Halloween line. This Christmas/Halloween separation corresponds culturally to a family/horror distinction. And the choice of one over the other—rather than both at once—worked not only as a branding exercise but also as an antidote to criticism.[30] The notion that Christmas and horror are incompatible is so strong that when *Gremlins* was given a restricted rating in the United Kingdom (a "15"), Warner's vice-president Julian Senior came to its defense with a simple statement: "I think it is a lovely Christmas movie."[31]

The discrepancy in approach between the filmmakers and the promotional team is critical. Where Spielberg and Dante seem to have been in search of children's horror—and the potential of their hunch was validated by the film's box office success—the team in charge of marketing and promotion seems to have been warier of the limits imposed by a PG rating. This not only suggests a cultural reluctance to pair children with horror but also reveals the constraints of the market: without an established genre identity or a clear rating, it was unsurprising that business people chose to speak the language they already understood and shared with consumers—that of the family film. As we will see in the next section, this caused problems greater than those it solved.

Two Thumbs Down

Whereas *Gremlins* marketing had attempted to sidestep the problem of genre hybridism, viewers confronted with the realities of the film (and primed by the marketing campaigns to expect something else) found *Gremlins* hard to stomach—much more so than *Temple of Doom*. As I will argue here, the difference was that, textually and ideologically, *Gremlins* took the form a horror film. That this identity came stamped with a PG rating was the real problem, raising questions not only about suitability but also about the stability of the cultural reference points of American audiences, including the definition of children's film and of the PG rating and also of innocence, childhood, and America itself.

The shift in tone between the violence of *Temple of Doom* and that of *Gremlins* is insightfully illustrated in Vincent Canby's review. Similar to what he had done for *Temple of Doom*, Canby warns parents about *Gremlins* not being "ideal entertainment for younger children" despite its PG rating—only this time he refuses to excuse the violence in the film. On the contrary, Canby describes *Gremlins* as "seriously mean," as a film which "[attacks its] young audience as mercilessly as the creatures attack the characters." He writes:

> I've no idea how children will react to the sight of a Kingston Falls mom, carving knife in hand, decapitating one gremlin and shoving another into the food processor, head first. Will they laugh when Billy Peltzer, the film's idealized, intentionally dopey, 20-year-old hero, is threatened by a gremlin with a chainsaw and then stabbed by a gremlin with a spear gun? Will they cheer when Billy blows up the Kingston Falls movie theater, where the gremlins, now resembling an average kiddie matinee crowd, are exuberantly responding to "Snow White and the Seven Dwarfs?"[32]

These are serious questions, brought forth from a genuine discomfort with the film's message. What we read here is not just a concern that the film's violence might be too intense but a specific concern about the domestic context in which this violence occurs: a mother brutally killing gremlins in the family kitchen; the film's hero graphically attacked by the gremlins he kept as pets; and lastly, the violent death of gremlins during the screening of a Disney film, after these same gremlins have been narratively equated to children. These are not simply instances of violence on screen; they are scenes of violence committed against children and, perhaps more disturbingly still, by children against the family.

Canby was not the only one to read *Gremlins* this way. The film itself emphasizes the links between gremlins and children (as in the *Snow White* sequence), as did the marketing campaigns. One of the posters for the theatrical release, for instance, depicts one of the gremlins as an American schoolchild (complete with baseball glove and Gizmo lunchbox) under the caption "See 'Gremlins' again before you hit the books!" The tagline in the main poster could equally read as a description of children, particularly in a horror film context: "Cute. Clever. Mischievous. Intelligent. Dangerous."

Though children have a history of monstrous representations in horror, understanding the gremlins as children is nevertheless particularly challenging because, as Canby reminds us in his review, these scenes are addressed at child viewers too—and, unlike in *The Watcher in the Woods*, the purpose of this otherness and horror is not merely cautionary. How will these children feel, Canby asks, when they see these depictions of themselves? And what does it mean that these representations have been sanctioned by us, the parents, adults, rating experts, and filmmakers?

Other critics addressed the same questions. See Alexander Walker's flaming review:

> [*Gremlins*] is a black adult joke at the expense of innocence, all the more disturbing because children have been lured to it in America by its "Parental Guidance" rating, though the kids with me in the cinema sat with the stiff, contorted limbs of coma victims as the movie turned from being a homely comedy into a house-of-horrors nightmare.[33]

Like Canby, Walker questions the film's suitability for young audiences, but he also clearly identifies the source of the problem: the breach of the boundaries set by the R rating on the horror genre and its unwelcome trespassing into the realm of "homely comedies," the PG rating. Walker presents the issue loosely as a concern over media effects but the root of his concern is obviously much broader, as it had been with Canby. As Walker himself states, "*Gremlins* snatches the security blanket away from everything that has been held holy in children's movies—home, family, Christmas, religion and even the beloved memory of Walt Disney."[34]

This is where *Gremlins* differs so radically and significantly from the other PG-13 instigators. It simply does not honor the sanctity of home, family, or any of the things understood as intrinsic to the family film and the PG rating. On the contrary, its message, as summarized by critic David Edelstein, is that "too many gizmos are rupturing the nuclear family; our children are out of control; Christmas kills."[35] This was not the message that audiences found in *Poltergeist* or *Temple of Doom*.

While *Poltergeist* revolved entirely around notions of childhood innocence, critics felt that the gremlins were "children as seen by those who don't like them. Little devils, we say."[36] And while *Temple of Doom* sought to create and elevate a family unit around Indiana Jones, *Gremlins* systematically destroys every family it creates. Note the flow of its narrative: the supposed patriarch, Mr. Peltzer, is not only far from a heroic type but also quickly reduced to a comic relief character, entirely dependent on his son Billy for basic survival. But Billy, too, is soon upstaged by his figurative son, Gizmo, who is in turn overpowered (if temporarily) by the gremlins, establishing a chain of fathers made redundant by their progressively less innocent children. Mother figures likewise degenerate, from strong Mrs. Peltzer to troubled Kate, to no mother at all with Gizmo and the gremlins.

There is a hint of a working family unit in Billy, Kate, and Gizmo, but, as Pauline Kael notes, the film's tone is too sarcastic to openly praise them, leaving audiences unsure whether Bill and Kate "are meant to be a charming pair or a spoof of dopey wholesomeness."[37] Cynicism is, in fact, the engine of *Gremlins*'s narrative, and it is sharply aimed at the notion that wholesomeness is at the heart of American identity. As Ebert put it, *Gremlins* "haunt[s] the whole tradition of Norman Rockwell's Christmas, American Hollywood movie,"[38] or, to use Pauline Kael's wording, *Gremlins* "defiles [a] vision of the good American life"; it defiles "Frank Capraland."[39] The most comical illustration of this target is the character of Mr. Futterman, a family man with unshakeable faith in American values. As he enthusiastically claims, the American way "can take anything!" Anything, that is, except gremlins, who later in the film take the wheel of Mr. Futterman's American-made plough and run it over its enthusiastic owner, his wife and their Christmas-decorated home. In many ways, this scene encapsulates the film's approach: it thoroughly paints a picture of America as idealized in a thousand family films before it but only so it can destroy it.

Many, if not all, of these provocations seem to have been meant as tongue-in-cheek commentary, but their presence in a children's film was nevertheless troubling to the majority of critics—as evidenced by the curious insistence on reading the film's tone as the result of a creative clash between Spielberg and Dante, despite such a clash having no basis in reality or rumor. Kael described Dante's tone as "(perhaps deliberately) uncertain"[40] while Vincent Canby wrote about the "schizoid" personality of this "wise-acre mixture of ... movie genres and movie sensibilities."[41] For Newman the film was "a struggle between the world views of Spielberg and Dante,"[42] and Edelstein, rather more bluntly, summed it all up as "Dante shitting all over Spielberg's never-never land, and Spielberg sugaring that excrement."[43]

The fabrication of this antagonism is important because the opposition is not between the persons of Dante and Spielberg but between what they represent: Dante for horror, the R rating, and anarchic ideology; Spielberg for the family film, the PG rating, and traditional family values. Ideologically, both *Poltergeist* and *Temple of Doom* fit neatly into the second of these categories, without ambiguity. But *Gremlins*, as a deliberately hybrid creation—as a children's horror film—sat uncomfortably on the fence, thus threatening the established order of both the horror genre (and the R rating) and the family genre (and the PG rating).

The contemporary difficulty in fully understanding *Gremlins*, its approach, or its audience makes it clear why the PG-13 rating was necessary. Remember Walker's pointed critique: films like *Gremlins* are "a black adult joke at the expense of innocence, all the more disturbing because [of their PG rating]." They are films that "[snatch] the security blanket away from everything that has been held holy in children's movies."[44] Again, the PG-13 rating was created not so the system could signal violence more precisely. It was, instead, to save this "security blanket," to preserve innocence, to rescue the family film and to maintain a Capraesque ideal of American life—in other words, to keep the meaning of the PG rating (and through it, of childhood) as intact as possible in the face of a changing culture.

Conclusion

When PG-13 was officially introduced, it became the clearest and most tangible marker that pre-adolescence had become part of America's cultural vocabulary. Though its specific details were still to be settled, the concept was no longer the abstraction it had been in *The Watcher* but a demographic with clear boundaries, and even a specific age as a cut-off point. Because of this, PG-13 was, in many ways, the end of these worries over innocence and suitability. The "unfair netherworld" between PG and R described by Spielberg was no longer a problem, and the set age of the rating made it clear to parents and guardians what kind of intensity to expect. PG-13 also helped establish a more cohesive identity for children's horror films by setting the standards for violence and intensity—though maybe not in the ways that might have been anticipated, as chapters 6 and 7 will explore.

But while PG-13 made this new childhood visible, it also made it impossible to ignore the repercussions of the broader cultural change it embodied. As the reception in this chapter showed, America was ready to accept different stages of childhood only insofar as the overarching ideal of childhood innocence did not perish—and, as it was soon apparent, this was more of a challenge than it first seemed.

A good summary of my argument here, and of these implications, can be found in Ebert's review of another PG-rated Spielberg film with close ties to the children's horror cycle: *The Goonies*, released one year after PG-13. "There used to be children's movies and adult movies," Ebert pondered. "Now Spielberg has found an in-between niche, for young teenagers who have fairly sophisticated tastes in horror." Ebert at once acknowledges the pre-teen audience, recognizes their affinity with the horror genre, and supports the shift toward establishing this intermediate level of intensity. Echoing Canby, he also goes to great lengths to praise this new and nuanced understanding of childhood:

> "Goonies," like "Gremlins," walks a thin line between the cheerful and the gruesome, and the very scenes the adults might object to are the ones the kids will like the best: Spielberg is congratulating them on their ability to take the heavy-duty stuff.... His technique is to take his thirteen- and fourteen-year-olds and let them act a little older than their age. It's more refreshing than the old Disney technique, which was to take characters of all ages and have them behave as if they were twelve.[45]

Optimistic as it is, Ebert's review also notes the thorns in this development. His doubt is revealed in the comment that closes the review: though *Goonies* is an exciting film, it "doesn't have the lift of a film like *E.T.* It has the high energy without the sweetness." Ebert then repeats his comparison of *Goonies* to *Gremlins* and contrasts the two with Spielberg's earlier work, *E.T.* and *Close Encounters*, films that "didn't simply want us to feel, but also to wonder, and to dream."[46] These are obvious references to innocence, and it is telling that Ebert could not leave them out but actually gave them a place of honor in his review. He is, of course, right: neither *Goonies* nor *Gremlins*, nor any of the other children's horror titles, engage the viewer in dreams of innocence. Their goal is explicitly the opposite, to move viewers away from the innocence of childhood and into the experience of adolescence.

Ebert's longing for innocent children's film is the symptom of a philosophical dilemma. On the one hand, he wants to accept pre-adolescence as a moment of increased maturity, and pre-teens as children to whom it would be improper to condescend, but, on the other hand, he still values innocence in childhood and mourns its loss. Ebert's review therefore encapsulates my observations in this chapter and foreshadows my claims to come. PG-13 was the result of important social changes, and it did solve the issues caused by ambiguity—but it also meant that change was now impossible to ignore and that all of its consequences would have to be immediately addressed. Some of these are plainly suggested by Ebert: does pre-adolescence mean the end of childhood? Is this it for the children's film? What will happen to values like innocence, and how will American identity adapt?

And there were other questions to resolve, namely in relation to the horror genre, its identity, and its cultural position. Up to this point, the genre had defined itself almost entirely in opposition to the PG rating. What were the possibilities, the rewards and, more pressingly, the dangers of an unrestricted rating? Would horror water itself down to fit into the mainstream? I will begin to address these questions in the next chapter, as I consider the immediate aftermath of the PG-13 rating and unravel any sense of resolution the present chapter might have established.

CHAPTER 3

Horror vs. Children: Confronting Young Audiences After PG-13

The period between the introduction of PG-13 in 1984 and the end of the decade was the most prolific of the children's horror cycle, producing iconic titles such as *The Gate* and *The Monster Squad* (1987), and other famous releases like *Invaders from Mars* (1986), *Lady in White* (1988), and *Little Monsters* (1989). This increase in output was in no small part a consequence of the new rating, which ended the suitability debate, but it also signaled that the industry had moved toward a recognition of pre-teens as a separate demographic and was now explicitly catering to them.[1]

In regards to children's horror, this meant discarding the Otherness template, along with its anxieties about childhood, and embracing hero characters with fears and hopes appropriate to a real child: coping with family dynamics, making friends, building a new adolescent identity, becoming more independent, and coming to terms with (or challenging) their lack of power in an adult-oriented world. These themes were, moreover, framed clearly within the context of pre-adolescence: they used young adolescent actors, mentioned the words pre-teen or tween, and displayed a stronger grasp of the appropriate level of intensity for this age (which was in turn supported by the newly-improved ratings).

In this new, more clearly-targeted form, children's horror posed few challenges to childhood and innocence, even as it maintained its hybrid genre label. From a horror perspective, however, its presence in the mainstream was now more uncomfortable than ever. Can horror really exist this peacefully in the "safe" domain of PG and PG-13? Once again, the real issue was not the quality or intensity of these films but the ratings system itself: in the process of answering previous questions about childhood and horror, the PG-13 classification radically altered the mechanism through which the horror genre gained its meaning, status, and legitimacy.

My focus in this chapter is the immediate fallout of PG-13's introduction. Primarily, my aim here is to understand how and why PG-13 developed an industrial and cultural identity in the late 1980s and to appreciate what this meant for popular conceptions of the horror genre. On a secondary level, this chapter also addresses the ways in which PG-13's identity was tied to newly-established ideas about childhood and pre-adolescence, and how these were circulated through children's horror. I make three intertwined arguments here.

The first refers to the film industry in a broad sense: I propose that PG-13 very quickly became established as a general mainstream category, with no attachment to any particular demographic. PG-13 thus became an updated version of the old PG rating: suitable for all general releases, as PG had been, but without negative connotations about immaturity or a lack of "edge."

The second argument refers to the horror genre specifically: I contend that horror fans rejected children's horror mainly because of its associations with unrestricted categories. There was significant tension particularly when children's horror was rated PG-13, as these titles clearly linked horror with both young audiences and the mainstream, and so corrupted the genre's values and authenticity.

Finally, the third argument concerns childhood: I note how much more precise notions of pre-adolescence became during this period, both as representations within children's horror and as part of the reception discourses around these films. This is the moment where "tweens" are acknowledged as their own demographic by both filmmakers and audiences—albeit not yet unanimously.

To support these arguments, the chapter will begin with an overview of PG-13's use between 1984 and 1989 across all genres to unveil trends in the MPAA's practice. Only after this analysis will I zoom in on horror and children's horror specifically, pointing out the paucity of PG-13 releases during this period and the similarities in their (negative) reception. The chapter's main case study, *The Gate*, is of special interest as its reception was interestingly split: negative views were directly linked to objections to mainstream horror (with little concern for childhood) while positive views were directly linked to an acceptance of a new childhood (with little concern for the horror genre). These opposing values systems were articulated—and their incompatibility eventually rejected—in the text itself, particularly when its narrative and aesthetics were interpreted in light of the director's stated intention for the film: to "empower tweens."

Establishing an Identity: PG-13 from 1984 to 1989

As far as public debate goes, PG-13's early years were distinctly unremarkable. Once introduced, PG-13 was as discreet as any other long-established classification, barely mentioned and hardly noticed. This is, in itself, fascinating. Could those heated controversies really vanish this easily? Was a new childhood so easily accepted? These first five years may have been low-key, but still their answer to these questions is a loud and clear no.

On the one hand, it is quite obvious that PG-13 was a rating wanted by the market. Not only did its numbers rise steadily until the end of the decade, it was also the rating given to the sequels of all PG-13 instigators: *Poltergeist II: The Other Side* (1986), *Poltergeist III* (1988), *Indiana Jones and the Last Crusade* (1989), and *Gremlins 2: The New Batch* (1990). But what these films also uniformly show is that cultural attitudes about childhood and suitability remained ambivalent. This point is clearly made in the reception to these PG-13 sequels, particularly the commercially successful *Last Crusade* and *Gremlins 2*.

In the case of *Last Crusade*, critics almost universally agreed on this film's message (wholesome) and audience (children and families)—exactly as if this had been a PG-rated adventure. The PG-13 rating is never mentioned. And, indeed, apart from a couple of scenes with rats, *Last Crusade* could easily pass for a PG—perhaps deliberately so. See Hal Hinson's sharp review:

> Clearly, with this relationship [between Indiana and his father] the filmmakers are attempting both to deepen the series and to redeem it (in their minds) from the ignominy of the darker, much-criticized [*Temple of Doom*]. [Spielberg] has been quoted as saying that there were only two reasons for him to make a third Indiana Jones picture and one of them was to fulfill a commitment to his friend Lucas (the other was to atone for the perceived sins of their second installment). As a result, [*Last Crusade*] seems swamped with the spirit of obligation.[2]

Though other critics did not explicitly read the film as an ideological correction to the controversies of *Temple of Doom*, their comments make it clear that the strategy worked. As Joseph McBride highlighted in *Variety*, not only was this a film about family unity, where "the principal love story is between father and son," its morality also made it "the best film ever made for 12-year-olds." McBride continues: "[This] is not a backhanded compliment. What was conceived as a child's dream of a Saturday matinee serial has evolved into a moving excursion into religious myth."[3] This sentiment was also expressed by Caryn James, who titled her review "Indiana Jones in pursuit of Dad and the Grail" and suggested that it "may well become the sentimental favorite" in the series.[4] Roger Ebert likewise praised the film's returning of the series to Spielbergian themes of innocence and adventure in childhood.[5]

Gremlins 2 similarly redeemed the *Gremlins* brand. Rarely labeled horror, the film was framed as a straight-up summer comedy, one purposefully constructed to remind audiences of the first film's humor and to downplay its horrors. As Ebert put it, *Gremlins 2* is only "a series of gags," even though "the microwave oven of the first movie meets its match this time in a paper shredder."[6] Hinson made a similar point:

> The tone ... is set even before the "actual" movie has started. In place of the usual credit sequence, the picture begins with the familiar telescoping Warner Bros. logo from the Looney Tunes cartoons.... What [Joe Dante] wants most of all is to create a kind of live-action Looney Tunes, a flesh-and-blood movie with a cartoon heart.[7]

Like *Last Crusade*, *Gremlins 2* is a PG-13 film which makes no attempt to capitalize on the freedoms that rating suggested back in 1984 in relation to ideological constructions of childhood, horror, innocence, and the boundaries of suitability. On the contrary, the discourse of these two films seems to reject, even to deny, the challenges posed about these topics by the previous films. Both sequels clearly work toward a redefinition of the cultural association between their franchise brands and PG-13, away from notions of controversy and unsuitable content and toward a wholly child- and family-friendly title.

Naturally, both *Gremlins 2* and *Last Crusade* were high-stakes cases. Had they been met with the controversy of their predecessors, that reception would have probably spelled the end of each franchise, not to mention been a hard hit for their production companies's wallets. Even so, these two examples represented the rule and not the exception in their use of PG-13. A glance at the rating trends of this period is enough to show that, from very early days, PG-13 was not envisaged as a half-way house between PG and R but rather as only a couple of steps down the road from a traditional PG. The vast majority of releases under this classification were comedies, family films, and teen films, and the classification warned only of mild language, rude humor, or brief sexuality.[8] PG-13 was also used to flag up violence and mature themes, but this happened far less frequently and in clearly defined generic contexts: sometimes science fiction and fantasy,[9] but more often prestige drama and war,[10] which tend to exclude child audiences from the start.

This association between PG-13 and general suitability became so thoroughly naturalized that the classification was virtually never noted in reviews, not even during the first years of its existence. PG-13 ratings were only mentioned in truly exceptional circumstances, when critics felt an obligation to reinforce its warning to parents. *Batman* (1989) is one of the few examples: "Take that PG-13 very seriously," cautioned Sheila Benson in her review, "this is where bad dreams are born."[11] Critic Jay Boyar was blunter still: "Go to Batman expecting anything but a horror show, and you're certain to be shocked."[12] Boyar's reference to horror here is doubly meaningful: it is not only a comment reinforcing the incompatibility of young audiences with horror but also a clue that PG-13 was associated with family entertainment primarily. This association is clarified even further in Ebert's review: "It's classified PG-13, but it's not for kids."[13]

PG-13's identity was thus as uncomplicated as it was unanimously accepted: in practice, not very different from PG. And, in spite of the controversies surrounding its introduction, PG-13 was, almost as soon as it was created, not a rating for teenagers but a rating for children—which is to say, a rating for everyone, a rating for the mainstream.

A Blessing and a Curse: PG-13 and (Children's) Horror

As expected, PG-13 was a boon to the children's horror cycle: *Critters* (1986), *Raiders of the Living Dead* (1986), *Monster Squad, The Gate, Lady in White*, and *Critters 2: The Main Course* (1988), plus a number of PG-rated titles. But children's titles aside, PG-13 was only very selectively used for horror. Virtually every PG-13 title of the late 1980s had ambiguous status within horror culture, the root of which can be traced every time to the problem of child audiences.

Discounting children's horror titles for the moment, most PG-13 horror films of the late 1980s were comedies,[14] some with obvious appeal to child audiences, such as *Killer Klowns from Outer Space* (1988) or *The Return of Swamp Thing* (1989), which also starred pre-teens. Non-comedic titles were so rare you can count them on one hand: *Cat's Eye* (1985), *Chiller* (1985), *The Wraith* (1986), and *Jaws: The Revenge* (1987). Trends in film production are not deliberate, fully orchestrated efforts; however, there is enough evidence to suggest that the lack of PG-13 horror in the late 1980s was not a coincidence but an active rejection of what was, for all purposes, a child-friendly classification.

Take *The Lost Boys* as an illustration. Originally, the film was conceived as children's horror, taking its inspiration from the children's classic *Peter Pan* and developing the idea of the lost boys as vampires since they could fly, did not age, and wandered the night. The script focused on the Frog brothers, "two chubby eight-year-old cub scouts," who faced and defeated a gang of 11-year-old vampires.[15] The production was set to be headed by Richard Donner, who had directed *The Goonies*, but due to circumstance ended up in Joel Schumacher's hands, who promptly changed the basic premise. Schumacher "hated the idea"[16] of children fighting vampires and so decided to age up all the characters, make the story sexier and gorier, and aim for an older teenage audience instead.

With these changes in place, *Lost Boys* became a firm R, miles away from Donner's original vision, which Schumacher described as a "sort of a cutesy, G-rated movie aimed at young kids."[17] While this statement is not entirely inaccurate, Schumacher's mention of the G rating is strange. He was surely aware that the G rating had long fell out of favor, and that Donner's intention was to make *The Lost Boys* as a companion piece to the *Goonies*,[18] itself a PG-rated film (PG-14 on television) pitched at preteens. The mention of the G rating is then quite deliberate, serving as a catch-all term for all unrestricted classifications. In suggesting only one distinction between ratings—unrestricted and restricted—and using the most innocuous of all ratings to serve as representative for the former, Schumacher's point is clearly made: there is only one appropriate rating for horror and it is Restricted.

Schumacher's views were not unique. One of the loudest voices against horror for young audiences in the late 1980s was critic Kim Newman. I have already addressed Newman's critiques in the introduction, but they bear repeating here as this is the specific period to which the critic is responding. His disapproval leaps out of the page in *Nightmare Movies*, a critical history of the genre:

> *House 2: The Second Story*, is even less coherent [than *House* (1986)] and tries even harder to be a kiddie comedy rather than a horror movie, despite its impressive 9ft-tall cowboy zombie. These movies—along with such big-budget, major studio films as *Fright Night* and *The Lost Boys*, and cheapies such as *Trick or Treat* and *The Gate*—reduce the genre to the level of *Scooby-Doo, Where Are You?* With children, adolescents or childish young men in the leads, and with one scene of knockabout looning for every dose of effect-dripping monstrousness, the films provide the MTV genera-

tion with something to watch every three minutes but are unable to get seriously scary, or even seriously funny. All they prove is nobody needs a safe horror picture.[19]

Newman's outrage at children's horror and other films mixing horror and humor is revealing. His personal definition of horror, shaped by the films and ideologies of the late 1960s and 1970s, does not allow for "knockabout looning," child protagonists, or young audiences. The presence of these elements is therefore not just wrong but shameful, reducing the genre to the status of a children's cartoon. There is something to be said about judging children's entertainment according to the values of adult audiences, but from Newman's perspective there is no mistake here: adult values are the only possible values on which to judge horror.[20]

Similar thoughts were expressed by other critics, too. In his review of *The Gate*, Andrew Dowler also suggests a very strict idea of what is and is not horror, even opening his piece with a lengthy distinction between "extreme horror" and "horror for people who don't like horror" (that is, the mainstream, easily available and consumable). After putting *The Gate* in this last category, Dowler has the following to say: "At worst, [*The Gate* is] flat and pointless. At best, though, there's nothing great, nothing to give any but the least experienced viewer a rush of real pleasure or thrill."[21] He takes the point further by contrasting *The Gate* with extreme (that is, "real") horror, using *Evil Dead II* (1987) as his example of what extreme horror should be—thus comparing a PG-13 children's film to an X-rated horror. The comparison seems a tad unfair but, like Newman, Dowler does not accept that horror can legitimately exist beyond his extreme/mainstream divide. His preconception of a default or correct demographic for ("real") horror impedes him from questioning if those "least experienced viewers" (that is, children) could perhaps be the very audience targeted by *The Gate*—much like Newman, who did not consider that what is "safe" for an adult might indeed be "seriously scary" (or even "seriously funny") for a child.

The kind of opinion expressed by Schumacher, Newman, and Dowler was not conjured out of thin air. They are a logical continuation of the problems explored in the previous chapters, and moreover a direct response to a growing trend in academic and critical thought of the mid–1980s. As I noted in the introduction, this was most famously articulated by James B. Twitchell, who argued in *Dreadful Pleasures* that horror is in essence a juvenile genre, fit not for adults but for children and teenagers.[22] Until 1984, the rating system had provided some protection against these criticisms because the R rating was a visible signal that a group of experts had declared the film not suited for child viewers. After PG-13, however, the landscape was apt to change, unless all horror champions assembled to save their beloved genre—which they did in full force during the 1990s, as the next chapter will explore. In the meantime, however, all of these tensions were articulated in children's horror titles, from conflicting notions of authenticity to debates about proper classification.

Quintessential Children's Horror: *The Gate*

It is useful to focus on a case study in order to properly unpack these struggles. And the most appropriate title also happens to be one the most iconic of the children's horror cycle: Tibor Takács's *The Gate*. It tells the story of Glen and Terry, two young pre-teens who find and open a gate to hell in their backyard. Glen's parents are away, naturally, and so it's up to the boys and Glen's older sister, Alex, to destroy the Demon Lord's minions and banish chaos from their house.

Though this synopsis might not suggest it, *The Gate* is an intense film. Its gore and violence easily matches, if not surpasses, that of *Gremlins*: slime and blood as expected, plus faces that melt and children who get strangled, stabbed in the eye, and forced into self-harm. Beyond this gore, however, is the emotional intensity of the narrative. Glen and Terry are exposed to traumas such as the deaths of a pet, a parent, and a close friend, and experience the distress of humiliation, abandonment, loneliness, and parental rejection. And they face these threats very much like a real child would—in tears. The striking honesty of this last detail is as significant as the film's serious tone, compensated at the end by a happy resolution in which traumas are overcome, relationships strengthened and, most importantly, all deaths reversed.

This combination of intensity and friendliness are a great part of what makes *The Gate* an interesting title, particularly as both characteristics come from the film's commitment to stay with Glen and Terry's point of view. This is where we first see the implementation of what would later become the base pillars for children's horror "formula" (see chapter 6): a focus on pre-teen main characters, moving away from the family unit as main theme (as had been used in *Poltergeist* and *Critters*); the use of narrative themes of empowerment, self-confidence, and closeness with friends and siblings; and the mixing of comedy with straight horror to reduce the film's overall intensity without downplaying its scares (a strategy used also in *The Lost Boys*).

One of the conditions (and results) of this blueprint is a more nuanced representation of childhood and pre-adolescence. *The Gate*'s focus on Glen's tears and his fear of disappointing his parents, or on Terry's grief over his mother's death are miles away from horror's usual representations of children as symbolic of adult anxieties. The film itself seems aware of this difference, in the way it parodies the motif of the Terrible Child and other horror tropes for the benefit of its young audience. In Takács's words, *The Gate* would make its audience "contemplate the idea of what is scary ... very much like a fairy tale, and I think that's why people can relate to it very easily."[23]

Indeed, *The Gate* resonated. It was a box-office hit both in the USA and in Canada, where it became the top grosser for its year of release,[24] all the while receiving no challenges to its suitability. Thirty years later, *The Gate* continues to resonate and is still remembered as a "cult hit"[25] and a "classic horror [that] traumatized a generation [of] junior horror fans,"[26] often placed above other children's horror titles of the period. Its continued popularity has already justified a special edition DVD release in 2009, endless online rumors of a 3D remake, and inspired other children's horror titles after this film cycle was over (see chapter 8) such as Joe Dante's *The Hole* (2009), *Stranger Things* and others.

But if it struck a chord with some audiences, *The Gate* was not without its challenges, all of which were articulated, as before, through production conflicts, rating discussions, and polarized critical reception. As I will now explore, *The Gate* represented a new kind of childhood and revealed horror's ambivalence toward young audiences.

"May the old devils depart!" The Gate's Approach to Childhood and Horror

Back in Chapter 1, I proposed *The Watcher in the Woods* as a very cautious first attempt to make child-oriented horror. Specifically, I noted how *The Watcher*'s use of 1970s motifs contributed to the othering of its young characters, which the film also portrayed as the only two faces of youth (young childhood and older adolescence), with no substantial mention of pre-adolescence. In many ways, *The Gate* provides a resolution to the central questions raised by *The Watcher*'s production: what is childhood, and what is a pre-teen? What role can a child play in a horror story?

Significantly, its answers are not presented as straightforward new truths but as an on-going negotiation—and the process is curiously personified in the clashing figures of *The Gate*'s writer and its director: Michael Nankin, the writer, seems aligned with a more traditional view of childhood and of children's role in horror, while director Tibor Takács was committed to the idea that pre-teens were a new audience for the horror genre. Though Takács's vision dominates the final cut, *The Gate* nevertheless seems to have ping-ponged between these two perspectives all the way through the production process.

The first significant clash between Nankin's tradition and Takács's innovation happened as soon as the director took on the project. Nankin's original script was not a child-oriented narrative, despite starring two young children (eight and nine years old). Takács knew he wanted to target pre-teens, so he aged the children up slightly. In the DVD commentary, Nankin expresses reservations about the success of the change, revealing that he "never quite felt like [he] really made the characters old enough." Takács retorts: "I always thought they were age-appropriate.... They're plain ten-year-old.... That's part of the charm of the movie, the reality of those kids."[27]

Already this is a significant disagreement, suggesting two opposing notions of what a child's "reality" might be: while Takács had no trouble evoking a clear image of pre-teens and of their liminal "reality," Nankin instead "lumped them in" with younger children—continuing to see childhood as a period segmented into only two distinct moments, early childhood and adolescence. If this position seems reminiscent of *The Watcher in the Woods* and 1970s horror, Nankin's personal stance on his child characters and their role in *The Gate* makes the connection even clearer:

> Everything they do is wrong. Everything they do they're not supposed to do, or is cruel, or is dangerous. And they basically get what they deserve.... I always thought horror movies become scarier if your protagonist deserves bad things. You're just waiting for them to get their come-uppance.[28]

This sentiment is reminiscent of film scholar William Paul's thoughts on children in the horror film, particularly the popular figure of the demonic child. For Paul, malevolent child characters engage the (adult) audience's notion of physical harm for the child's own good and so focus the drama on the pleasure the adult viewer finds in the discovery of evil in the child as well as in its eventual punishment.[29] This description applies not only to the Terrible Child films of the 1960s and 1970s but also to the treatment of both main characters in *The Watcher in the Woods* and to the vision of *The Gate* that Nankin describes above.

Other elements of the story point to this tradition as well, such as the discovery that Glen's tree-house (a symbol of childhood) was built on a tree literally rooted in hell. It is through the destruction of this tree, and thus through the symbolic unraveling of Glen's childhood innocence, that the demons are let out to destroy not just Glen but everyone around him too. This view of children as menacing both because *and* in spite of their innocence echoes *The Watcher in the Woods* and is clearly linked to the themes and preoccupations of adult-oriented horror.

The characters of Glen and Terry also seem to have been built in a way to match these Terrible Child assumptions. Terry is described in the film as confused, angry, and destructive, traits explicitly attributed to his lack of adult supervision, and is visually represented as the opposite of a wholesome child: dark colors, death imagery, and an affinity for heavy metal and the occult. His special relationship with the dark side is further explored in one of the film's later plot points, in which Terry becomes a demon and turns against Glen—a twist meant by the writer perhaps as a warning to susceptible children about the effects of keeping bad company.

This idea of Terry as a bad influence is matched by Glen's extreme vulnerability. Like Ellie in *The Watcher*, Glen stands in for the notion that children are especially susceptible to corruption and cannot be trusted to know right from wrong. As Glen himself admits, he would jump off a bridge if Terry did. But while Terry seems unaware of his damaged condition, Glen is hyper-aware of his. *The Gate*'s narrative hinges precisely on his overwhelming feelings of guilt, which lead to a simultaneous fear of and desire for punishment. This emphasis on guilt was deliberately planted in the script by Nankin, who often refers to it in the DVD's commentary to describe Glen's emotional state—even when other feelings, such as anxiety or fear, would have seemed more appropriate, as for instance during one of the first encounters with the demons.[30]

Nankin does not clarify why Glen should feel guilty, but the narrative suggests a somewhat masochistic understanding of childhood as something inherently bad. This is obvious particularly when the demons take the shape of Glen's parents, a scene Nankin describes as his "favourite."[31] The sequence is one of the climaxes of Glen's encounters with the demons and comes at a point when he feels particularly despaired. When he sees what he thinks are his parents outside the house, Glen runs into their embrace with relief—only to hear his demon-dad roar, "You've been bad!" Demon-dad then attempts to strangle Glen to death, who defends himself by pushing his fingers into Demon-dad's eyes until his head erupts in a pulpy mess. Glen looks at his hands in shock and horror: they are covered in his father's blood.

Nankin describes this scene as "five really good ideas: the parents come home, you've been bad, dad tries to kill you, you kill your father while your mother laughs."[32] This description suggests strong negative emotions:

the guilt of having non-filial thoughts and of disappointing your parents, as well as the fear of punishment and of humiliations—all of which seem to have been central to Glen's character from the writer's perspective, and all of which fit the view of children as Other in a horror context.

Tibor Takács also names this scene as one of his favorites but explains its meaning in very different terms:

> Glen sees his mom and she starts laughing at him, and then his dad tells him, "You've been bad." And then Glen tries to push him away but his face turns into like an old pumpkin, and everyone runs back in the house. All of those moments together really encompassed that feeling of "enchantment" that I wanted this movie to have. It all came together beautifully.[33]

The word choice here—enchantment—is crucial because its dissonance opens the door to an entirely different reading of Glen's emotions and his character arc. The ending to this "You've been bad!" sequence is not mentioned by Takács here, but it's nevertheless a good illustration of what this enchantment might mean. The sequence's symbolic patricide embodies Glen's anxieties about disappointing his parents, and his feelings are illustrated by the blood we see on his hands at the end. However, after Glen runs back inside the house, he looks at his hands once more and is surprised (along with the audience) to see no blood—his blame has been lifted. In Takács's vision, the "You've been bad!" sequence does not affirm guilt or evil but innocence.

Takács continually leads Glen to this same conclusion of hope and blamelessness. Another powerful illustration of this view comes at the end of the film, after Glen has defeated the Demon Lord. Immediately, the dark clouds dissipate and a ray of light shines through, illuminating Glen like a redeemed sinner. His body language likewise suggests a new sense of self: chin up, chest out, a confident stride, and a smile on his face. Moreover, Glen's encounter with the Demon Lord is significant in deeper symbolic ways, as explained by the director:

> The other scene that I have always really liked is when Glen and the big Demon Lord have a moment with each other. This was a really pivotal moment in the movie to me, because not all horror movies have it. A lot of great horror movies do have that scene in it, where the protagonist and the antagonist get to stare each other down, and they both realize that they're somehow connected by fate, or maybe, in some ways they're the same. I always thought that was a really powerful moment in the movie, and really love how it came out.[34]

What Takács suggests here is that Glen's realization that he might be the same as the Demon Lord is not an indication that Glen is evil. On the contrary, although this might point out that some parts of his character need correction, the comparison is almost overwhelmingly positive: the Demon Lord is strong, powerful, and independent. What Glen understands in this encounter, then, is not only his potential to embody these characteristics but also his potential to channel them in a different way. In other words, this scene affirms children's agency in the face of life and its dangers—in real life as well as in the symbolic world of horror stories.

This is, ultimately, Takács's argument in *The Gate* and it almost entirely subverts Nankin's more traditional perspective. For the director, the film's intent was to tap into "nostalgia about childhood and, if you're a kid, your experience as a kid" but it was important that it not be "mean-spirited," a characteristic Takács felt was overpowering in horror of the early 1980s[35]—and, we might add, of the 1970s and even the 1960s as far as representations of childhood go. As he repeatedly stated, *The Gate* was not a film about children being demons or worrying that they might be; it was about the ways in which children can overcome these fears, it was about children "empowering themselves,"[36] just as Glen and Terry do when faced with the challenges of puberty and independent existence.

Whose Genre Is It? *The Gate, The Lost Boys, The Monster Squad*

Given the novelty of its approach, some strong ambivalence was to be expected in *The Gate*'s reception—but this resistance was contained within horror criticism. When *The Gate* was read as a children's film primarily (and even when read explicitly as a children's horror film) by critics less invested in horror's cultural capital, the consensus was overwhelmingly positive. As I will now argue, the discrepancy between general and horror-specific reception to *The Gate* is evidence of two things: the cultural recognition of pre-teens as a demographic for whom horror is appropriate (also acknowledged in the text itself); and the beginning of horror's rejection of child audiences and of the PG-13 rating.

Let us first recall Takács's creative vision: *The Gate* was meant to be an "enchanting movie [instead of] a hard-edged slasher film," which had "always [been] intended for tweens" and not general audiences.[37] This description matches the readings of the critics with no attachment to horror. For instance, Gordon Walker felt that this "charming fantasy-fable about love" had a "shamelessly positive" message "to and about young people."[38] And Johanna Steinmetz described *The Gate* as "perfectly adapted to living room viewing," and repeatedly compared it to fairy tales. "This is good-natured terror," she wrote, also emphasizing the film's "several messages about the value of love, self-sacrifice and the Bible," as well as the "struggle by the kids to control their own demons, the temptations to yield to peer pressure and to disobey their parents."[39]

But, as Takács frequently lamented, this was not how everyone read the film. "At the time," he recalled in an interview, "people were always comparing *The Gate* to *A Nightmare on Elm Street* [1984] or something where to me the films had a completely different type of audience."[40] Or, as the director put it elsewhere, referring to retrospective audiences: "Sometimes people forget it's a PG-13 movie for kids [and] try to match it for gore and intensity against R-rated 80s horror classics. It's really a different animal."[41] Takács's own explanation for this confusion was the lack of cultural agreement about the pre-teen demographic (which surfaces even in Takács' clashes with Nankin). As he stated in interview, "People really never talked about tweens as an age group back then. Now Disney specifically caters to them quite a bit. At the time, though, people just lumped tweens in with teenagers."[42]

Takács's point echoes my arguments in this book, but this confusion over target audiences was actually a minor point in *The Gate*'s mixed reception because the critics who misread the film's target were all part of a specific subsection of horror critics and fans. My suggestion is that what made *The Gate* hard to read was not its focus on child audiences but its refusal to choose between them and the horror label.

The kind of comparisons made between *The Gate* and other contemporary titles are evidence of this suggestion. As Takács points out, these comparisons appear to have been made strictly on the basis of genre association, disregarding each film's specific themes and modes of address. See for instance how *The Gate* was described as "yet another tussle with devilish gremlins"[43] or the mention of villains who could be "relatives of *Gremlins*."[44] While these comparisons are not absurd, Takács has a different view:

> I never really thought about *Gremlins* the movie or referenced it during the making of *The Gate*. *Gremlins* felt more like an adventure movie than a horror film.... I thought it didn't focus on the characters it was about, the gremlins. *The Gate* is about Glen and his imagination. Not the minions.[45]

In other words, for Takács the critical difference between *Gremlins* and *The Gate* was perspective: one focuses on monsters, the other on children and their reality. For those reading *The Gate* primarily as horror, however, this difference seems to have been difficult to accommodate—as seen even more explicitly in the frequent comparisons to *A Nightmare on Elm Street*:

other than their horror affiliation, there aren't many points of contact between this PG-13 film about children and that R-rated film about teens.

Some of this confusion comes down to my earlier point about the identity of the PG-13 rating in the late 1980s. Takács' position is that PG-13 is a rating for children, and he seems to have relied on this classification as a way to signal his film's target and intension. As Takács has revealed in interview, the rating of *The Gate* was a point of contention between himself and the producers, who believed R would have been both an appropriate and desirable rating for a horror film.[46] But for Takács, PG-13 was the only option "or it wouldn't make any sense." In the director's view, the concept of children digging up a hole to hell was "strictly the fantasy of an eleven-year-old. I don't think many fifteen or sixteen-year-old were going to be thinking about that."[47] From this perspective, not only would an R rating keep his intended audience away, but it would also wrongly signal the thematic focus of the film. Thus a PG-13 would serve as a signal for pre-teen-friendly themes, such as adventure, family and personal empowerment in films like *The Gate*, while an R would flag up reprehensible behavior such as promiscuous sex or drug use in franchises like as *Nightmare on Elm Street* or *Friday the 13th* (1980).

What Takács dismisses here, however, is that ratings and intensity are not the only discourses surrounding a film's reception. As I mentioned in Chapter 2, marketing campaigns rely on shorthand brands, names, and icons to signal the generic affiliations of a film and adjust audience expectations. Fortunately or unfortunately for Takács, *The Gate* clearly signaled its affiliation with horror—and did so without any counter-points to suggest it also was a children's film. The trailer, for instance, features the young actors clearly, but it also draws disproportionate attention to the teenage characters, who play a very secondary role in the story. Moreover, its highlights are the horror scenes and the scary special effects, both of which would not be out of place in an adult-oriented trailer; and, aside from one line, there is no humor to suggest this as a family comedy (indeed, it is not one).

This explains why *The Gate* was always acknowledged as a horror film, and also why it was then quickly labeled a bad horror film (much like the other PG-13 horror films mentioned earlier in this chapter). Newman's criticism, for instance, stemmed from his recognition of *The Gate* not as a pretender but as a legitimate, if substandard, example of horror. The same was true for Dowler's comparison between this film and *Evil Dead II* and also for other critics, whether they referred to the "rather routine horror-film scaffolding"[48] or labeled it "another horror movie made by people who have seen too many other horror movies."[49] Most tellingly, *The Gate*'s horror affiliations were often explicitly connected to childhood and child audiences: "cheap rip-off" of *Poltergeist*[50] or "hopelessly copycat ... basically powdered Spielberg on Zwieback toast and Stephen King on a stick."[51] These critics seem not to notice *The Gate*'s intentions to target and empower young people, nor to recognize its attempt to tailor its intensity and themes to a level appropriate for that audience, because the guiding light for their readings is a definition of horror as a genre that does not include young audiences—regardless of other cultural perspectives, regardless of a new cultural concept of childhood, and regardless of the stated intent of the individual text under analysis.

It's helpful at this point to return to *The Lost Boys*, that children's film turned R-rated horror mentioned earlier. While Joel Schumacher had been right on the money that a focus on teens and R-rated content would make his film successful among horror fans and critics, his decision did not go unnoticed by reviewers outside of the horror sphere, who emphatically lamented Schumacher's decision to not realize his film's full potential. As Dave Kehr put it, "The issues raised by vampire movies seem most pressing during adolescence, and 'The Lost Boys'—or, at least, the original story by Janice Fischer and James Jeremias—does an imaginative job of translating those issues into contemporary teenage terms." Later in his review, Kehr accuses Schumacher of not developing the psychological center of the tale provided by Sam, the pre-teen character, in order to focus instead on shocking visuals, which were a great part of the film's campaign for the R rating.[52]

Similarly, Rita Kempley noted how *The Lost Boys* still had "more in common with 'The Goonies' than with really first-rate vampire lore." She continued: "It's an off-key ... mix of teen romance and preteen adventure that's at its best when it focuses on the kid brother [Sam], [and is] weakened when the filmmakers pander to older-teen tastes by inserting video love interludes."[53] These comments are evidence of a distinct cultural awareness of pre-teens as a social group and film audience. Both in relation to *The Lost Boys* and *The Gate*, these reviewers champion the notion that pre-teens deserve stories of their own, stories that speak to the anxieties of early puberty without the interference of a more mature perspective (both thematically and in relation to the film's intensity). On a deeper level, this positive, uncomplicated reception by critics who did not specialize in horror is also strikingly accusatory: there was nothing outlandish about "different animals" like *The Gate* or the original idea for *The Lost Boys*. They could work, and did work, on their own terms—it was only the horror pundits (never acknowledged by these general-interest critics) who could not accept them.

Further evidence of this tension can be found in another children's horror of this period, *The Monster Squad*. Though generally less well-received than *The Gate*,[54] *Monster Squad* was also read by non-horror specialists as a film "so clearly intended" for pre-teens that this "the only age group likely to find it scary."[55] Thirty years later, we now have evidence that children not only watched this film but found special meaning in it—and it is their memories that prop up *Monster Squad*'s reputation as a cult classic today, as they do for *The Gate*. Note, for instance, this passage in one of *Fangoria*'s "Tales from the Video Store" features, where staff writer Ken W. Hanley remembers watching *Monster Squad* at the age of seven:

> I felt like I was watching something more important than a movie where kids were pit against the Universal Monsters. The dialogue felt more realistic than either the kids, or even the horror movies, that I'd seen previously. The kids from *The Monster Squad* were funny, mischievous and at times antagonistic towards one another, but they were always equals. There was an exceptional feeling of empowerment as a kid watching *The Monster Squad*, as if there was no role you could not fill with the right amount of courage. [This film] was both food to my imagination and to my pride as a child.[56]

Hanley's use of the words empowerment, courage and pride (pride as a child, no less) are reminiscent of Takács's insistence that horror could be about "tweens empowering themselves." Indeed, Hanley's description of *Monster Squad* is entirely focused on its appeal to children, and it encapsulates much of what made children's horror a successful trend in children's media of the 1980s and 1990s. Yet this was not how contemporary adult horror critics read it. See Newman's review:

> [This is] a wholly charming homage to the great days of Universal and Hammer.... Rather than update the classic themes, Dekker waxes nostalgic about the days when such monster rallies were common and stages several big action climaxes the way Universal would have done if they'd had the money and effects resources back in the 1940s.[57]

What is striking about this comment is that, although persuasive, it flips *Monster Squad*'s target audience: away from contemporary children and toward contemporary adults who remember watching Universal films as children. As Newman himself put it in a different, more recent review of the same film, "*Monster Squad* appeals to cinephile as well as teen sensibilities."[58] There is more than a hint of irony here, as Newman acknowledges children's affinity with horror in his generation while sidestepping the issue for those who came afterwards. But his reading is nevertheless effective at reframing *Monster Squad* because once a film is hailed as intelligent homage, it is no longer a mere children's film. Indeed, Newman never suggests *Monster Squad* as safe or childish, as he had done for *The Gate*, in spite of the two films sharing the same target audience. This is because, in spite of its child protagonists, child-oriented themes, and address, *Monster Squad* can be made to fit a pre-existing view of horror as a strictly mature genre, whereas *The Gate* cannot. In other words, while the first title can be shaped into submission, there is no option but to reject the second.

Similar points could be made about other children's horror features of the period, and there, too, we would find alternative readings by adult fans preoccupied with maintaining the cultural status of the horror genre. Rejecting these children's films, or alternatively reframing them, achieves the same end goal: the preservation of horror's boundaries and its separation from child audiences. What we have here, then, is the beginning of a struggle over the ownership of the horror genre, which the next chapter develops in great detail.

Conclusion

The events of the late 1980s mark an interesting twist in this narrative of the children's horror cycle. What had so far been framed in public and critical debate as a challenge to traditional childhood and the limits of suitability now revealed other implications: was a total reimagining of the horror genre part and parcel of these new cultural agreements?

As the children's horror cycle became more cohesive in form and address, the films noticeably begun to worry less about adult audiences. Instead, their narrative and thematic focus was increasingly child-oriented and often accompanied by new takes on horror's established tropes and motifs, such as the Terrible Child, popular in the 1970s but parodied in *The Gate*. As I argued in this chapter, these changes were not a stab at horror's legacy but part of a necessary adaptation to a pre-teen audience. Removing otherness, focusing on childhood anxieties, and reducing intensity all worked not to diminish the narrative's horror but to better target an audience of children and young teenagers. The biggest shift we see from *The Watcher in the Woods* and *Gremlins* to films like *The Gate* is a secure grasp of target audience—suggested, among other things, by the use of the PG and PG-13 classifications.

As pre-adolescence as a concept comfortably settled into American culture, there were some important side-effects: to target young people so openly, and to do so without incurring public suitability charges, was also to legitimize children as audiences for horror. As the reception to *The Gate, Monster Squad*, and the production of *The Lost Boys* demonstrate, this acceptance of child audiences was perceived as a threat to the genre's cultural capital and strongly opposed by a majority of horror critics and gatekeepers. My point in this chapter was that the real issue was not with the children necessarily but with what they signify, the mainstream.

On this point, the PG-13 rating posed a considerable threat. A genre predicated on its restricted identity could not easily accept a rating that, for all intents and purposes, is open to all audiences. Before PG-13, clever marketing and public controversy drove attention away from the possibility of horror for children—as the previous chapters explored, titles like *The Watcher in the Woods* or *Gremlins* were either dismissed or reframed within popular (and horror-specific) debates as rating mistakes or abnormalities. But after PG-13, with the pre-teen audience firmly established, it became harder to ignore the suggestion that horror had indeed left its restricted niche.

The ramifications of this suggestion became much more obvious during the 1990s. It is in that decade that the small complaints seen in this chapter morph into a full-blown genre-wide backlash against all unrestricted classifications. How and why that came to be is the subject of the next chapter, where I also explain how a fight for legitimacy was the beginning of the end for children's horror cinema.

Part II

NEGOTIATION

THE PLOT THICKENS. In Part I, I presented children's horror and the history of pre-adolescence's "making" as a linear chain of cause and effect events: from the first awareness of a new childhood to the controversy of catering to the hybrid demographic of pre-teens, and eventually to the establishment of pre-adolescence as a concept in American culture, both in its understanding of childhood and in its film audience breakdown. In many ways, this first decade of children's horror is the decade where pre-adolescence erupts—and though this was a fierce rupture, it happened in a relatively contained space. It is only in the 1990s that the shock waves were really felt, as the notion of an in-between group began to clash with the wider culture in a number of unexpected ways.

Again, the children's horror trend provides a perfect window into these clashes. There are two important changes in it during the 1990s: first, the film cycle ended; and second, the trend continued outside of the cinema. Both of these events were the result of simultaneous industrial and cultural shifts, including the acceptance of the pre-teen as a separate social group (and audience) in American culture, and a return to the segregation of children and horror, with direct impact on rating choices—and, indeed, on cultural constructions of the medium of cinema itself.

Chapter 4 addresses horror's response to pre-adolescence and argues that the genre's rejection of youth in the 1990s was an attempt to protect horror's identity and subcultural capital. Chapter 5 focuses on parenting culture's response to pre-adolescence and argues that its rejection of pre-teen independence was mirrored in the themes and representations of family entertainment, resulting in a wider association between pre-teens and the innocence of childhood. Together, these two chapters explain the end of the children's horror film cycle by pointing out the ways in which pre-adolescence became understood as a subsection of childhood rather than of adolescence. The two chapters also chart the development of another key argument in this book: the industrial and cultural transformation of the cinema into a medium for mainstream entertainment in the 1990s, as opposed to a generalist medium for differentiated audiences, including children and pre-teens, as it had been before.

Chapter 6 then presents the culture's response to these changes, arguing that it was in the smaller sphere of children's culture, and away from cinema, that pre-adolescence was allowed to maintain its liminality and, as a result, an unproblematic connection to the horror genre.

CHAPTER 4

Backlash:
The R-Rated 1990s

Establishing pre-adolescence as a concept in American society may have irrevocably transformed the concept of childhood, but it was still only half the story. There were deep implications to this transformation across the culture, and new tensions revealed themselves as soon as the 1990s rolled around. As Chapter 3 explained, the cracks had already begun to show within the horror genre, as the consequences of welcoming young audiences affected the genre's cultural capital as well as its identity and meaning more generally.

This fight over horror's boundaries intensified in the early 1990s, as horror remade itself into a restricted and mature genre once again. This was accomplished in great part through a return to the values of the past, as embodied in the canonization of 1970s-era productions, which had been unquestionably adult, and the rejection of the tropes of the 1980s, when horror had been the most child-friendly. The strategy worked to dampen the enthusiastic growth of the children's horror cycle. The few titles we find in this period are almost as ambiguous in their audience address and generic claims as those of the early 1980s; ultimately, this translated into the eviction of child-oriented titles from the genre altogether.

This chapter makes two central claims. First, I argue that the shape of the horror genre radically altered in the 1990s in response to the attack posed to its boundaries (and therefore to its cultural position) by pre-adolescence and the PG-13 rating. And second, I argue that this cultural backlash against child-oriented horror was part of a broader cultural shift regarding the uses and purposes of the medium of cinema itself. This second argument will become clearer in the next chapter, where I explore how industrial and cultural trends of the 1990s reduced the cultural value of child audiences.

To develop these points, I have divided this chapter in two. The first half takes a step back from children's horror and offers a bird's-eye view of horror more generally. Through this review of the key titles of the 1990s and their reception, I demonstrate that this backlash against the ethos of the 1980s did not just transform the contents, themes, and aesthetics of cinematic horror but also its critical framing and industrial presence. I especially want to highlight that a significant part of this response included the outright dismissal of every connection to childhood: child heroes did not exist, and child characters were badly accepted even when Othered as supernatural villains.

More pressing still, child audiences became anathema. Virtually all horror titles—and certainly all key titles—of the 1990s were rated R, and, in an intensification of what happened in the late 1980s (see Chapter 3), PG-13 releases were continually denounced not as bad horror but simply as not-horror, both in critical opinion and in their own marketing campaigns. This is a critical turn of events. The discrediting of PG-13 as a valid horror classification not only snubbed the children's horror film cycle but also rendered its challenges and questions pointless, as if stating definitively that children and horror cannot be put together.

The second half of this chapter then takes a case study to demonstrate the obstacles posed to children's horror by this situation. *Tim Burton's Nightmare Before Christmas* exemplifies the impossibility of claiming generic hybridism in the early 1990s: to appeal to horror audiences it needed to downplay its child appeal and to appeal to general audiences it needed to maintain its Burton brand, which required the opposite. The (very successful) solution was to distance *Nightmare* from both horror and children's film and, using the film medium to heighten sophistication, to present it instead as an art curiosity (and, much later on, as a Christmas family film). The strategy was successful but it illustrates children's horror's return to a limbo state of indistinctive address and ambivalent generic claims—which, inevitably, spelled its end in the cinema.

Restoring Horror's Maturity: Back to the 1970s?

As Steffen Hantke notes in *American Horror Film*, the 1970s (and its adjacent periods, the late 1960s and early 1980s) are a romanticized moment in horror film history, its productions constituting the majority of the genre's canon. In this section I will argue that this standard (as well as the preoccupation with generic decline that came with it) is not a modern development but was in fact an established part of the genre's culture as early as the late 1980s. Indeed, the values of 1970s horror, namely its maturity and restricted character, were the very cornerstone of 1990s horror in response to the genre's child-friendly front in the 1980s. I'll begin this argument with a focus on critical opinion and reception, before moving on to ratings and representations in the next sections.

Criticism does not always highlight the 1990s as a period of extreme maturity and sophistication in horror. David Sanjek's overview, for example, reads the period as one of castrated, derivative films, which led the genre away from the political work of people like Clive Barker and George Romero. The problem, as he saw it, was that horror tailored itself to teenaged audiences, who "are more interested in observing the genre rearticulate itself rather than [calling] attention to the social, cultural and ideological fissures and fault lines that the form represents."[1]

In relation to the *Nightmare on Elm Street* series, Sanjek notes how the original film (1984) developed complex themes of everyday horror and family nightmare, which had developed in the genre since the 1960s. In the sequels (1985, 1987, 1988, 1989, and 1991), however, "the familial superstructure gave way to an emphasis upon the spectacularity of special effects and the effete manner with which Freddy savagely terminated the life of another individual."[2] This supposed degeneration is even more prominent in 1990s hits like *Scream* and *I Know What You Did Last Summer* (1997), which "virtually abrogate any discussion of family. All [of these] films focus primarily on the isolated and self-involved world of teenagers."[3] In other words, teenage audiences have trivialized the genre and obscured its political mission—much like the Code had tamed horror before the ratings system. As critics like Sanjek argue, it is because horror of the 1990s tried to reach these unsophisticated audiences that it was forced to let go of the challenging ideological critiques which had made the genre great in the late 1960s and 1970s.

Hantke explains this rhetoric of a genre in crisis as a means of preserving cultural capital: horror fandom "must defend itself against production and distribution strategies that ... expand the audience demographics ... with the result that no clearly discernible segment of the market remains the sole property of hardcore fans."[4] Thus, Sanjek's attack on teenagers and the supposed superficiality of the films made for them is another way of asserting ownership of the genre and its boundaries. We see this move in the contemporary criticism of the 1990s, too—albeit in very different shape. Sanjek may have read the decade as infantile, but critics contemporary to that period were mostly exuberantly positive, praising 1990s' titles for their maturity and sophistication. And, significantly, they seem to have been using the exact same gold standard as Sanjek: the 1970s.

This difference in assessments is explained through context. Sanjek, writing as an academic in the year 2000, understood the genre politically and intellectually as a whole movement, and was sensitive to what he perceived were the bigger patterns in the shape of horror during the 1990s. The critics and filmmakers of the period, however, were responding to the more immediate shifts in the genre's landscape, namely the popularity of children's horror and the introduction of PG-13 in the 1980s. The significance of these "smaller" changes is made explicit in the reviews and interviews of the period, as I explain in this chapter, but ignored in existing academic studies. In any case, both judgments of 1990s horror (as either "good" or "bad") are driven by the same desire to control the genre's boundaries and, specifically, to do so by rejecting the legitimacy of young audiences (children for 1990s critics, teenagers for Sanjek).

This drive is explicit in the marketing, production, and reception of 1990s horror, which directly positions these texts close to the valued canon (and in opposition to the 1980s) through an overt return to art aesthetics, intellectualism, and maturity. If the 1980s had seen an explosion in children's horror titles and teen slashers, the 1990s mostly replaced these trends with other icons (big budgets, reputed stars, and literary gravitas), in order to change its image from childish to sophisticated. Tellingly, it was in this period that a horror film, *Silence of the Lambs* (1991), first won a Best Picture Oscar (as well as Best Director, Best Screenplay, Best Actor, and Best Actress), setting the tone for what the genre would or could be in this decade.

As Mark Jancovich has noted, *Silence of the Lambs* is a good example of how generic labels are used to ascertain cultural capital and legitimacy within critical discourses.[5] Vincent Canby of the *New York Times*, for instance, does not refer to *Silence of the Lambs* as horror but as suspense thriller and suspense melodrama. This labeling seems closely related to Canby's highlighting of the film's artistry, the director's subtlety, and the dialogue's qualities as "tough and sharp, literate without being literary."[6] But if the exact position of *Silence of the Lambs* has been debated, the film nevertheless shares many similarities with other horror titles of the period. Canby's review stresses what would be praised during this decade in the genre: *Silence of the Lambs* "is clearly the work of adults."[7] This statement, written in obvious approval, effectively summarizes the zeitgeist of 1990s horror—this was a genre transformed, mature, sophisticated and prestigious, and above all, not for children.

The point is illustrated by a quick glance at the decade's output. It's hard not to notice the enthusiastic revival of classic monsters, the emphasis on literary adaptations, and the deliberate linking of horror productions to art aesthetics and quality pretenses, whether through auteur directors or star-studded casts, often with a proven record of Academy approval. And if these seem like desperate production gimmicks, it must be noted that, for the most part, critics did buy the message. Take for example *Mary Shelley's Frankenstein* (1994), a film that might not seem an obvious part of the horror genre but which critic Hal Hilson defined as "a contemporary highbrow version of [an] ageless horror classic."[8] Another good example is Francis Ford Coppola's take on the vampire in *Bram Stoker's Dracula* (1992). *Variety* labeled it a film of "extreme adult nature," on account of it being "faithful to its literary source," with "grand romantic goals" and a "serious tone."[9] Canby also appreciated Coppola's maturity: *Dracula* "transcends camp to become a testimonial to the glories of film making as an end in itself," he wrote and added, "It's as if Mr. Coppola were saying: 'You want a horror film? You got a horror film.'"[10]

These affirmations of sophistication and maturity actively shaped the narrative approaches of the period. The werewolf, for instance, moved away from its long-standing associations with puberty and youth and became instead a metaphor for the yuppie crowd and adult office workers in *Wolf* (1994), a film described by *Variety* as "decidedly upscale."[11] Roger Ebert's review is particularly clear about the film's transformation:

> *Wolf* is both more and less than a traditional werewolf movie. Less, because it doesn't provide the frankly vulgar thrills and excesses some audience members are going to be hoping for. And more, because Nicholson and his director, Mike Nichols, are halfway serious about exploring [the topic].... The tone of the movie is steadfastly smart and literate.[12]

Ebert's comments are revealing, at once denouncing young audiences as "vulgar" influences on the genre and praising *Wolf* for its mature take on its subject matter. But *Wolf* is not alone in maturing the genre's approach to classic teenage monsters. The vampire was stripped of its *Lost Boys* adolescent image and made erudite and glamorous in *Interview with the Vampire* (1994)—"an intelligent ... reading"[13] of Anne Rice's novel, according to Todd McCarthy[14]—and the ghost, too, was transformed in critically-acclaimed titles like *The Sixth Sense* (1999) and the romantic *Ghost* (1990). The serial killer, made popular by the slashers of the 1970s and 1980s, went from babysitter murderer to intellectual in *Silence of the Lambs*, *Se7en* (1995), and the supernatural *Candyman* (1992), which Ebert praised for "scaring me with ideas and gore, instead of simply with gore."[15]

It could be argued at this point that these responses are the exception, that they come from generalist critics, and that these films did not truly represent horror in this decade. Indeed, as Sanjek's overview indicates, the bulk of horror-specific criticism targeted not these mature films but the teen slasher revivals. But here again I must point out the disparity between retrospective academic (and fan) readings and popular contemporary reading by emphasizing the proximity of the 1990s to the "threat" of children's horror.

Slashers of the 1990s were simply not received like their 1980s counterparts by contemporary audiences. On the contrary, critics often noted favorably how the new franchises were of a different breed, dedicated to correcting the excesses of the previous decade's slashers by returning to the virtues of the 1960s and 1970s.[16] This correction applied not just to their increased narrative complexity, striking aesthetics, and perceived artistic merit but also to a clear effort to sublimate their teen focus through the deliberate construction of this audience as one of sophisticated connoisseurs.

One of the most immediate examples here is *Wes Craven's New Nightmare* (1994), widely read by critics as a return to form for horror. For critic James Berardinelli, the genre had "been badly hamstrung by poor films, and [slashers] have been at the forefront of the decline. Therefore, it's somewhat ironic that one of the most intelligent and creative efforts to come along in a while bears the *Nightmare* theme, title, and signature villain." The review continues, ominously prescient: "Any copycat features spawned by this movie will hopefully take a cue ... and favor quality of scares over quantity of blood."[17] For the most part they did. The hit blockbuster *Scream*, for example, was described in *Variety* as "more intelligent than the norm" and a "sophisticated parody,"[18] terms also applied to other popular franchises, such as *I Know What You Did Last Summer*, which was read as "a polished genre piece with superior fright elements ... just clever enough to rise above the usual fodder."[19]

This "norm," the "usual fodder," refers here not to the general output of horror in the early 1990s but rather to the standard of slashers in the late 1980s. The positive responses to *New Nightmare*, *Scream*, and other slashers of the 1990s were almost always framed by an acknowledgment that the 1980s had been a low point and that the genre had peaked in the 1970s. Owen Gleiberman spells out this attitude in his review of *I Know*

What You Did Last Summer: "By the end of the '80s, teen-horror films ... had descended to a level of ragtag ineptitude depressing to behold. [*Last Summer*] is not of that lowly ilk; it attains a level of solidly mediocre trash competence."[20] Though his wording is not the most flattering, Gleiberman approvingly links the franchise to the past, comparing it to films of the 1960s and 1970s: "[the villain] stands ramrod straight, in the square-shouldered psycho tradition of Jason Voorhees, Michael Myers, and—where they descended from, after all—Norman Bates."[21] Even if Gleiberman does not consider *Last Summer* a masterpiece of horror, he nevertheless respects it as an example of the genre primarily because of its rejection of the 1980s and desire to return to horror's better past.

This kind of attitude is important to highlight because it explains why the focus on teenage audiences was not a significant issue to 1990s critics. The nostalgia for the 1970s fostered in the neoslashers of the 1990s was a much more important characteristic of these films, and it promoted associations with maturity, artistry, and sophistication. Consider Lawrence Van Gelder's response to *I Know What You Did Last Summer* in the *New York Times*: "Like Mr. Williamson [writer of this film and of *Scream*], Jim Gillespie, the director, respects the conventions of the genre. He devotes time to establishing the characters, spaces out the surprises and provides knowing aficionados with time to relish [the film]."[22]

The key word here is respect, which implies that these "knowing aficionados" are the correct audience for horror—in spite of whatever other audiences with whom they might be lumped together. Mick LaSalle's review is even more explicit on the matter: "Teenagers looking to scream will find things to enjoy in 'I Know What You Did Last Summer.' But audiences looking for another 'Scream' will be disappointed."[23] LaSalle's comment is not just a remark on which of these franchises is the better example of horror; it is also a rejection of the claim that teenagers own slashers, even when those films openly court them. The same sentiment can be found in Ebert's review of *New Nightmare*, where he made a clear distinction between the film's appeal to "serious fans of horror," who are "going to love this movie," and its "strangely intriguing" appeal to "general audiences."[24]

In spite of existing critical disagreements over the political, intellectual or aesthetic qualities of this period, 1990s horror embodies a clear backlash against the juvenile reputation the genre had acquired in the 1980s. The rejection of 1980s values—and, crucially, of its "default" audience of young people, which, it should be remembered, included young children—is central to each film mentioned in this section and to its critical reception.

This drive away from young audiences continues to be explicit beyond critical reception. The following section addresses ratings specifically while the one after focuses on representations and themes.

Embracing the R Rating

What do all the titles in the previous section have in common besides having been received as sophisticated, adult-oriented horror? They are all rated R. With very few exceptions—and despite PG-13's availability—R was the only horror rating of the 1990s: from the philosophical *Jacob's Ladder* (1990) to the ground-breaking *Blair Witch Project* (1999), and including titles like *Night of the Living Dead* (1990), *Brain Dead* (1990), and *Army of Darkness* (1992), or even *Natural Born Killers* (1994), *From Dusk Till Dawn* (1996) and *Blade* (1998), plus titles like *In the Mouth of Madness* (1995), and *Sleepy Hollow* (1999)—all were rated R. Not to mention others like *The Vagrant* (1992), *Copycat* (1995), *The Night Flier* (1997), *Deep Blue Sea* (1999), *End of Days* (1999), *Ravenous* (1999), and *Stir of Echoes* (1999)— also rated R. Plus, of course, all the neoslashers, from *New Nightmare* and *Scream* to *The Faculty* (1998), *Urban Legend* (1998) and *Final Destination* (2000), along with their many sequels—all rated R, too.

The list of R-rated horror films of the 1990s could go on and on, as virtually all horror releases of the decade were rated so. This overwhelming rating preference adds important evidence to the argument I put forth in the previous section: in the 1990s, horror film actively sought to disengage itself from the associations with child audiences built in the 1980s. And what could be more mature than a restricted rating? What could more clearly send the message that children are not a desired or legitimate audience of horror than a rating which keeps them out?

Before I go on, I want to address an immediate challenge to this claim: the R rating is not, has never been, and perhaps will never be, a deterrent for young audiences, nor do all American theatres enforce it strictly. Indeed, even I claim that the R rating cannot exclude a film from the children's horror trend, as in the example of *The Lost Boys*. But as this same example illustrates, the R rating does have a certain weight because Schumacher refused to take on the project unless he could age it up (and sex it up) to an R rating. In this instance, the director's aim was explicitly adolescent; the R rating functioned as a not-so-secret signal to teens that this film was going to be an edgy experience, without restricting its distribution as much as an X or NC-17 would have done.

But although this connection between the R rating and teen audiences does exist in industrial and popular conscience, the main point here is that this link is accomplished through a deliberate distancing from young child viewers: R becomes the teen rating because it is *not* the children's rating. Indeed, the only unchanging characteristic of the R rating is that it excludes children; whether it then becomes associated with teens, as in *The Lost Boys*, or with adults, as in *Bram Stoker's Dracula*, is dependent on other factors.

This is an important point because it challenges the notion that teenage audiences have been a threat to the cultural legitimacy or even the quality of the horror genre. On the contrary, the problem has always been *children*. Even in a critique like Sanjek's, the problem with teenagers is that they supposedly have the minds and tastes of children, are preoccupied with themselves and disengaged from political realities. Likewise the real fear of mainstream acceptance is not that young audiences might dumb horror down but that legitimating their presence and aiming for the widest possible audience has often meant stripping horror of its oppositional cultural function.

The notion that horror could be a genre so unquestionably "safe," to use Kim Newman's term, that even children could consume it is anathema to many horror critics and enthusiasts. The 1990s obsession with the R rating illustrates this rebellion clearly. Whether these films excluded teenagers from their marketing and narratives (as in *Wolf*) or whether they embraced them but reconstructed them as mature connoisseurs (as in *Scream*) is a distinction less important than their common denominator: the irrevocable rejection of child audiences and the mainstream culture they represent.

One last point needs to be addressed before closing this section: what about the PG-13 releases? Though a very small minority, they nevertheless existed alongside the R-rated titles I've been discussing. But even these titles attempted to comply with the view of horror constructed by the more numerous R releases before being rejected in critical reception. Take *The Island of Dr. Moreau* (1996) as a first example. This film subscribes to the expectations of 1990s horror (based on classic horror literature and featuring the star power of Marlon Brando and Val Kilmer), but it was firmly rejected as a horror title: "cheap thrills," wrote *Entertainment Weekly*, comparing it unfavorably to the classic 1930s version, which still remained "a really creepy creep show."[25] Another critic, Peter Stack, dismissed it even more clearly, not only stating that "nothing ever gets very scary" in it but also removing its horror badge and calling it instead "a Hollywood movie."[26] For a second example, consider *The Haunting* (1999), another film which seems to fit 1990s criteria for horror. But Ebert's verdict was that it did not, "alas, succeed as a horror film" even as it "succeeds as a film worth watching."[27] Mick LaSalle was, again, much more direct: "There's no excuse for 'The Haunting.' ... A 1963 adaptation of the book was scary and intelligent. The only thing scary about the new version is realizing that someone keeps giving director Jan De Bont money to make movies."[28]

In critical opinion, then, the issue with *The Island of Dr. Moreau* and *The Haunting*, two PG-13 films with an established link to classic horror, was that they did not update the material properly and instead made themselves tame—the expectation being that any horror film of this period should be the opposite. We see this assumption in other PG-13 releases of the 1990s. Films like *Jurassic Park* (1993), *Godzilla* (1998), *Sphere* (1999), and *The Mummy* (1999) could all have made a claim to a horror label, yet to go for the R would have killed their blockbuster appeal, so they were instead marketed and received as action, adventure, and science-fiction. Similarly, *Anaconda* (1997), a film which broke the 1990s mold both by being rated PG-13 and by not having a sophisticated attitude toward the genre, toned down its horror connection by amplifying its low-budget camp aspects. Hence it was not horror but something in "the great tradition of cinematic cheese." LaSalle declared it "so desperate and silly that here and there, it's a lot of fun"[29] while Lisa Schwarzbaum described it as a "direct-to-video-type title."[30] That Schwarzbaum also distinguishes *Anaconda* from *Scream* in her review confirms how emblematic of the horror genre the latter had become and how distant *Anaconda* was in turn.

If these examples confirm my suggestion of 1990s horror as a genre assumed to be mature, restricted and sophisticated, there is nevertheless one exception worth noting: *The Sixth Sense*. On the surface, this title seems to contradict everything I have just argued: here is a PG-13 film, read not only as horror but as quality horror for a discerning audience. Instead of a contradiction, however, *The Sixth Sense* is a sign of what was to come in the 2000s, a decade in which PG-13 established itself as the de facto mainstream classification, something which I address in more detail in the conclusion of this book. *The Sixth Sense* also marks the end of the themes and narrative tropes popular in 1990s horror, as I will explore in the next section.

Strictly No Children Allowed (Not Even Demon-Children)

A line in *Variety*'s review of *The Sixth Sense* perfectly summarizes the 1990s attitude toward children in horror: "the positioning of a child at the center of otherworldly goings-on ... could spell sleeper status."³¹ This prediction speaks volumes about the assumptions around the horror genre at the end of the decade, even if *Variety* turned out to be quite wrong in this instance (as I noted above, a sign of change to come). Throughout the 1990s, children are anathema in horror: invisible as audiences, impossible to find as heroes, and so unfashionable that even the Terrible Child motif fell out of favor.

In the remarkably limited horror releases focusing on children or childhood in this period—all rated R, needless to say—the overwhelming trend is the open rejection of the themes made popular in the 1980s. Children's perspectives and pre-pubescent anxieties are ignored, and pre-teens rarely feature, swapped out in favor of younger children who usually appear as embodiments of otherness in films such as *The Unborn* (1991) and *Mikey* (1992). The presence of these othered, evil children, however, should not be taken as unproblematic evidence of the continued cultural resonance of their themes, as films about evil children tended to be met with overwhelmingly negative critical reception, even when they were products of popular franchises or reputed directors.

Children of the Corn II: The Final Sacrifice (1992), for instance, was deemed "so poorly conceived that its symbolism has no internal logic,"³² and John Carpenter's *Village of the Damned* (1995), a remake of Wolf Rilla's classic of the same title, provoked tedium and laughter instead of fear. "Fans and students [of the original] ... likely will be bored," wrote Peter Stack. "[T]he trademark glowing eyes from the first film are now in color like shining marbles and seem rather silly.... It takes almost no time at all for the alien kids to look entirely uninteresting, partly owing to the nerdy way they're dressed."³³ This sense of *Village of the Damned* as a film removed from the reality of the 1990s continued in Richard Harrington's review for the *Washington Post*, in which the critic wondered if Carpenter had "lost his mind or just his talent," and reviewed the film as dull and "populated by actors we already tend to speak of in the past tense."³⁴

This reading of the Terrible Child as an outmoded figure seems to have come out of cinematic boredom as much as growing social resistance, even repulsion, to the notion of children performing evil acts. *The Good Son* (1993) is a perfect example: starring *Home Alone* (1990) prodigy Macaulay Culkin, it was reviewed negatively by nearly every critic in the United States. For Hal Hinson, for example, the film not only "degenerates into a campy mess" as soon as "the demon-seed plot kicks in" but was also morally objectionable: "where were the responsible adults when this thing was made?"[35] The query was echoed by Ebert: "Who in the world would want to see this movie?" Ebert is especially clear about his distaste of the film's morality:

> One of the reasons the movie feels so unwholesome is that Macaulay seems too young and innocent to play a character this malevolent.... You want to confront the filmmakers who made him do it, and ask them what they were thinking of. For that matter, what were Culkin's parents thinking of...?[36]

The repulsion *The Good Son* elicited from critics and the lack of seriousness with which *Village of the Damned* was received are two sides of the same coin: in the 1990s, evil children in film were not only a thing of the past but also in serious bad taste. Not only had horror changed, general attitudes toward children and childhood had also shifted, notoriously toward a model based on notions of innocence. This again is illustrated in Ebert's review of *The Good Son*:

> The movie is rated R. Market surveys indicate that kids want to see it, probably because it stars their "Home Alone" hero. This is not a suitable film for young viewers. I don't care how many parents and adult guardians they surround themselves with. And somewhere along the line, a parent or adult guardian should have kept Macaulay out of it, too.[37]

Similar views are suggested by Janet Maslin of the *New York Times* in her review of *Village of the Damned*. "Don't take the children, not even if they fix you with ice-cold stares and try to make you do their bidding," Maslin wrote with some humor, even as she acknowledged that the same motifs might once have been very enticing for young audiences: "With its baleful little villains, 'Village of the Damned' is even creepier to watch as a parent than it was to see as a child."[38]

This critical swing toward the notion of horror as a dubious influence on children was articulated beyond film reviews; it was also the subject of media guides and books for parents.[39] This shift is more than a simple comment on horror before and after PG-13. It is also closely related to other shifts in American perceptions of the child in the 1990s, namely a return to the notion of children as vulnerable beings, spurred by the growing popularity of attachment parenting styles. This is an issue which I will address in much more detail in the next chapter, where I focus on transformations around the concept of childhood. For now, however, I have established the general climate of the 1990s as far as the horror genre in film is concerned—mature, restricted, and uninterested in young audiences—and so it is time to turn my attention to the children's horror trend and its position in it.

So What of Children's Horror?

Given such a hostile climate children's horror was inevitably transformed and three important things happened in the trend at the start of the 1990s. First, children's horror distanced itself from the horror genre. Second, children's horror grew closer to the family film genre. And third, children's horror moved away from cinema as a medium. These things happened roughly simultaneously but can also be read as responses to one another, as I explore in this Part II. In the remainder of this chapter, my goal is to show how the transformation of horror into a mature genre very quickly resulted in the suppression of the children's titles. Indeed, my first pieces of evidence are the lack of obvious examples of the cycle at the decade's turn and the way most of these, like *Jurassic Park*, *Jumanji* (1995), and *Casper*, eschew their horror links from the start in favor of family film connections, a significant move which the next chapter analyzes.

But there is one remarkable exception, which also marks Disney's second struggle with horror: it is *Tim Burton's The Nightmare Before Christmas*, a film with a history almost as strange as that of *The Watcher in the Woods*. The next section retells this history and highlights the new points of tension in Disney's relationship with horror while the section after that explores the way *Nightmare* carefully navigated horror's new antipathy toward child audiences.

Disney vs. Horror, Round Two:
The Nightmare Before Christmas

One of the most famous pieces of trivia about *The Nightmare Before Christmas* is how it almost never came to be. According to director Henry Selick, *Nightmare* remained halted because it was "too crazy for Disney in those days [the 1980s]."[40] A more accurate explanation, however, would be that in those days Disney was understandably reticent about horror projects. Live action children's horror was one thing, but animation made it much harder to signpost a pre-teen audience target because of the medium's association with children and families as well as with the studio's traditional output. And yet today, Disney is nothing but proud of its brand association with *Nightmare*. As I will now explain, this shift is evidence not of a broader acceptance of children's horror or of a transformation of the Disney brand but of the opposite: *Nightmare* could only be accepted as a legitimate Disney film once it shed its horror associations.

Before *Nightmare,* Burton worked as an animator in the Disney team, occasionally given the freedom to pursue individual projects. In Burton's words, his vision and the Disney brand were "a bad mix"[41] from the start. Recalling his first short, *Vincent* (1982), a stop-motion film very close in spirit to *Nightmare,* Burton has noted how Disney "seemed to be pleased with it, but at the same time kind of ashamed.... [T]hey didn't know what to do with it."[42] His next project, the short film *Frankenweenie* (1984), fared slightly better—in part, I contend, because it was live action, and therefore much closer to Miller's other children's horror efforts of the period. The short was even selected for theatrical release alongside *Pinocchio*, but its surprise PG rating gave Disney cold feet—unsurprising given the commotion around *The Black Cauldron,* also rated PG, that same year. As Burton put it, Disney "freaked out" and *Frankenweenie* "met with the same response as *Vincent* in a way, which was 'Oh, this is great, but we have no plans to release it. *Ever*.'"[43]

The same fate should have awaited *Nightmare Before Christmas.* Especially after *The Black Cauldron*'s disaster, Disney no longer had an appetite for horror so Burton's idea for *Nightmare* was vaulted indefinitely. Burton soon left and went on to become extremely successful with *Peewee's Big Adventure* (1985), *Beetlejuice* (1988), and the blockbuster hit *Batman.* By then, Disney's Touchstone label had also officially launched and because it gave the studio an outlet for risky projects Disney approached Burton with an offer: to finally make *Nightmare Before Christmas* in return for his next film, *Ed Wood* (1994).[44] Burton agreed, and *Nightmare*'s production began, with director Henry Selick at the helm.

This could have been the end of the story, but it soon became apparent to all involved that, in spite of Touchstone's safety net, Disney had very little faith in *Nightmare Before Christmas*. It was "kind of a stepchild project," Selick revealed. "They never felt [it] was a Disney film." The studio's "biggest fear," Selick continued, was that the core audience, that is children and their families, would hate the film and not come to cinemas to see it. "It was very much, 'We don't have high expectations. It's kind of too dark and too scary.'"[45] With Ron Miller gone, *Nightmare*'s horror bent was unlike anything else the studio was invested in at the time, such as the traditionally wholesome *Beauty and the Beast*. As Selick concluded, the film "had no relationship to what Disney's identity was, so they didn't develop it."[46]

Which is not to say they didn't worry about it. As critic Jeff Strickler notes, the public was aware that Touchstone was part of Disney, so "it took nerve to make such a complete break from the warm-and-fuzzy genre to something that can be as outrageous as this is in spots.... One imagines that Disney executives lost more than a little bit of sleep worrying about *The Nightmare Before Christmas*."[47] Strickler was not wrong. In a flashback to the days of *The Watcher in the Woods*, Jeffrey Katzenberg (then-chairman of Walt Disney Studios) and other Disney executives continuously provided Selick and his team with suggestions aimed at softening the film's tone—all of which were promptly rejected by Burton, who distance-supervised the whole production.[48]

Undeterred—and taking another page from Miller's book—Katzenberg took the damage-control procedures further. To the press, he repeated various disclaimers: "We know it's not for 3-, 4- and 5-year-olds.... There are some images that are too scary for really young ones."[49] In marketing, the strategy was more aggressive still: children were simply not targeted—even though pre-teens had been identified by Disney's own marketing team as one of the film's biggest audiences (more on this in the next section). In fact, aside from a small line of toys, Disney did not employ any of its trademark promotional tactics for animated and family films, such as the integration of a potentially chart-topping pop song or deals with children's meals at fast food restaurants (an omission since rectified).

The release strategy was also understated—and woefully matched to audience responses. *Nightmare* opened modestly on a handful of cinemas, then spread to around 500 screens and, on Halloween, to just over 1,600 cinemas across the United States. But its earnings were impressive: the film topped the box office two weekends in a row before being withdrawn by Disney (reluctantly, one imagines) to make way for the studio's planned big holiday release, *The Three Musketeers* (1993).[50] As Paul Sherman reported, "the half-hearted merchandising deals" also proved insufficient for consumer demand, though perhaps with a happy consequence, as they "caused much of the original merchandise to become instant collector's items."[51]

Not only was the film popular, it was also received as appropriate for children—despite its PG rating, still uncommon for animated features at this time.[52] Critics called it "fun for the whole Addams family,"[53] "in no way mean-spirited,"[54] and moreover reassured "concerned parents" that "ultimately, things will be put right.... Jack and his Halloweentown collection of strange friends are oddly charming [and] Jack (with whom the viewer identifies) is genuinely unaware of his transgressions. If Jack's a bad skeleton, he's an innocently bad skeleton."[55] Occasionally, critics also pointed out the differences between *Nightmare* and the rest of Tim Burton's work: his "taste for jokey malevolence is much less troubling here"[56] than it had been in *Batman*, a film harshly criticized for its tone.

The film's continued popularity eventually led to a change of heart on Disney's part. In 2001, Jack Skellington was presented as Disney's prodigal son at Disneyland, where the classic Haunted Mansion ride was made over with a *Nightmare Before Christmas* theme for the holiday season—a tradition that parks across the world have maintained to this day. Equally significant was the abandonment of Touchstone's label in 2008, when the digitally-remastered collector's edition of the film was released. Touchstone's name, logo and labels had been present in home releases and merchandise until the year 2000 but were from this point onward completely removed and replaced by Disney's name.

Today, *Nightmare*'s brand is both that of a Christmas film and that of a Disney classic. Like *Gremlins*, *Nightmare* has now lost most of its horror associations, making it the most successful Disney children's horror title but also one seldom recognized as such. The next section focuses on the initial promotion and reception of the film, to show just how distant this framework was from the original intentions, which were guided almost entirely by the new expectations of horror and by an understanding of cinema as a medium primarily for adult audiences.

Fitting In: Art and Intellect, Not Children and Horror

Even if the themes and narrative of *Nightmare Before Christmas* suggest it is a children's horror film, it is also true that it has always tended to be thought about in different terms: dark fairy tale, gothic animation, art film, and others along these lines. These associations arose from a carefully constructed production and marketing strategy on Disney's part. In this section, I will suggest how the promotion and reception of *Nightmare Before Christmas* played by the new rules of horror in the 1990s and how as a direct consequence *Nightmare* became something that was neither horror nor children's horror and, for a while, not even a children's film.

During the film's production, marketing research revealed three potential audiences for *Nightmare Before Christmas*: "the preteen set" first, followed by two other groups, namely "people drawn by Tim Burton's reputation, and adults attracted by the film's artistic and experimental nature."[57] But the first audience, pre-teens, posed some issues. Though its existence was now more tangible than it had been in the early 1980s, its boundaries were still up for debate—and certainly where Disney was concerned, the fear was that getting the pitch wrong would jeopardize Eisner's strategy of reasserting the studio as a beacon of family and innocence. This was especially the case as the rest of the industrial landscape seemed to no longer favor the niche hybrids of the late 1980s like *The Gate* but preferred an increasing separation of genres: children's films got friendlier (see next chapter) and horror more restricted.

The final decision, then, was to ignore pre-teens as a potential audience and capitalize on the other targets instead: *Nightmare Before Christmas* was presented as a horror-themed curiosity for a discerning audience, fitting in with the expectations of 1990s horror and sidestepping the problem of children and suitability altogether. The film's PG rating posed no problem and in fact helped the cause because it was as still an unusually high classification for an animated film of this period.

Other branding strategies followed. The most significant was the attaching of Burton's name to the film's title: *Tim Burton's The Nightmare Before Christmas*. The addition caused some confusion about who directed the film, which persists popularly to this day, but Selick has conceded that "it was probably a good decision. [T]here was *A Nightmare on Elm Street*, so I think they wanted to differentiate from that—and also get Tim's audience in the theater."[58] Indeed, the addition of Burton's name gave potential audiences an immediate and clear indication of what to expect and, as Selick pointed out, also what not to expect: Burton's name forged associations with art, aesthetics, and innocence, not gruesome teen-oriented horror.

These associations were cultivated by Burton himself, who consistently explained his interest in horror (specifically classic and gothic horror) in terms of its intellectual and emotional depth. For example, the director has written about his ability as a youth to "make direct links, emotionally, between that whole Gothic/Frankenstein/Edgar Allan Poe thing and growing up in suburbia,"[59] a claim which not only positions him as a thinker but also distances him from negative stereotypes of the unintelligent, possibly damaged, young horror fan. Whenever Burton links horror to his personal life, his associations are not with extreme horror but with art and the innocence of a child's mindset: "those movies, just the poetry of them," Burton writes, "and this larger-than-life character [Vincent Price] spoke to me in the way Gary Cooper or John Wayne might have to somebody else."[60]

While this framework elevates horror's artistic merits, Burton also paradoxically refuses to take the genre as seriously as some scholars and critics have done. "I always found more humor in horror [than in comedy]," he has said in interview. "One of my favorite things was in the original

'Frankenstein,' where we have this hunchbacked, twisted man with an absurdly short cane walking up this expressionist stairway and, halfway up, he stops to pull up his sock."[61] In a similar manner, Burton has frequently downplayed the obvious horror influences in his work. For example, he discredited the idea of a direct link between *Frankenweenie*'s imagery and that of James Whale's *Frankenstein* (1931) and *The Bride of Frankenstein* (1935) despite the clear similarities, instead attributing his visual choices to influences in his real life.[62] And, in response to a comment about *Vincent* appearing to be inspired by *The Cabinet of Dr. Caligari* (1920), Burton not only rejected that link but connected the film to children's classics instead: "it probably has more to do with being inspired by Dr Seuss. It just happens to be shot in black and white, and there's a Vincent Price/Gothic kind of thing that makes it feel that way. I grew up loving Dr Seuss."[63]

This persistent emphasis on childlikeness, art, and intellectualism is what allows Burton's use of horror to be read as parody, homage, inspiration, or even just horror, depending on the viewer's persuasion. This is remarkable branding, as it gives Burton the best of both worlds: respected by horror champions for recognizing the genre's importance but also accepted in the mainstream for highlighting the values of innocence and childhood. Moreover, because Burton frames childhood and innocence as abstract concepts and explicitly rejects the idea of making films for children, the prestige of his brand is not diminished by associations with "lesser" children's entertainment.

The strength and flexibility of Burton's name guided readings of *Nightmare Before Christmas* in critical reception as well as the promotion. Note Desson Howe's review for the *Washington Post*: "[Burton] pulls adult minds down to the surreal darkness of childish imagination—where the real nightmares are. But through Burton's eyes, these dark dreamscapes aren't bad places at all. In fact, they're quite wonderful."[64] Or, as Janet Maslin put it in the *New York Times*, "It is Mr. Burton's peculiar gift to find benign mischief in that kind of [horror] spectacle."[65] Indeed, the film was frequently described as "macabre humour and tongue-in-cheek horror"[66] or as a number of "fright gags, ... mock-scariness," imbued with the certainty that "older viewers should be thoroughly in sync with Mr. Burton's comic tastes."[67]

This distinction—older viewers, not children—was echoed by a number of other reviewers. "Although [*Nightmare*'s] soul is sweetness itself," wrote Kenneth Turan in the *Los Angeles Times*, "its surface is disturbing and intentionally so, and its clever and satiric sense of humor is undoubtedly pitched to adult tastes."⁶⁸ Thus, even as he questions the film's contents, Turan concludes that the film's legitimate audience was, undoubtedly, not children but adults. This is an important difference from the way Canby and others framed the suitability of *Temple of Doom*. Whereas an in-between audience of teenagers or older children had been identified then, with *Nightmare* there seems to be no thought given to pre-teen audiences. Some of this can be explained through a shift in attitudes toward pre-teens, which the next chapter will develop. But part of it was also a response to Disney's efforts to promote *Nightmare* as a film for a discerning adult audience.

The premiere at the New York Film Festival, for instance, surrounded *Nightmare* with the prestige of an art film, drawing critical attention to its aesthetic triumphs. Part of this attention naturally focused on Burton's auteur status: the *Washington Post* described the filmmaker as "Oscar Wilde ... raised on E.T.A. Hoffmann, the Brothers Grimm and the expressionistic German films of the prewar period such as *The Cabinet of Dr. Caligari*"⁶⁹; while *Variety* staff described the sets and backgrounds in *Nightmare Before Christmas* as "surreal takeoffs on 19th-century engravings and etchings" and noted that "the characters inhabiting them are endlessly inventive, as in a Bosch painting."⁷⁰

A great many critical notes on *Nightmare*'s imagery also highlighted the film's use of stop-motion animation. Most critics spend several paragraphs in their reviews explaining the processes of stop-motion, a technique unfamiliar to a large portion of audiences at the time, with special emphasis on the "painstaking skill"⁷¹ involved in this "labor-intensive process,"⁷² as well as the "enormous"⁷³ achievement represented by this film and how it was "a major step forward" for stop-motion animation.⁷⁴ Significantly, the technical side of *Nightmare* was discussed in ways that stressed adult enjoyment and admiration, as in comments like the one made by Turan that "at maximum efficiency, the *Nightmare* crew could turn out no more than 70 seconds of finished film per week,"⁷⁵ or Bill Jones's remark on the advantage Burton gained by virtue of having to wait a decade to produce this film as he could then make use of better technology.⁷⁶ The use of "sophisticated computers,"⁷⁷ which now allowed the camera to be moved as well as the puppets in front of it, was also noted by other critics who remarked on the cinematic qualities of the film and the flexibility of Selick's camera which, as Quentin Curtis put it, "swoops and swirls, as if it were on loan from Brian De Palma."⁷⁸

This "revolutionary application of stop-motion animation"⁷⁹ was not only critically praised for having "revitalized"⁸⁰ the practice but was also contrasted favorably to Disney's animation formulas: *Nightmare* was, in McCarthy's words, "something refreshingly different" for those "with an aversion to conventional animation."[81]—by which he meant adults, not children. Turan also reflected on the ways *Nightmare* was "not a cartoon like *Aladdin* [1992] or *Beauty and the Beast*"[82] while Betsy Sharkey of the *New York Times* called it "an anomaly in the Disney animation equation," and likewise stressed how it was light-years away from *Aladdin* and *Beauty and the Beast*, two of the studio's most successful films at the time.[83] Sharkey also noted how the "highly stylized look and the technical advances represented by *Nightmare*" were "quite distant" from cel animation, which she described as being "as familiar as an old shoe to most adults and children."[84]

Not only was it read as higher quality, stop-motion was also described as a more authentic technique, far "more personal"[85] than drawing. Notions of greater authenticity also came across in the way Selick and Burton discussed stop-motion with the press. Burton talked about it being "handmade" and as possessing "more weight, more of a place,"[86] as well as "a funkiness and roughness"[87] in comparison to cel animation. Selick likewise described it as "infinitely more difficult than cartoon animation."[88] In making these comments, critics and filmmakers positioned *Nightmare* as a special kind of animated feature: not old-hat Disney, accessible to all, but rather a niche product, restricted in its appeal to an educated audience of adults. Or, in other words: not harmful, but not for children either.

This separation from child audiences, constructed equally by Disney and the contemporary critics, is my main point here. It demonstrates how the window of possibility had begun to close for children's horror films as the prestige and cultural value of young audiences decreased in the 1990s, and it furthermore suggests that the meaning of the cinema itself was affected by these changes, namely through being used as a vehicle for prestige releases only.

Conclusion: The End of a Film Cycle, the Start of a New Era

This chapter's title implies some aggression, and I hope that the reason for it has been clear in the analysis—the separation between children and horror was indeed made final during this period. But I should stress again that this segregation happened only in the cinema. The emphases on restriction, maturity, and intellectualism were universal rules in the

1990s not for the horror genre generally but for theatrical horror film only. The reason for this should be no mystery to the reader of this book: during the 1980s, it was mainly in cinema that children's horror made waves, and this was also the only medium in which categories of maturity (ratings) were firmly entrenched. The shift described in this chapter is thus a direct response to the changes in 1980s' horror film.

That this response was so strong in film should make clear one of the biggest implications of the arguments made in this chapter, namely that this preference for the R rating functioned as a way to police the boundaries of *both* the genre and the medium. I will continue to develop this point in the next chapter and, more directly, in Chapter 6 when I explore how children's horror continued to be a popular trend even after its removal from film. For now, however, I do want to develop the impact of re-constructing the cinema as a medium not-wholly-friendly to child audiences. I obviously do not mean that children were no longer targeted (on the contrary, the 1990s are one of the most family-friendly periods in film history), but rather that they were no longer valued as an individual audience. Instead of targeting only pre-teens, as films of the 1980s had done, the trend in the 1990s was to target them alongside other audiences—hence creating the wide-reaching "family audience." Anything more niche than that had to find its place in other media, most notably television, where there was built-in audience segregation and pre-established suitability agreements (see Chapter 6).

For an example of this shift at work, we need only to look at the children's horror output from this point onward. Consider, for instance, the titles produced by Disney in the 1990s and 2000s. For theatrical release, the studio produced *Hocus Pocus* (1993) and *The Haunted Mansion* (2003), both family films with a humorous slant. For its television channel, however, Disney produced *Tower of Terror* (1997), *Under Wraps* (1997), *Halloweentown* (1998), *Don't Look Under the Bed* (1999), *Mom's Got a Date with a Vampire* (2000), *Halloweentown II: Kalabar's Revenge* (2001), *The Scream Team* (2002), *Halloweentown High* (2004), and *Return to Halloweentown* (2006). Though these titles vary in their uses of humor, they match what had been done in the film cycle at the end of the 1980s more clearly than either of the theatrical releases (in particular *Tower of Terror* and *Don't Look Under the Bed.*)

This preference for straight-to-video and television as a medium for children's horror is also reflected outside of the Disney brand. Children's horror (or horror-inspired) television series in particular flourished in the 1990s: *Round the Twist* (1989, 1993, 2000, 2001), *Are You Afraid of the Dark?*,

Eerie, Indiana (1991–1992), *Tales from the Cryptkeeper* (1993–1999), *Bone Chillers* (1996), *Nightmare Ned* (1997), and *Freaky Stories* (1997), among others, including the notable *Goosebumps* (1995–1998). Book series likewise multiplied: *Graveyard School* (Tom B. Stone, 1994–1998), *Shivers* (M.D. Spenser, 1996–1998), *A Series of Unfortunate Events* (Lemony Snicket, 1999–2006), and the two *Creepers* series (Bill Condon & Rob Hood, 1996–1997; Edgar J. Hyde, 1998–2010), among many others.

The 1990s thus pose an interesting paradox, in that the decade marks both the end and the beginning of children's horror: the end of its film cycle, in which some of its biggest cultural battles were fought, and the beginning of its golden years, when it quietly dominated children's pop culture. Horror's "backlash" against child-oriented texts is an important factor here, but there is still one piece of the puzzle missing, and one that implicates cinema's cultural meanings: the re-making of pre-adolescence as part of attachment culture and its subsequent influence on Hollywood's template for family entertainment. This shift is what the next chapter explores, before I turn my attention to children's horror after the film cycle in Chapter 6.

CHAPTER 5

The Final Conflict: Children's Horror Meets Family Entertainment

Although mainstream horror's disowning of child audiences triggered the end of the children's horror film cycle, it was family entertainment that delivered the kiss of death. As seen with *Nightmare Before Christmas*, the obstacle to children's horror in the early 1990s was that horror's new reactive identity had made it much harder to successfully establish an explicit link between horror and child audiences. But there was a way around this, suggested by Hollywood's increasing reliance on the family entertainment model: what if the films did not target children exclusively?

Broadening children's horror appeal to include the elusive family audience allowed the cycle to continue into the 1990s, but its shape was deeply altered in the process. Titles like *The Witches, The Addams Family, Jumanji, Casper,* or even *Jurassic Park* retained their connection to the horror genre and continued to target their narratives openly at young viewers, but they weren't children's films in the way their predecessors had been. Part of the family entertainment compromise was that these films needed to target adults equally, so they all include major adult characters in their narratives and often focus on parent/child teams. Their narratives are still about childhood for the most part but the requirements of their form demanded that the issue be seen not from a child's perspective exclusively; rather, the family's perspective (and often, the parental perspective) is emphasized throughout.

This highlighting of family togetherness worked not only to designate the film's target audience; it also significantly softened the horror elements through the inclusion of more humor and a stronger focus on childhood innocence and traditional family values, as opposed to pre-teen independence. Naturally, the introduction of these new elements was not without side effects. Children's horror films of this period are so different in tone and address to their predecessors that they were never perceived as a significant part of the horror genre—even the most traditional horror critics spent no time discrediting these titles, in sharp contrast to what had been the case with *The Gate*. Instead, children's horror films of the early 1990s were read and are remembered still as comedies, adventures, and fairy tales—in other words, as family films.

The assimilation of children's horror into the family film label only intensified as the decade progressed. Hollywood's emphasis on family entertainment grew, meaning that mainstream releases increasingly had to consider broad audiences (and, therefore, dominant ideologies). As a result, the defining factors of children's horror were lost: the children's bit, because it now targeted families; and the horror bit, because innocence was seen to deserve protection (and, in any case, horror wanted nothing to do with children).

This chapter chronicles this decline to highlight how, even at its end, the children's horror cycle was again tangled with a number of important industrial and cultural shifts. The first of these has already been suggested in the previous chapter: during the 1990s, the value of child audiences plummeted while the value of family audiences (meaning adults) rose. This affected Hollywood's production choices, transforming the cinema into a medium almost exclusively adult-oriented with profound implications for the children's horror cycle (and, as Chapter 6 explores, for children's media more broadly).

The second important shift concerns American views of childhood and pre-adolescence. On the one hand, the early 1990s were a period of clear resolution on the topic of pre-adolescence. The understated but crucial commonality of the films of this period, whether in the children's horror cycle or not, is that they treat the pre-teen as its own social group, distinct from young children and teenagers. These portrayals were not only consistent, with each pre-teen very much like the one in other films, but were also received widely without challenge. On the other hand, however, there was a clear cultural return to notions of childhood innocence, which once again made children's horror the hub of (some) controversy. This was sometimes targeted at the films' intensity and expressed in critical reception but mostly it circulates in the films' own narratives, which try to negotiate the pre-teen's position halfway between maturity (as endorsed by pop culture in the 1980s) and innocence (as promoted, vigorously, in parenting philosophy of the 1990s).

In this chapter I argue that family entertainment of the 1990s, under which the children's horror cycle now fit, circulated a clear but reconfigured image of pre-adolescence, adapted to the attachment perspectives of the period and much closer to the ideals of childhood innocence than before. To make this claim, the chapter addresses two important turning points in the film cycle: first, the transition away from expectations of children's film in the 1980s and toward those of family entertainment in the 1990s, illustrated by *The Witches*; and second, the completion of this assimilation process, illustrated by *Casper*, the last children's horror film. Before this analysis can take place, however, I must outline the cultural and industrial landscape of Hollywood in the early 1990s, much as I did for horror in the previous chapter, so as to introduce the new players—family entertainment and attachment parenting—and their relationship to one another during this period.

Family Values: A New Hollywood for New Cultural Attitudes

Many authors have examined the 1990s as a period of great change in Hollywood's working models. One of the best analyses comes from Robert C. Allen, who brings together a number of factors to show how and why Hollywood fundamentally changed the way it made and marketed films from the 1990s onward. As Allen puts it, "the emergence of Hollywood's version of postmodern family entertainment is a cultural response to separate—though interlaced—demographic, technological and social phenomena: the 'echo boom,' the VCR and the postmodern family."[1] These three elements expanded a film's potential markets but also altered the definition of film audiences, which was now no longer limited to the people watching a film in cinemas when it was released.

Because of this change in goalposts, Hollywood developed a new golden standard for its production, the family film. These films were defined primarily by their cross-generational appeal, which made them the best candidates for expansion beyond the cinema and into the ancillary markets of home video, merchandise and promotional tie-ins. According to Allen, these economic priorities also infiltrated the content of the films, making them ambivalent and ideologically uncommitted. He writes:

> As the production and marketing logic behind a substantial fraction of Hollywood films shifted ... and as the nuclear family fractured into increasingly diverse social groupings, it became less and less in Hollywood's interest to align itself to any particular configuration of the family or any equivocal set of "family values." "Family" for Hollywood basically meant those markets more effectively exploited by films that were not rated R.[2]

This is where Allen and I part ways. Though I agree that the term "family audience" was always loosely defined I also contend that, as far as representations and ideology went, Hollywood was strongly committed to one specific version of the family, namely that which was promoted in wider culture: the Boomer/Millennial family whose dynamics abided by attachment parenting philosophies.

As Allen himself notes, one notorious effect of the echo boom was the emergence of a "cultural 'preoccupation with parenting' for the first time since the 1950s."[3] This has been well-documented by other scholars, and as these authors have pointed out, the 1980s and the 1990s embodied a very sharp turn in the values that guided parenting advice. Notions such as the sanctity of children, their vulnerability, and the necessity of absolute attachment were not just the guiding principles of parenting culture in the 1990s they were also dominant principles of general culture—which, of course, included Hollywood.[4]

I have argued this position in much greater detail elsewhere and so won't labor it extensively here.[5] My point for the purposes of this chapter is that the paradigm shifts in Hollywood's business model in the 1990s must be understood not only in terms of technological advances but also in relation to its cultural context. The introduction of VHS and the subsequent mass expansion of a film's markets were certainly a big influence in Hollywood's direction during this period—but the desire to maximize profits by not ruffling any feathers was not manifested in apolitical, non-ideological content. Rather the opposite: its content mirrored dominant values, specifically the belief that children are precious and indisputably at the heart of the family.

This position made economic sense because there was very little to disagree about. Whether American families were organized in the traditional way (white, Christian, middle-class, married parents and two children) or whether they were more diverse, reflecting more postmodern ideals, these families were still likely to be united by their beliefs about childhood and the child's role in the family. Indeed, this shared agreement over the centrality of children underpinned a great deal of American culture of the period, including politics.[6]

Where did these beliefs about childhood and the family come from? Discourse around the family pervaded the culture generally, but its core can be traced to the sphere of parenting culture, where a new doctrine called attachment parenting was making waves. Attachment parenting is based on the attachment theory of John Bowlby and the scientific observation that infants tend to do better when they develop a secure relationship with their principal caregiver. Bowlby's studies on the matter go as far back as the 1950s, but it wasn't until the 1970s that the theory took hold, transforming a number of cultural practices related to the care of infants, notoriously in the case of orphans and others in institutional care. Its influence on parenting manuals and broader childrearing advice began in the 1980s, with authors such as Aletha Solter, and continued into the 1990s with T. Berry Brazelton and others. The most famous author, however, is William Sears, who not only incorporated attachment into a new parenting philosophy but also coined the term attachment parenting.

As the name implies, attachment parenting revolves around physical and emotional proximity between parent and child, achieved through practices such as extended breastfeeding, co-sleeping, and baby-carrying. Though Sears describes these practices as natural, he also acknowledged in his first book that they clashed with parenting advice from previous decades, that his way of parenting was "rather foreign to the ... mind-set we've all been exposed to."[7] But they did take hold, and boomed particularly in the 1990s. In 2012 *Time* magazine ran a profile on Sears, naming him "the man who remade motherhood"[8] and not without hyperbole—the principles behind attachment parenting, whether articulated by Sears or by one of the many other experts with similar views, effectively reshaped not just the practices of parenting but also the dynamics of American family life.

As Sears notes in one of his books, parents following his advice now "orchestrated their lifestyle and working schedules to incorporate their baby. Parenting, work, travel, recreation, and social life all revolved around and included baby—because they wanted it that way."[9] These new dynamics were, moreover, not restricted to a child's infancy, and attachment parenting practices go together with another famous concept of the 1990s: the Soccer Mom, she who "paces the sidelines of her children's games, [wearing] T-shirts emblazoned with slogans like 'I don't have a life. My kids play soccer.'"[10] As described in the *New York Times*, "Soccer moms of the 1990's were the 'supermoms' of the 1980s. Many of them have kicked off their high heels and replaced them with Keds to watch their kids. If you are a soccer mom, the world according to you is seen through the needs of your children."[11]

Not every family practiced attachment in this way, of course. But the appearance of these terms in the general culture at this time is not irrelevant. On the contrary, this newfound dedication to children, and the specific attached way of doing so, is an important part of 1990s America—and it was accordingly circulated in the films of the period. As Peter Kramer argues, Hollywood in the 1990s was notorious for its "obsessive concern ... with family issues,"[12] resulting in what he calls family-adventure movies, which not only featured families on screen but worked as a sort of cultural therapy to bring the families in the audience closer together. These trends assert the cultural power of a very specific set of values and expectations about the family and its dynamics, as well as their significance.

Therefore, it is particularly significant that the only point of tension in these family-centered films is the figure of the pre-teen. As I have been arguing, the idea of pre-adolescence gradually took form in American culture throughout the 1980s and was more or less fixed by the end of the decade. On-screen pre-teens become a strikingly coherent group in the 1990s: a specific age (usually twelve), with a certain look, and a distinctive set of interests and characteristics—and no longer played by very young children or much older adolescents. But while this acceptance of pre-adolescence as a liminal space between childhood and adolescence fit the cultural climate of the 1980s, it clashed head-on with the dominant ideology of the 1990s.

The reason why is easy to see: attachment parenting promoted a view of all children (not just infants) as innocent and deeply vulnerable. Moreover, the entire family dynamic, and particularly the relationship between parent and child, was based on this assumption and the need for continued attachment—in other words, continued dependency. What I want to stress here is that Hollywood family entertainment was founded on dominant views and therefore worked from this pre-existing understanding of the family. Its texts portray pre-adolescence in ways that "corrected" or reconfigured that concept, turning it away from ideas of independence and toward traditional childhood again.

The rest of this chapter addresses two films that show how this conflict over pre-adolescence was played out and negotiated through the children's horror cycle: first, *The Witches* for a picture of the emerging cultural split over the issue; and then *Casper* to observe a transformation in the ideology of children's horror and, with it, the end of its cinematic existence.

A Short-Lived Truce: *The Witches*

The Witches is the first children's horror title of the 1990s but in many ways it still feels like a 1980s production: it pitches a child protagonist against supernatural evil, often portraying real peril and several dark plot details. These elements come from the film's source material, a 1983 novel by Roald Dahl, the British author famous for his subversive approach to children's literature. But *The Witches* also embodies the less controversial cross-generational approaches favored by Hollywood in this decade. It is less an "old-fashioned" children's horror and more a family-friendly take on Dahl's novel—an interesting balance between the past and future of children's horror on film.

This period between two moments—the rebellion of the 1980s on one hand and the restraint of the 1990s on the other—is what the next two sections explore. *The Witches* walked a line between accepting a new view of childhood, in the tradition of children's horror, and wanting to return to a previous ideal of innocence, as dictated by the business imperatives of 1990s' Hollywood (family entertainment) and the growing cultural hold of attachment ideologies. In reality, the "correction" of pre-adolescence began almost as soon as the concept was culturally accepted, as we see in the production and reception of *The Witches*.

The next section examines the changes made to the source material, which brought it in line with expectations of family entertainment by softening the horror and relying more heavily on the concept of innocence. The section after that analyses the disparity between critical opinion and box-office results, which I read here as a cultural rejection of *The Witches'* correlation of pre-adolescence and independence.

From Children's Horror to Family Entertainment

The Witches is a novel much like the rest of Roald Dahl's work: there is violence, horror, cruelty and grotesque imagery, all tied up with a less-than-happy but still positive ending. Though the book is witty, its tone is undeniably dark, with several instances of real peril as well as a subversive take on the power dynamics between children and adults, a recurring trope in Dahl's work. Dahl subversively positions his stories on the side of children, often portraying adults as incompetent or cruel, their authority arbitrary, and their rules unnecessary. Underpinning these choices is not just creative spirit but a very particular view of childhood: Dahl repeatedly acknowledges the astuteness and resilience of children and builds his narratives around the affirmation of these qualities.

Dahl's children always win—even when they lose. In *The Witches*, for example, the main character Luke is turned into a mouse by a witch. Although he defeats her in the end, there is no cure for his condition, so Luke must accept and adapt to life as a mouse. Not only does he succeed, he also finds happiness in this new situation, as it means that he and his beloved grandmother now have the same amount of time left to live. This kind of stoic approach is not uncommon in Dahl's stories and suggests a strong belief in the abilities of children to thrive in the face of sad, scary, or otherwise "unsuitable" events. This philosophy also parallels the views promoted in the children's horror films I've been discussing in this book: children are not just attracted to horror but can use it in ways that encourage personal growth. Dahl's children win for the same reason that Glen and Terry manage to close the Gate, and that Billy and Gizmo are able to defeat the gremlins: they are forced to become independent agents, with full responsibility over their actions.

Dahl's particular view of childhood was not simply philosophical; it was also political. The writer no doubt believed children were clever but his fierce loyalty to them was also part of his disregard, even disrespect, for established authority and cultural expectations. Dahl's subversive character might have been charming in his fiction but in the real world the author was frequently derided for his abrasive communication style and often offensive views. *The Witches* is a famous example: upon receiving the manuscript, the editor suggested toning down the portrayals of women, which he felt were unnecessarily harsh. Dahl's response? "This is a book for children and I don't give a bugger what grown-ups think about it."[13]

This defiance worked in the publishing business, where Dahl had status equivalent to a cinema auteur, but when it came to adapting *The Witches* to the screen it was Hollywood calling the shots. The film version is still led by Dahl's voice but at every crucial plot point it is quickly drowned by that of the director, Nicolas Roeg, and his producers. As a result, the film version of *The Witches* is much more receptive to "what grown-ups think": it reforms the witches, reverses Luke back into a boy, and even avoids some of the harder moments in the story, such as the death of Luke's parents. In the book, these deaths are thoroughly spelled out; in the film, however, it is left for the viewer to work out—or not. As Caryn James notes, "this information is so subtly handled ... that children might not realise what has happened."[14]

These changes could be read as a taming of Dahl's views, but more importantly they were a crucial step in making the material work in the context of 1990s Hollywood. The *Witches* film was collectively loved by critics, in great part because it conformed to expectations of family entertainment, such as cross-generational appeal and a story with (mostly) uncontroversial views. Critic Desson Howe makes this clear when he stresses that *The Witches* "takes care of [the grown-ups] too. In this extended good time of a fairy tale, there's something for everyone."[15] James does the same when she proclaims it "a fanciful film for savvy children and a witty, well-made movie for their parents."[16]

These qualities were, moreover, clearly signaled by the film's PG rating. As I explored in the previous chapter, after PG-13 was introduced, the PG rating became ever more established as the default family film rating. And this is how critics read it, noting *The Witches*'s appeal to both children and their parents, and stressing the film's benevolence as well as its educational potential. For Rita Kempley, the film was "beguiling.... If fairy tales reach coping, then 'Witches' gets a poisoned apple for a job well done."[17] For Michael Wilmington, the film was not only "a cockeyed delight," but "the kind of literate, imaginative children's fantasy we see too rarely ... both childlike and knowing, sophisticated and magical."[18]

When reviewers noted the story's horror slant, it was therefore framed within the context of family entertainment. Note Caryn James' opener: "*The Witches* resembles a brilliantly told bedtime story, though the teller of this children's tale may well be the slightly cracked relative who can't judge when scary stories become nightmares."[19] Or even Michael Upchurch's estimate that, for "precocious first-graders with a warped sense of humour and an appetite for chills, thrills and spills, nothing could be better" (in a review titled "*The Witches* is a Delightful Mix of Wickedness and Magic"). These passages suggest an acceptance of horror as a suitable genre for children, a view which other critics are quick to spell out in full. Roger Ebert, for example:

> The best children's stories are the scariest ones, because to kids they seem most likely to contain the truth.... Roald Dahl's children's stories always seem to know that truth, and the best thing about Nicolas Roeg's film of Dahl's book *The Witches* is its dark vision—this is not only a movie about kids who are changed into mice, it's a movie where one of the mice gets its tail chopped off.[20]

These positive reviews highlight a moment of important resolution. *The Witches*, a film more intense than many of those made in the 1980s, is here not only accepted but unchallenged, because childhood is now perceived differently. In James's words, "There is a truism that modern children lose their innocence early. *The Witches* is an engaging film for them."[21]

An important detail to note here, though, is that part of *The Witches*'s critical success, and the reason it could associate horror and children in the way it did, is that it didn't try to be a horror film. On the contrary, it fully took on the label of family entertainment and stayed within its confines. In this way, *The Witches* is a good example of the kind of harmony that was possible in the 1990s—what could have happened to *The Nightmare Before Christmas* had it taken the family route. As the next section will show, however, there were other complicating factors to *The Witches*'s genre identity.

How Dark Is Too Dark?

Although *The Witches* was generally received positively, the praise was not universal. Dave Kehr describes it as "disappointingly insincere" and "excessively sober" and clarifies his reasoning in this way:

> Instead of adapting the boy's point of view, which might have produced a children's adventure as strange and memorable as "The 5,000 Fingers of Dr. T" or "Invaders from Mars," Roeg chooses to place himself out of the story, emphasising instead the campy elements of Anjelica Huston's extravagant performance.... Roeg's giggly, condescending approach to the story strips [Huston's] character of any real menace and the film of any real suspense.... [I]t's a film that doesn't believe enough in itself.[22]

In other words, Kehr expected *The Witches* to be more radical. More, perhaps, like previous examples of children's horror—an association made clear by his reference to *The 5,000 Fingers of Dr. T* (1953), a precursor of this trend, and *Invaders from Mars*, another 1953 film, remade in 1986 as part of the children's horror cycle. This expectation, so strongly articulated, is evidence of the cultural changes happening around children's horror in the 1980s, namely the notion that children's film could be both intense and appropriate. But what is more interesting here is that, in 1990, Kehr was in the minority. Most other critics, even those who enjoyed *The Witches* and declared it a suitable family film, had some doubts about its intensity. Take, for instance, this short blurb in the *Boca Raton News*:

> A horror-adventure movie for kids. Its horror comes more from how Anjelica Huston and her fellow witches look (hideously grotesque) than from their plot to turn all of England's children into mice. A fine performance by Mai Zetterling is a major plus. Rated PG: may frighten faint-hearted children.[23]

Given the review's strict space constraints, its single-minded focus on the film's suitability is significant. Not only is the entire blurb preoccupied with relaying information about the film's intensity, it only deviates to mention the things that might counter it, such as Zetterling's performance as the kindly grandmother (and reformed witch), or the facetious nature of the witches's plot. This focus on suitability also features prominently in the reviews of critics less pressed for space. Even when these reviewers enjoyed the film and did not find it unsuitable, they nevertheless mentioned the film's darker moments, often at length. Wilmington, for instance, wrote:

> [W]hat [Roeg]'s done is put disturbing flesh on Dahl's fancies [so] that the movie takes on an unnerving pulse and threat. The setting becomes overwhelming, the evil palpable.... In a way, *The Witches* summons up other, scarier child-in-hotel horror movies, like Bergman's *The Silence* and Kubrick's *The Shining*, plus other Roeg movies where innocents are lost in perverse, dangerous worlds.
> All this shouldn't be taken as a warning that this PG movie is too dark for most children. It's no grimmer than the Brothers Grimm.[24]

The interesting thing about this excerpt is that even though Wilmington stresses his comments are not meant as a warning, warn is exactly what they do. The passage is also marked by a noticeable shift in tone, which turns suddenly uneasy in what is otherwise a very upbeat review. A similar cloud hangs over James's review in the *New York Times*: "the film begins by clobbering viewers with an uncomfortable dose of paranoia and death," she writes, also noting that "it certainly goes too far when Luke's parents are killed in a car crash." Like the worried *Boca Raton* reviewer, James is quick to reassure parents that *The Witches* soon moves away from "these harsh realities" and that "Mai Zetterling ... provides the film's much needed and appealing human soul." But she ends her review on an ambiguous note:

> There is a truism that modern children lose their innocence early. "The Witches" is an engaging film for them. "The Witches" is rated PG. Its ideas—witches everywhere and parents who die—are probably scarier than the images, though the witches at their ugliest are horrific sights. This is not a film for very small children.[25]

While James acknowledges that a significant cultural change has taken place in the concept of childhood, she seems unsure whether this is a positive change after all. And James is not alone in this view. Ebert, who describes *The Witches* not as a family film but as a "so-called children's film," also warns that it "might be too intense for smaller viewers," a note he follows by a pregnant comment on modern childhood: "(although some of them these days seem hardened to anything)."[26]

Were these doubts shared by American audiences? *The Witches* was certainly a critical success, but audience response was in fact only lukewarm: the film didn't have spectacular box-office success in its first weekend, and its returns failed to pick up in the following weeks.[27] This is surprising given the film's established credentials—Roald Dahl, Jim Henson, Anjelica Huston—but could be conceivably explained by Dahl's sabotage campaign, launched in the press after the author learned of changes made to his story, in particular the new ending. He called the film "utterly appalling,"[28] proclaimed that the studio "had completely missed the point,"[29] and launched into a stormy battle to disassociate his name from the film, going as far as publicly discouraging audiences from seeing it. "I want it known I wouldn't allow a child to see it, let alone encourage one to do so," he said to a reporter.[30] As loud as Dahl might have been, I am not persuaded of his influence on this matter—particularly as his novel *The Witches*, the 22nd most banned book of the 1990s, had not been universally loved either.[31] Instead, I read the film's underwhelming box-office proceeds as another side of the doubts articulated in the critical reviews above. That is, parents in the would-be audience found it hard to reconcile the film's artistic charms with its potential horrors.

This suggestion gains strength when parenting culture of the time is considered. As explored earlier in this chapter, the messages that targeted parents in the late 1980s and increasingly in the 1990s were rooted in attachment principles and, as such, were part of a specific ideology about children and childhood. The values of independence and agency, which had reigned supreme from the 1970s, were now not only questioned but effectively overturned and replaced by notions of innocence and vulnerability. We see an awareness of this shift in the doubts expressed in the reviews above, all of which seem precariously balanced between the two conflicting views of children. But we see it also in the attitudes expressed about children in horror, such as Ebert's damning review of *The Good Son* cited in the previous chapter, and indeed, the horror genre's entire shift toward the R rating.

It's important to note here that these were opinions expressed by professional critics, who may or may not have been parents. Nevertheless, parents are very likely to comprise a significant portion of the audience for a family film—and those parents would have been keenly aware of the shift toward attachment, as they were themselves the main target of these messages.

As I noted at the start of this section, these conflicts are present around *The Witches* but they are subtle. Nevertheless, it is clear that what began here continued to grow as the decade went on and cultural attitudes moved further away from viewing children as resilient beings and toward seeing them as innocents. The next section will expand on the influence of attachment culture, as well as explore how, in conjunction with the business imperative of family entertainment, it eventually sealed the fate of children's horror on screen.

Closing the Cycle: *Casper*

While *The Witches* suggested a new change in attitudes toward children and their entertainment, *Casper* confirms this paradigm shift. It is not only built on the Hollywood family entertainment model but also frames itself as a film about family and for families: clearly targeted at adults alongside children and presenting a wholesome PG narrative about childhood innocence and family togetherness. This framework severely limited the intensity of *Casper*'s horror but not its narrative emphasis: though *Casper* is the softest title in the cycle, it is also one of its clearest illustrations of cultural anxieties about pre-adolescence.

My key point with this case study relates to the new focus of these anxieties. While the films of the 1980s circulate anxieties about changing conceptions of childhood and attempt to establish the identity of the pre-teen group, *Casper* and the other films of the 1990s accept this transformation and focus instead on negotiating how it affects other pillars of American culture, namely the ideal of family as defined by attachment philosophy. Significantly, the textual exploration of pre-adolescence no longer comes from the perspective of children but aligns with the whole family as a unit (and is often guided by the parental point of view). Thus, while pre-adolescence is still represented as a point of tension (and a hook for the horror framework), the child's quest is no longer in pursuit of identity and agency but family harmony. This change affects representations as well as ideology in the texts and is an important part of why, from this point onward, pre-adolescence acquired more traditional associations with childhood, innocence, and vulnerability.

The analysis will first focus on *Casper*'s general lack of association with the horror genre and note how it addresses and resolves the conflicts present in *The Witches*. After this, I will scrutinize *Casper*'s particular use of horror tropes to explore issues around pre-adolescence and attachment philosophy.

Toning It Down

One of the most distinctive features in *Casper* is its tone: soft, and thoroughly sentimental. This tone can be explained by the general approach of the decade's family films but should also be understood in the context of the children's horror cycle and of the cultural and industrial shifts I have been discussing—particularly as *Casper*'s tone was explicitly built on associations with innocence and fairy tales and is what sublimates the film's use of the horror genre.

This is visible across the film's reception. The innocuous nature of the film was unanimously agreed upon, as critics noted the way it "load[ed] on the fairy-tale allusions"[32] and how even the more menacing details seemed to pose no threat at all, not even "our friendly villains"[33] (consisting of "an evil though essentially harmless heiress"[34] and her comic relief assistant) or even Casper's "wacky"[35] (or, at worst, "inhospitable"[36]) uncles, whom a creative reviewer describes as "the *Snow White* dwarfs meet *Gremlins* meet Robin Williams' Genie in *Aladdin*."[37] The *Gremlins* reference may seem out of place here since the two films are diametrically opposed in tone and attitude. But it is evidence that *Casper*'s horror inspirations were still recognized by contemporary critics, even as they were also sublimated by the film's stronger emphasis on childhood innocence.

Casper overtly references a number of fairy tales, most notably *Snow White*, *Cinderella* and *Pinocchio*—all of which are also classic Disney films, connected to the studio's renewed image as champion of childhood and family in the 1990s. This link was an integral part of director Brad Silberling's vision[38] and it pervaded every element of the production. As composer James Horner revealed when commenting on his soundtrack's tone, *Casper* aimed to be "a modern fairy tale" by focusing on that "lost quality of youth or childhood that [Casper] can never recapture."[39]

This lost quality is understood explicitly as innocence. Casper's character and appearance are clear, if ghostly, embodiments of this theme. Note the way critics describe him: his "obsequious and bubble-headed"[40] nature, his "Walter Keane eyes that bat up and down like Bambi's"[41] and his "lovable ... baby face and big blue eyes"[42] make Casper an "adorable creature,"[43] a "cuddly, floating baby-head from the next world."[44] This childlike, even baby-like, aesthetic carries over into his actions, especially those motivated by his puppy love for Kat. Casper's displays of affection are exaggeratedly child-like, from cartoonish expressions and inflated romantic sighs to his naive attempts at seduction, such as shape-shifting into a muscular superhero.

Kat's character also complements this focus on innocence. Although she functions as a more realistic portrayal of pre-adolescence and therefore her actions are slightly more evocative of real-life budding sexuality, her character still hinges on ideals of platonic, innocent romance. Kat and

Casper's relationship is defined by a series of chaste interactions (going to a Halloween party together, a slow dance, a shy first kiss) and led by friendship, with no suggestion of sexual chemistry, budding or otherwise. This, too, was frequently noted by reviewers, who often preferred to describe their coupling as a close friendship rather than a romance, sometimes comparing them to Elliot and E.T.[45] The majority of reviews refer to Casper's longing "to make friends with"[46] Kat and note how they "become fast friends,"[47] or how their "friendship"[48] develops until they become "best friends."[49]

Given these very strong narrative themes, there was no ambiguity about the film's target audience. Critics wrote of watching this "sweet children's movie"[50] in "a theatre packed with 300 happy 8-year-olds,"[51] described it as "an engaging fantasy for very small children,"[52] and noted how its "appeal for small children"[53] was built on "performances for the under-twelve audience."[54] In other words, even if critics realized *Casper*'s use of horror aesthetics and themes, it was still positioned entirely as family entertainment, with not a thought given to the horror genre.

Again, the film itself carefully assured this reading. Even if its use of horror premises (the exploration of anxieties and fears) is serious enough, *Casper* is playful and often tongue-in-cheek in its use of horror aesthetics and tropes. The canted angles, dramatic organ music, and stormy night scenes are deliberately over the top, thrown in not to create an atmosphere of horror but as jokes for the audience's amusement. The Whipstaff Manor set is a particularly blatant example of this approach. The rounded angles, bold swirly lines and warm colors, plus comically excessive cobwebs and dust make the Manor look less like a Gothic haunted house and more like a parody of one. As one of the characters put it, "This looks like Dr. Seuss threw up" (a line tellingly cut out of the first edit "for the fairness of young viewers"[55]).

Like the insistence on the value of innocence, these playful aesthetics flag *Casper*'s affiliation with child audiences and family entertainment. The lack of real peril, the rejection of frightening situations, and the humor all have a deliberate function: to neutralize, and therefore oppose, associations with the horror genre. And this worked in tandem with the film's obvious alignment with the dominant attitudes of the period: not just the understanding of horror as a genre not suitable for children, but also of childhood as a period of innocence. By adopting this perspective, *Casper* effectively avoided the ambiguity and rejection *The Witches* faced at the start of the decade, but the necessity of these compromises also illustrates the diminishing space children's horror could claim in the landscape of 1990s cinema.

Soothing Family Anxieties

Given the evidence presented in the previous section, and my insistence on this cycle's serious approach to its horror affiliation, can *Casper* really be considered a children's horror film? In some ways, this question is prompted by *Casper*'s place as the last film in the cycle, reflecting the usual ambiguities of texts in that position. What is important to highlight, however, is that like all other titles in this film cycle, *Casper* still uses horror to make sense of pre-adolescence and still targets this process at young audiences. There are important differences, of course. *Casper* assumes pre-adolescence and pre-teens are concepts fully established in cultural and industrial discourses, and it moreover fully embraces the family audience. And, significantly, it also acknowledges that the onset of puberty affects not just the child but the entire family. *Casper* is a marker not just of how the door was closed for theatrical children's horror but also of the last significant cultural dilemma around a pre-adolescence: in an age of attachment values, could this move toward independent childhood break up the family?

This fear is what's behind Silberling's insistence that "emotional healing" was at the heart of *Casper*.[56] The "emotional wounds" that intrigued the director are explicitly addressed in the film's use of horror symbolism, particularly death and liminality (in the form of ghosts and ghostliness), which represent pre-adolescence: just as the child must leave childhood ("die") to enter adolescence, so, too, must parents let go of their child to welcome their teenager. Death (that is, puberty) affects all characters in *Casper* and is, in each case, linked to fears about the destruction of parent/child bonds and the dissolution of the family unit.

For Casper, puberty is represented by his own death and is associated with isolation, loneliness and separation from his father. For Kat, puberty is symbolized through her friendship with *Casper*, and it is through this relationship that Kat confesses her fears of abandonment, of forgetting and being forgotten by her family.[57] Both Casper's and Kat's anxieties reflect the danger of losing one's childhood identity, particularly as this is what parental love is seen to depend on. This same anxiety is mirrored by their parents, whose fears are based on the assumption that a child's love for their parents hinges on their need for protection, a need puberty and its resulting independence would remove.

This is quite clearly worked out in the film's narrative, particularly as the film contrasts different parental responses to this problem: refusal to accept the situation, represented by Casper's father, and an irresponsible eagerness, represented by Dr. Harvey. The film's message is ultimately to strike a balance between the two, but one keeping in line with attachment philosophy.

Note how it all plays out. When Casper recounts his death/puberty to Kat, he focuses on how deeply this affected his father: "I got sick. My dad got sad." The viewers also learn that after his death/puberty, Casper's father became consumed with bringing him back—symbolically, back to childhood from adolescence. This was an impossible pursuit, but one the film also portrays as deeply unhealthy to the relationship between the two, keeping them forever disconnected from one another and also impeding Casper's complete maturation, leaving him stuck as a ghost.

Dr. Harvey's approach is also presented as destructive to all involved. After drinking too much in an attempt to forget his wife's death,[58] Dr. Harvey has a fatal accident. The film's approach is too hopeful to make this mistake final, so he comes back as a ghost—however, the newfound freedom of this state means he forgets his previous life almost entirely, including his daughter and his responsibilities toward her. Kat is devastated, but eventually her demonstrations of filial love, affection, and continued need for emotional closeness (one might say attachment) remind Dr. Harvey of their bond.

This moment is the film's emotional climax, and it speaks directly to the question of pre-adolescence and attachment values by soothing the anxieties of both parent and child about this transition. Adding another layer of meaning, the film brings Dr. Harvey back to life using Casper's father's invention (itself a product of parental love). The mystery and treasure of Whipstaff Manor is then revealed—not gold but love, specifically the love between a parent and their child—and with it, the film's message and philosophy: pre-adolescence may be the beginning of the end of childhood but it is not the end of innocence or of an attachment-focused relationship; family will always remain.

The "emotional healing" and "emotional wounds" emphasized by Silberling are thus quite clearly related to fears over the way puberty might change a child's relationship with the family. In interviews and in the DVD commentary, Silberling repeatedly framed *Casper* as a film about parenting and the preservation of good relationships between parent and child. He spoke, for instance, of Dr. Harvey's fear of "not being quite up to speed on what it is to raise a daughter" and his tendency to "panic, as any parent would, about not having the skills to parenting."[59] Though Silberling generalizes here, Dr. Harvey's anxieties are actually quite specific in the text: he doesn't know how to respond to Kat's transition out of childhood. He is confused about which words to use with his daughter (she wants to "hang" with her friends, not "play"), does not seem to be in tune with his daughter's preoccupations (looking "date-nice," not "cute"), and when he displays his affection by kissing her on the cheek, Kat's response is "I hope no one saw that."

The solution to Dr. Harvey's problem is eventually dispensed by his dead wife, who comes back as an angel. Kat is "growing beautifully because of you," she reassures him, and adds, "Don't pick up the extension every time she gets a phone call, french fries are not a breakfast food, and don't ask her to wear a t-shirt under her bathing suit." In other words, the key to parenting the new Kat is to allow her to grow up—without relinquishing innocence and attachment.

Conclusion

Here is where the children's horror film cycle ends. As I've been arguing, this cycle was a vehicle for expressing contested shifts in attitudes about childhood and horror, prompted by the emergence of pre-adolescence. What this chapter and the last have shown is not that these questions found definitive answers but that they were placated—at least within the boundaries of the cinema medium.

The previous chapter made this case for the horror question: are children a legitimate audience of the genre? It only makes sense to ask if there's any room for ambiguity—but an emphasis on the R rating and other strategies removed this ambiguity, so the question needs not be asked anymore. A similar process took place for the childhood question: is there an audience between young children and teenagers for whom some intense content might be appropriate? In reality, the need to verify suitability no longer existed in the context of 1990s Hollywood because the dominant production model, family entertainment, demands suitability for even the youngest children in the audience. So this question needs not be asked, either.

There was, nevertheless, some cultural resolution in this process, and it refers specifically to pre-adolescence. Throughout the decade, the preteen is not just present but easily recognizable across Hollywood's features: he is the "skinny preadolescent boy" in *Beethoven* (1992)[60]; she is Christina Ricci getting her first kiss from Casper; he is Kevin, home alone and indulging in "some preteen risky business: videos, sundaes and sled rides."[61] As I argued here, the idea of pre-adolescence as a significant transition and of the pre-teen as a distinct social group is so deeply established in American culture by this time that other related anxieties became central. The most significant of these related to the family, and whether pre-adolescence could destabilize the attached dynamics promoted in parenting culture, but even this was relatively short-lived—attachment philosophy quickly prevailed.[62]

Without this anxiety to address, or the space to explore either of its previous questions, children's horror was no longer a viable film trend. As I also argued in the previous chapter, it's important to stress how this was related to vital transformations in the cultural and industrial situation of the cinema medium. The core premise of a business model primarily based on family entertainment was that most of its product should be both suitable and entertaining for all audiences—much as it had been in the days of the Code. Consequently, smaller niche audiences (such as children, or pre-teens in isolation) were no longer profitable, and so ceased existing as distinct or significant targets.[63]

Children in particular, central as they were to Hollywood production, were always conceived of as being attached to an equally-important, at times even more important, adult audience. The point was well illustrated by Felicity Dahl, when asked about *The Witches* and its film adaptation: "What makes Hollywood think children want the endings changed for a film, when they accept it in a book?" The answer, of course, is not that children want these changes but that their parents might, and they—not the children—are the main target in family entertainment. And again in *Casper*, a film which was well-received primarily because it combined family entertainment and (soft) horror to address a question of interest to adult audiences.

Cinema itself quickly became a signal for this form of address, reconstructed as a medium for generalist, mostly adult, audiences. This transformation is why the children's horror film cycle ended—but also why the trend was able to continue in different media, which preserved their child-oriented spaces. The next chapter takes a close look at these protected spaces, and explores how and why the children's horror trend still thrived in the 1990s.

CHAPTER 6

"Viewer beware ... you're in for a scare": The Horror of Puberty, Televised and Serialized

With its film cycle dead and buried, children's horror changed gear. This shift into other media was timid at first; a title here and there, mainly restricted to children's fiction (*Creepers*, *Bone Chillers*). But soon the trend expanded to television, with various live-action (*Eerie, Indiana*) and animated shows (*Nightmare Ned*), adaptations (*Goosebumps*) and originals (*Are You Afraid of the Dark?*), as well as straight-to-video and television films (*Tower of Terror*), plus toys (*Boglins*) and games (*Atmosfear*). By the mid-decade, horror had filled every crevice, nook, and corner of children's culture, becoming one of the most notorious trends of the period.

In many ways, this expansion beyond cinema was inevitable. A new idea of childhood had been fully integrated into American culture, for one, meaning that the pre-teen audience was easier to identify and target, therefore leading to massive expansion in children's media and entertainment. While these are industrial changes, they also correspond to a cultural soothing of the tensions around children's horror: because it now worked from dominant cultural expectations about childhood, its representations and levels of intensity were widely perceived to be appropriate, and because it was positioned exclusively in child-oriented markets, it was not judged against the expectations of adult-oriented media.

This chapter explores how leaving the cinema behind and expanding into other media transformed children's horror from a problematic trend into a benevolent (and wildly successful) one. In the process, I aim to confirm the arguments I made in the previous two chapters—that in the 1990s cinema became a prestige medium for adult audiences primarily, and that the concept of pre-adolescence was softened by the cultural dominance of attachment-style families. In addition, I make two new points:

First, I argue that the popularity of children's horror outside of cinema circulates a return to the status quo: horror and childhood were strongly re-established as antagonistic cultural notions. Second, I argue that this reinforced antagonism locked children's horror inside the confines of children's culture, making it invisible in mainstream pop culture but also nourishing the development of the trend's greatest emotional and cultural strength, its laser-focus on children's anxieties over puberty.

The chapter begins with an examination of the distinctions between the cinema and the more narrowly targeted children's media industries. I focus specifically on how these differences affected the horror genre, to point out a sharp contrast between the cinema's insistence on restriction and other media's embracing of diverse audiences. I then take the *Goosebumps* franchise as a case study, noting the deliberate way it avoided mixed-audience outlets and linking this respect for the limits of children's culture to its uncontroversial reception. Lastly, I closely analyze the *Goosebumps* "formula" and argue its significance as a window into America's notion of pre-adolescence, including the ways horror might be especially appropriate for this demographic.

Meanwhile, in Other Media: The Children's Market Welcomes Horror

In the previous chapter I detailed Hollywood's move toward a family entertainment model and explained how this resulted in a more homogeneous medium directed at a single (if rather broad) audience. As I suggested, this business model was a characteristic of the medium not one of the period. Indeed, virtually every other medium of pop culture moved in the opposite direction during the 1990s: toward an ever-clearer fragmentation of audiences and therefore an increasingly varied and differentiated output. It was in those spaces that children's horror truly thrived, with television and publishing deserving special mention for the way they cultivated not just the children's market but the horror niche as well.

Let us begin with publishing, as its example is straightforward. Children's literature has been established as a market separate to general or adult-oriented literature since at least the nineteenth century (this market split is in fact a big part of what makes certain texts recognizable as children's fiction and not general fiction featuring children), but the strength of children's fiction as a market in its own right rather than a niche was especially notoriously in the 1980s and 1990s. It was the time of the echo boom and more children meant a greater demand for children's books. But it also meant that variety, not just quantity, was in the industry's favor. Different kinds of books could reach different kinds of children and therefore assure profit. This is why the 1990s were especially rich in new formats, such as the gamebook[1] or, indeed, the children's horror novel.

To be sure, children's literature had never been strangers with horror, but the relationship was different in this period because horror became a specialized genre within children's literature, as opposed to an intrinsic and more general part of its content, as it had been in the times of violent fairy tales, folk stories, and cautionary novels. Not only that, horror also became one of the most popular genres of the period: the *Goosebumps* series, of course, but also countless others, beginning with Alvin Schartz's famous *Scary Stories to Tell in the Dark*, a popular series of three illustrated books (and audiobooks) of adapted folklore and urban myths. Schartz wrote other collections of scary stories for children based on popular mythology and horror retellings, among them *In a Dark, Dark Room and Other Scary Stories*, published as part of HarperCollins' "I Can Read!" series in 1984. *Short & Shivery* by Robert D. San Souci was another very popular series of retellings and adaptations, which ran between 1987 and 1998.

Although these examples are folk retellings and therefore tie back to the previous ways in which children's literature used horror, the market also craved new original fiction featuring contemporary children in contemporary settings. Popular authors here include the obligatory Christopher Pike, whose *Slumber Party* (1985) is often (erroneously) credited as the start of the children's horror trend,[2] but also Betty Ren Wright (*A Ghost in the House*, first published in 1991 and reprinted in 1995, plus other titles) and Mary Downing Hahn, who, among many other titles, wrote *Wait Till Helen Comes* (1986), winner of the Young Reader's Choice Award and other prizes, and *The Doll in the Garden* (1989), also a repeat award-winner. There was also a trend for bringing back hit tiles of the 1970s, as was the case with J.B. Stamper's *Tales for the Midnight Hour*, which was first published in 1977 but followed by sequels in 1987, 1989, 1991 and 2005. Sequels, series, follow-ups and spin-offs were particularly popular: R.C. Welch's *Scary Stories for Sleep-Overs* (1991) had nine follow-up collections (1992–1999), for instance, while the series *Scary Mysteries for Sleep-Overs* spanned four volumes plus three spin-off novels by Allen B. Ury between 1996 and 1997.

The examples of successful children's horror fiction are many, and it would be impossible to list them exhaustively, particularly as many popular series spawned dozens of individual titles.[3] This expansion in horror is evidence of my claims here about the children's horror trend, but I also want to stress that it was not an isolated success; it was part of a more general expansion in the children's market. A large and increasingly specialized output, whether in horror or other genres, could only be accommodated within a market big enough and profitable enough to prize a variety of products.

The proliferation of children's bookstores, dedicated exclusively to the promotion and consumption of children's fiction, provide further evidence not just of this market boom but also of its cause: the phenomenon of children's bookstores began in the late 1970s and faded away in the late 1990s[4]—the period of the echo boom and of Millennial childhood. The popularity of dedicated children's bookstores also tells of a change in associations with children and their place in society. Their reading used to be considered a private matter and the concern of educational institutions and spaces, such as book fairs, libraries, and schools—in much the same way as it used to be a niche portion of the general publishing business. After the 1980s, however, children and their entertainment (not just their education) moved to the public sphere, becoming an openly commercial endeavor but also claiming some visibility and legitimacy in the space of mainstream culture.

These changes—overt commercial goals, audience fragmentation, and an increasing demand for variety of product leading to abundant horror content—are also clear in the television industry's developments during this period. The 1980s and 1990s are commonly known as American television's TVII period, characterized by network expansion and branding strategies—and a sharp contrast to the business model of TVI (mid–1950s to early 1980s), that of a few channels broadcasting to an undifferentiated mass audience. Network expansion and aggressive branding meant that television was no longer broadcasting but narrowcasting: many channels, often specialized, to many small audiences. This model was amplified even further with the advent of digital technology in TVIII (1990s–present day), where each (niche) channel uses its (niche) brand to quickly identify, separate, and reach its own (niche) audience.

This industrial template worked in favor of child audiences. Because there were more channels and therefore less pressure on schedule space, children's content quickly expanded from Saturday morning into weekday afternoon and weekend blocks, and from there into entire dedicated networks. These channels then built their identity and brand on the kind of audience they targeted, often stressing their uniqueness by relying on oppositions. It was not enough to advertise their focus on child audiences, they needed also to highlight that they did *not* focus on adult audiences—the reverse of what film horror had done in the 1990s.

Nickelodeon is a great example of this branding strategy. The channel began in the late 1970s under the name Pinwheel but was quickly rebranded as Nickelodeon in 1979, becoming the first all-children's network on American television. The first five years were modestly successful, but it was only in 1984, after Geraldine Laybourne's team took over its management, that Nickelodeon entered its golden age and began to really make history. According to Laybourne, Nickelodeon used to have a reputation for being a "goody two-shoes, baby network" on account of the "conventional thinking" behind the brand and its inclination to "tell kids what to do."[5] What Laybourne is saying here is not that Nickelodeon didn't have a brand, but that this brand retained the thinly-veiled educational intentions of the defunct Pinwheel and was therefore too close to the interests of parents and adults to highlight the uniqueness of their target audience, pre-teens.

Laybourne wanted to do things differently. "A lot of television has a low view of its audience," she commented in interview, "but we didn't think we could get anything by with kids."[6] In elevating child audiences like this, Nickelodeon not only separated itself from other children's channels but made clear that its commitment was to this demographic alone, to the exclusion of all others. Furthermore, Laybourne's team tailored Nickelodeon's brand to closely match the interests of pre-teens. The channel then became not just about gentle rebellion against adult authority but also rooted in such values as agency and independence, which were key to America's cultural view of the pre-adolescent years.

The content had to match the brand, so Nickelodeon exclusively backed productions that emphasized children's interests and promoted them over those of other audiences, especially adults. Game shows like *Double Dare* (1986–1993) and *Guts* (1992–1996) and comedy shows like *Salute Your Shorts* (1991–1992) and the animated *Ren & Stimpy* (1991–1995) reinforced the kind of youth rebellion and independence Nickelodeon stood for, but they also aimed to create a collective pre-teen identity, with its own sense of humor and cultural references which were separate from the wholesome world of Disney and other bastions of childhood innocence. The same applied to other children's networks and productions.

Much like children's publishing, children's television was now a full market needing quantity as well as variety of content—thus setting the scene for children's horror once again. As with fiction, the examples are too many to list, but a select few from across channels can illustrate its breadth: *Are You Afraid of the Dark?* (YTV), *Eerie, Indiana* (NBC) and *Eerie, Indiana: The Other Dimension* (Fox Kids, 1998), *Aaahh!!! Real Monsters* (Nickelodeon, 1994–1997), *Tales from the Cryptkeeper* (ABC) and *New Tales from the Cryptkeeper* (CBS, 1997), *Courage, the Cowardly Dog* (Cartoon Network, 1999–2002), and others.

What the publishing and television industries have in common is also what the film industry increasingly lost from the 1990s onwards: a business model based on audience segmentation. The pre-teen market can only exist if it is kept separate from the general (adult) and family markets because meeting the needs of those wider audiences will tend to override the notion of a distinct pre-teen identity. As Nickelodeon demonstrates, the most successful way to reinforce a pre-teen identity, with its own values and culture, is precisely to oppose it to other groups: young children *as well as* families and adults. This is not viable if niche audiences are not profitable, as they increasingly were not in film.

Industrial differences aside, film, television, and publishing still shared the same cultural context, and therefore their children's horror texts are part of the same sociocultural shifts. Note the parallels between the key years of the cycle and the most significant publications, for example: the *Scary Stories to Tell in the Dark* trilogy was published in 1981, 1984 and 1991, respectively the years of the film cycle's start, the introduction of PG-13, and the first struggles with the film medium. Likewise, even the most cursory glance at the other titles mentioned in this section will reveal that the vast majority of the other texts was published or released after the PG-13 rating was introduced and therefore only after pre-adolescence had become an acknowledged concept in American culture. In other words, there is a clear continuity between the film cycle and the rest of the trend, a point that will become clearer as I move into my case study analysis in the rest of the chapter.

Building an Empire: The *Goosebumps* Franchise

If children's horror has one title to rule them all, this is without question R.L. Stine's *Goosebumps*. The franchise is one of the biggest icons of children's culture in the 1990s, described as a "generational touchstone" in *The Wire*[7] and recently named one of the "cultural artifacts that induce Proustian flashbacks in millennials" in *Newsweek*.[8] The books in particular remain dizzyingly successful, with over 300 million in sales, translations into 32 languages,[9] and two Guinness records (best-selling children's book series of all-time in 2003, and most prolific author of children's horror fiction novels for Stine in 2011).[10] Critics have dubbed Stine "the Enid Blyton *de nous jours*"[11] and "Stephen King for children"[12]—though he is in reality a better-selling writer than King,[13] counting in his sales history feats such as authoring nearly all of the top 20 best-selling paperback children's books in 1995 and 1996.[14]

This is unquestionable success, and given the arguments of this book, a feat that is not hard to understand. Not only did the film cycle prepare the way for series like *Goosebumps*, Stine and his publishers, Scholastic, were also lucky enough to be presented with an expanding market and a new, very sizeable and still underserved demographic. Stine should be credited for some of the series' success—as I argue later in this chapter, his "formula" captures pre-adolescence in significant ways—but *Goosebumps* must first be understood as a product of the new children's industries. Every step the franchise took, including its genesis as a book series, was guided by an editor or producer's insight into the new pre-teen identity and the pre-teen market.

The commercial savvy behind *Goosebumps* has always been acknowledged by Stine, in a mix of modesty and cynicism. "It was never my idea," he has repeatedly said about his career as a horror writer. "An editor said, 'I need a scary novel for teenagers. Go write a book called *Blind Date*.' She even gave me the title." As if to make the point clearer, Stine quickly added that he did not even believe in this project, but that he "was at that point in [his] career where you don't say no to anything." So he wrote the book. "[A]nd it was a No.-1 bestseller in *Publishers Weekly*. I'd been writing 20 years and had never been on that list. I'd struck a chord with kids."[15]

In spite of this success, the idea for the next project, *Fear Street*, did not come from Stine either: an editor "suggested that I write a teen horror series—and I said it was a bad idea."[16] Sales proved the opposite but still, when the opportunity arose to write a new series, one aimed at younger children this time—the one which would become *Goosebumps*—Stine was skeptical; he "thought it was a bad idea to compete with *Fear Street*."[17] In Stine's own words, "the real truth" is that "like most everything I've ever done in my career, I wrote [*Goosebumps*] because someone asked me to."[18]

Even if Stine maintains this perplexed façade over the success of his books, his comments suggest that his editors were anything but clueless about the market's fluctuations. The same applies to book's adaptations for television. According to Margaret Loesch, then-president of the Fox Children's Network, the *Goosebumps* show (YTV/FOX Kids, 1995–1998) was greenlit because she saw its potential to fit the demands of the children's television market: "I saw a group of five or six kids sitting on the floor, with their noses glued in these books, and not only that, but they were passing them around, asking each other if they'd read this one or that one. And even more interesting, it was a mixed group, boys and girls, which is rare."[19] With her support, *Goosebumps* went on to take over the programming slot reserved for *Mighty Morphin Power Rangers*, "by far the highest-rated children's program on television" in the mid–1990s.[20]

The *Goosebumps* paperbacks had been "staples of fourth graders' backpacks,"[21] but after the television series, the franchise grew so big the backpacks themselves were soon branded with the *Goosebumps* logo. The market overflowed with *Goosebumps* collectibles, toys, board games and video games, stationary, party goods, posters, costumes, bedding and apparel from baseball caps to sneakers, plus the VHS releases of the television episodes and their re-issued tie-in books. There was also a temporary Disney theme park attraction, as well as special campaigns with popular food and drink companies, among them Pepsi, Taco Bell, Frito-Lay, Hershey, General Mills, and KFC.

None of this was unplanned expansion, though—all of these promotions, deals, and merchandising items were targeted at pre-teens exclusively. Even at the height of the franchise's popularity, "not many people over 13 [knew R.L. Stine] except teachers, parents, booksellers and publishers."[22] And even these adult exceptions were never immersed in *Goosebumps*, but rather perceived it through the children they were close to—like the mother who wrote to Stine saying she liked his books "because they give my kids shivers but not nightmares,"[23] or the radio interviewer who "actually did watch [*The Haunting Hour*, a follow-up series]. Because I have ten-year-old boys,"[24] or even one of Stine's recent editors who claimed to knows his work "well" because "her ten-year-old son devours his books 'like crack.'"[25]

Audiences under the age of eight were just as unimportant as those over the age of thirteen, and likewise ignored in all campaigns. As the *Goosebumps* director of brand management explained in an interview, "Once that fifth-grader goes to school assembly and sees a kindergartner in a *Goosebumps* shirt, it's all over."[26] This statement reveals not just a clear intention to narrow-target the franchise at pre-teens but also an understanding that this targeting could be accomplished by highlighting this group's identity as separate from both adults and younger children. As a critic noted when describing the franchise, "fourth grade—that's the demographic bull's-eye."[27] Any format or decision which could dilute this target was simply not pursued.

There were other nuances to this marketing strategy. The next section focuses on how the horror genre was presented while the one after examines how the *Goosebumps* brand remained successful in spite of changes in the entertainment industries.

Controversy? What Controversy?

Even if *Goosebumps*'s strict targeting meant that it never came close to crossing the boundaries of pre-teen culture, its promotional campaigns still had to contend with the parents and educators who enabled pre-teens to engage with the *Goosebumps* brand. In this section I will address the way Scholastic's marketing campaigns were strategically split into two layers: one for children, which emphasized horror, and a second for their related adults, which did the exact opposite. My claim is that this tactic allowed *Goosebumps* to deflect nearly all suitability challenges while still retaining its authenticity as horror—but only as far as its target audience was concerned.

This promotional strategy goes a long way toward explaining *Goosebumps*'s reputation as not-horror outside of the children's sphere. Its "horror-cheese specifications"[28] weren't taken seriously by contemporary critics, and the few scholars interested in the series mentioned horror only to explain what *Goosebumps* was not. The famous horror covers were labeled "faux-gruesome"[29] by Timothy Norris, while Kimberley Reynolds was of the opinion that these stories were only "what [young readers] refer to as 'horror.'"[30] As Reynolds put it,

> Though [children's horror] texts [such as *Goosebumps*] imitate the narrative voice associated with traditional horror—strong on suspense, intimating impending crisis, trying to create a sense that something dreadful is just about to happen—they are in fact primarily concerned with showing many childish fears to be unfounded.... The certainty and sense of control produced by such texts are precisely the opposite of the reactions inspired by horror, or any other kind of fiction designed to create a feeling of fear in readers.[31]

This view was shared by Reynolds's collaborators and is still pervasive in some critical opinions today. But if this condescending reception had a lot to do with these authors's view of horror and their motivations for championing a stricter definition of the genre, it is also true that it was an opinion endorsed by Scholastic. The child-oriented elements of marketing might have advertised chills and thrills, such as the tagline printed on every *Goosebumps HorrorLand* book ("The all-new, all-terrifying series from the master of fright!"), but the branding directed at adult "consumers," that is parents and teachers, painted a much more sedate picture. Because these "consumers" were not expected to actually consume the series, the marketing directed at them was much more abstract about the actual contents and tone of *Goosebumps*. Moreover, it was produced with the explicit goal of pre-empting and evading anxieties about horror and suitability.

In Scholastic's Guide to Parents, for example, *Goosebumps* is described as "the beloved classic thriller series where kids triumph over evil," featuring "spooky (and funny!) tales."[32] The absence of key words such as "all-terrifying" and "master of fright" used in the child-oriented marketing is notorious, as is the omission of the word "horror." Instead, the emphasis is placed on safety, mystery, and humor—a move that comes at the expense of accuracy in describing the books' contents. In reality, children do not always triumph in *Goosebumps* stories, and even those who do are often put through distressing moments. Likewise humor is mostly absent from the plots and is confined to jokes the characters might tell each other, or to small details outside of the narratives, such as the titles (*It Came from Beneath the Sink!*) or the tag lines on the covers ("It's warm! It's breathing! And it doesn't do the dishes!").

This same portrayal of the series as not-entirely-horror was enforced by Stine in interviews. "You don't want kids to think [these stories are] true," the author said. "I try to make sure they know it's all crazy and silly."[33] Stine also frequently emphasized his lack of faith in horror and fear in general, claiming that horror makes him laugh.[34] Similar to Tim Burton's claims of the same attitude (see Chapter 4), the suggestion is not only that he does not take his scary books seriously but also that his intentions in writing them are not malicious. As one of Stine's frequent lines goes, "I never intended to be scary; I only wanted to be funny."[35] To stress the point further, Stine has also frequently expressed strong disapproval of the more extreme and violent iterations of horror ("I hate slashing. I hate the torture kind of horror films"), preferring ones "that have a good surprise" and are "clever."[36]

All of this is evidence of smart marketing on Scholastic's part, who assumed—correctly, judging from the contemporary critical reception—that adults would only know the surface of *Goosebumps*. The real draw of the series was saved for young eyes only: as the books' famous tagline went, "Reader beware ... you're in for a scare!" Adult non-readers, meanwhile, had no need to beware and could focus instead on the other famous slogan for the series, "Reading is a scream!," which was stamped on every book and on some of the merchandise (primarily stationery and other school supplies).

This second slogan also tackled a second important concern around children's popular fiction (and horror): its lowbrow position and therefore its suggested low educational value. Literacy—not suitability—was at the heart of the only known *Goosebumps* controversy. When the series made the list of most challenged books of the 1990s,[37] several districts across the United States held hearings on whether *Goosebumps* books should be banned from their school libraries. From a distance this might have looked like a challenge of the series's violence, horror, and high number of dead children, but what was actually at stake was the series' place on children's reading programs.

As one pro-ban parent put it in a letter to her school district, "These books do absolutely nothing to edify our children, or to promote decent morals, or kindness to one another."[38] Another argued the point in even clearer terms, claiming that *Goosebumps* did not meet "district values for educational value" and stressing how "amazed and appalled [she was] that the only way [parents] can get [children] to read [is to] let them read this type of garbage."[39] These concerns were not restricted to parents. In the words of a less sympathetic critic, Stine was nothing but "a literary training bra for Stephen King."[40] The comparison is enlightening: what might seem on the surface to be about horror and morality reveals itself here to be just as heavy with anxiety over lowbrow reading habits, literacy, and educational prospects, all of which are part of the negative discourse surrounding King's books.

Literacy, in fact, featured heavily in both sides of the *Goosebumps* debate.[41] Even the most reluctant school principals, teachers, and librarians recognized and valued the series' power to motivate young readers: some counted *Goosebumps* as "good books to get started with," others did not exclude them but encouraged children to "read other genres and more 'quality literature,'" while others still opposed bans but limited children's reading of *Goosebumps* to "a brief period on Fridays" or classified it as strictly recreational reading.[42] As both sides seemed to roughly agree that *Goosebumps* books could be good in moderation, the debate over book banning was ultimately short-lived, with many schools voting to keep them available and some continuing to use them actively in the classroom.[43]

Not only was this controversy brief, it is now only a footnote in the franchise's history, seldom mentioned even in the most complete retrospective critiques. This is evidence of the strength of Scholastic's marketing tactics, which framed *Goosebumps* in the ways that mattered most to each of its audiences: horror authenticity for the core pre-teen target and literacy for the parents. There was little attempt to blend the two, and the result was a franchise that registered as legitimate on both counts: legitimate horror, and legitimate children's fiction.

Staying Put: Children's Culture Over the Mainstream

Together, the previous two sections clarify the foundations of the *Goosebumps* franchise and of its success: a strong narrow target and an acceptance of the market's pre-existing framework for children's media, including the existence of internal suitability agreements and the centrality of educational aims. What I want to argue next is that these factors, initially driven by the market conditions, also became an integral part of the *Goosebumps* brand, dictating its format as well as shaping its content—so much so that when the market changed again in the late 1990s to favor broad-reach content, the *Goosebumps* franchise could not adapt to the new expectations while staying loyal to its own brand.

The market shift started in publishing and followed much of what had happened in film from the start of the 1990s: though child readers were still valuable, books that appealed to family audiences were increasingly taking precedence. The best example here (indeed, the watershed moment) is the cross-generational success of J.K. Rowling's *Harry Potter* series, which brought contemporary children's fiction into the mainstream. Because adult readers were associated not just with profit but with cultural prestige, they quickly became an important target, taken seriously and accounted for in promotional campaigns, merchandise, and even the characteristics of the books in question: from increasing length, to a reliance on prestige hardback editions, and including more mature content, even if these books still came under the children's fiction label.

Stine has not been shy about voicing his discontent with the new status quo. Children's books, he said, "used to be a paperback business [but] they don't want that [anymore], now it's all hardcover series. And everything's a trilogy."[44] On a different occasion, Stine was even more explicit: this industrial shift "ruined publishing" for him because hardcovers "are all publishers want now. The monthly book series are over."[45]

To an extent, Stine's criticism is justified. Monthly series did indeed decline in quantity and popularity since the advent of the *Harry Potter* cross-over model, in great part because they could not sustain their appeal when audience targets were broadened. The first problem was the content: because they were tailored to young readers, the narratives were simpler and often focused on matters of childhood that would seem trivial to older readers. The second problem was that the format lacked prestige: paperbacks were cheap, sometimes even disposable, and associated with lowbrow reading tastes. In the context of children's culture, these problems had not been problems at all. On the contrary, as Stine also points out, the paperback format was associated with a sense of agency for the child consumer: "I like one a month; kids are waiting for the next one. I also liked it because kids could afford it. They'd come into a bookstore with five bucks and buy four different books."[46]

Here is where the *Goosebumps* brand becomes deeper than a good combination of market factors. The sense of agency Stine refers to is a big part of the series's "formula," and it goes hand in hand with the sense of empowerment the stories instill in their young readers. The *Goosebumps* books were not simply consumables but a representation of puberty and the pre-teen experience, closely tailored to the tastes, values, and anxieties of the franchise's narrow demographic.

All of this will become clearer in the next section as I dissect the books's themes and representations; my point here is that the franchise's alignment with the pre-teen demographic and rejection of all other groups affected its content (and was affected by it in turn). The *Goosebumps* brand was therefore closely tied to the franchise's cultural meaning as defined by its target demographic, and it could not easily be changed, much less opened to outsiders, without betraying its own brand values.

There seems to have been an implicit understanding of this in the way *Goosebumps* navigated the changes in markets—it stayed just as it was. The book series remained a monthly paperback (with the single exception of a special commemorative hardback edition for the series's twentieth anniversary). The extent to which this was an unusual decision is seen in the way critics described the *Goosebumps 2000* series, which ran from 1998 to 2000: it was a "relic"[47] of different times, holding on to a "doomed" format.[48] The same attitude extended beyond the book series. There was no prestige boxset of television adaptations, only the same VHS releases of the show's two-parter episodes, with each story released as a separate video.

And, of course, there was no tie-in movie.[49] The official explanation for this is that producers "never had the right idea."[50] But a more likely reason why a *Goosebumps* movie did not happen in the 1990s was that the cinema was not a good medium for a pre-teen-oriented brand—both because of horror's rejection of child audiences (Chapter 4) and because of Hollywood's reliance of family audiences (Chapter 5). The incompatibility between expectations of film and the *Goosebumps* brand is particularly evident when we consider its "formula" and the proximity between its tone and that of *The Gate* rather than later children's horror films like *Casper* and *Nightmare Before Christmas*. To adapt the series into an R-rated horror film was out of the question, and to make it fit the family entertainment model would require changes so significant to the *Goosebumps* ethos it would barely be recognizable in its brand.[51]

Once again, we might read market savvy in this decision to bypass the opportunity for cultural prestige and bigger profits in favor of keeping the brand intact—the *Goosebumps* franchise is, after all, still going. But more importantly, this continued cultural presence highlights just how deeply the *Goosebumps* brand is connected to the pre-teen demographic—not many book series have resonated this deeply and continued to resonate, unchanged, with batch after batch of pre-teen. The next section explores why this is so.

Monstrous Puberty or, When Is a Formula Something Else?

I've spent most of this chapter making the case that the *Goosebumps* franchise should be understood as a product of the markets of its time, particularly as an example of what a focus on the pre-teen audience exclusively could produce, and how it facilitated uncontroversial approaches to children's horror. But, as I have also been suggesting, *Goosebumps* cannot be understood on market terms alone. The key to its brand, and an important reason for its success, was the way it used horror to serve a significant emotional and cultural purpose specific to its pre-teen audience: soothing anxieties about the onset of puberty.

The first evidence of the emotional, cultural, and social work done by the *Goosebumps* series comes from the mouth of the children themselves. As they repeatedly told Stine in their fan letters, their enjoyment of *Goosebumps* was not simply because they "like to be scared!"[52] but ran much deeper, amounting to almost a compulsion. Some letters demonstrated a desire to live the stories fully ("When you die, can I take over your series?"),[53] while others showed this engagement to be so deep they overlooked any flaws ("I like your books, but how come the endings never make any sense?").⁵⁴ A particularly insightful letter, incidentally Stine's favorite, came from an outraged and enthralled fan: "I've read forty of your books—and I think they're really boring!"⁵⁵

This kind of fan reaction has not been entirely overlooked by critics and scholars, but it has been understood superficially. Timothy Morris, for instance, who has written one of the few existing studies of the series, was quick to dismiss the contents of the novels, which he sees as "above all a formula,"⁵⁶ in order to turn his attention instead to the craze around them, wondering if "all that will come out of reading *Goosebumps* novels is a mindless, soul-deadening consumerism."⁵⁷ For Morris, the "dynamic of reading and collecting is ultimately of more cultural importance than anything in the 'content' of these series. The way we buy and save these books may effectively be their content."⁵⁸ While collecting was very much a part of the *Goosebumps* phenomenon, the suggestion that the series's actual contents are irrelevant is unconvincing, particularly given the relation between format, audience target, and content that I have explored in the rest of this chapter.

There is, however, an interesting passage in Morris's analysis: a very brief mention that the *Goosebumps* books provide a "fantasy [of preadolescence] for eight and nine year olds."⁵⁹ He does not pursue the observation further, nor does he connect it to the audience's compulsive habits of consumption. But this is an important link to make, and it is the foundation of the argument I want to put forth here: this aspirational vision of pre-adolescence is not just a minor aspect of the *Goosebumps* franchise but is in fact at its deepest core. Acknowledging that anxieties over the onset of puberty are the central (maybe even the only) theme of *Goosebumps* is significant not just because it explains why and how the series was able to resonate so strongly even before the franchise exploded but also because it clarifies why the *Goosebumps* "formula" eventually became the blueprint for all children's horror to come after it.

There is plenty of evidence that puberty is the *Goosebumps* engine. The horror in the books always comes, after all, in the form of changes to physical and emotional stability, always to twelve-year-old protagonists, and to both sexes in equal measure. The most explicit example of the metaphor is *My Hairiest Adventure*, in which Larry grows unexpected hair and undergoes physical changes that he is embarrassed to discuss with his parents. He does open up to Lily, a friend going through the same, and the narrative then hints at the beginnings of romantic feelings between the two. In this story, as well as others, physical changes are presented to the characters as an inevitability. They are, in fact, explicitly presented as a rite of passage (*Welcome to Camp Nightmare*) and as part of the process by which the *Goosebumps* children discover their true identity—whether as monsters (*The Girl Who Cried Monster*), vampires (*Vampire Breath*) or other creatures (*The Ghost Next Door*).

However the horror (that is, puberty) is delivered, any attempts on the child's part to avoid it are promptly punished. In *Be Careful What You Wish For*, the inescapable nature of puberty's suffering is made explicit through the cursed wishes given to Sam. All three backfire horribly, particularly the last one, when Sam wishes for Judy, her nemesis, to be given wishes, too, so they can ruin her life instead. Unfortunately for Sam, Judy's first wish is for Sam to "fly away," which turns her into a bird. *Calling All Creeps* presents another version of the same idea. In this story, Ricky wants to get back at his school newspaper editor but accidentally makes himself the target of the lizard aliens known as Creeps. Making the best out of a sticky situation, Ricky appoints himself the leader of the Creeps and turns the entire school into his slaves—if you can't beat them, join them. *You Can't Scare Me* offers another variant of this philosophy of embracing things as they are, when Eddie and Hat finally admit that their attempts to scare Courtney will never be successful and accept that "life just isn't fair." And a darker version of the same principle is seen in *Bad Hare Day*, where Tim is so elated to finally be in a real magic show that he does not seem to mind that he is only the magician's rabbit, about to be decapitated in the name of show business.

Though it is monstrous and imposing, puberty is in the end always presented as a positive force in *Goosebumps*. This is apparent not just in the narratives but also in the sort of monsters that Stine chose to use and those he avoided. "I don't get zombies," the author has said, explaining why he did not write about them. "They're so unsophisticated; they just stagger forward and try to eat people, and you just hit them with a shovel or shoot them."[60] The zombie has been reimagined in recent horror texts but in the 1990s it was still mainly defined by an unpleasant physicality and general lack of mental and emotional vitality. In classic films such as *Night of the Living Dead*, the zombie seems to embody human degradation, with few redeeming characteristics that Stine could highlight within the context of a puberty metaphor.

Other classic monsters had completely different associations. The vampire's body stays able, often even in ways superior to a human, and the ghost firmly holds on to its memories, transcending all limitations of the physical body while remaining human. Even the mummy is usually revived in order to pursue noble human emotions such as love and honor. This makes them a much more suitable metaphor for puberty because maturity does not diminish the human body, it develops it. So in *Goosebumps* puberty always means life, even when it brings death to its characters—as in *Casper*, the child must die so that the teenager can live. Tellingly, when Stine eventually added a zombie story to *Goosebumps HorrorLand* in 2011 it was titled *Why I Quit Zombie School*.

This positive outlook is reinforced by the *Goosebumps* children's ability to adapt to their new situation. In the "Werewolf of Fever Swamp" television episode, Grady is upset about the family's move to Fever Swamp. In words that could also easily apply to puberty, he complains, "I don't feel right about this place.... It just feels so weird." His father's response is also revealing: "You see these deer here? Up until a couple of days ago they had never seen a swamp before. Now your Mom and I get to study how they're gonna adapt. Because believe me, they will. It's just natural to adapt. Pretty soon they're gonna love it here. And so are you."

This inherent ability of a child to cope and adapt is further suggested by the stories's structure both in the gradual progression of the scares and in the twist endings. The unresolved resolution of the typical *Goosebumps* story parallels the progression of puberty in real children while also affirming their ability to respond to progressive challenges. In "It came From Beneath the Sink," for instance, the evil Grool becomes Kat's responsibility for the rest of her life. Her constant attention is needed, lest the Grool become unhappy and turn evil again, yet Kat does not see this as a burden, however; she simply adapts to a new routine. When at the end of the story she is presented with the Grool's cousin, the Lanx, her screams might suggest terror but the narrative has already reassured the audience of Kat's power to adjust to any challenge.

As they learn the skills to adapt, *Goosebumps* children are often left alone, with parents strategically removed from the conflict or playing the part of unbelievers. This is a common trope in children's narratives but it also parallels real life, in which parents often remain outsiders to a child's emotional struggles over puberty. If they "literally cannot see"[61] the monsters, as a critic pointed out, this is not because they are dim but because these monsters do not exist in their world; their puberty is long over. Like *Casper*, however, *Goosebumps* also treats puberty as a catalyst for a closer relationship between parent and child, even when the reverse seems more likely. Some of the books and most of the television episodes feature scenes in which the main character emphatically tells their parents they love them, and this love is even used as the solution to some curses: in "The Haunted

Mask," Carly Beth can only release herself from the evil mask when she recognizes her mother's token of love.

This theme of family togetherness also extends to siblings and cousins, as in "Night of the Living Dummy 3," in which siblings Trina and Dan must learn to trust and work together with their cousin Zane to defeat Slappy and his mob of living dummies. To my knowledge, there is only one *Goosebumps* story where this kind of reconciliation does not happen. In *The Cuckoo Clock of Doom*, Michael lives in constant torment and humiliation because of his younger sister, Terrible Tara. As a way to get back at her, Michael tampers with Dad's new cuckoo clock, accidentally reversing time and causing him to age backwards into oblivion. Michael is eventually able to restore normal time progression but in the process erases the year of his sister's birth, wiping out her existence. The story ends with Michael being much happier in his life without Tara and voicing very ambiguous thoughts about whether he should go back for her. Interestingly, *Cuckoo Clock of Doom* is considered by Stine one of his least scary books[62]—perhaps because simply ignoring a challenge is much easier than adapting to it.

All of these characteristics which equate *Goosebumps* with the anxieties of puberty are also what have led critics to disparage the series as one based on formula alone. I do not deny that there is a formula to Stine's writing, one based on cliff-hangers, twists, and a set narrative construction—but as I argue here, this structure is also the result of a deep understanding of children's emotions and anxieties, focused on one of the most significant moments in a twelve-year-old's life: his or her transition into adolescence.

Conclusion

When *Goosebumps* peaked, so did the children's horror trend. In 1997, the book series went on hiatus, and the television show was cancelled the following year, a shift accompanied by a sharp reduction in the number of other children's horror titles. There was a short second wind as the millennium turned, with *Goosebumps 2000* and a new series of *Are You Afraid of the Dark?*, but ultimately the 2000s were unremarkable in their children's horror output. I end my timeline here—even if this was not the end for children's horror.

Back in 1995, Stine famously predicted that "in 10 years they won't be buying these books anymore."[63] He was right that his series didn't realize the same level of popularity again, but children's interest in children's horror has never truly waned—and neither has the market's interest in responding to it. *Goosebumps* books are still coming out, plus a number of other series inspired by Stine's work, and the same happens in television and video, where old as well as new shows continue to be offered on demand, particularly on digital platforms like Netflix. What children's horror became after its peak popularity was something much more interesting than a trend—it transformed into an inconspicuous part of everyday children's culture.

I want to reflect on this observation, as it underlines the significance of my claims in this chapter and this book more broadly. The previous chapters were concerned mainly with the way children's horror was perceived as a cultural threat, whether because it presented childhood in a different way or because it violated the agreed boundaries of the horror genre. As I worked my way through the chronology of the film cycle, I noted how the texts and their reception revealed a growing awareness of pre-adolescence as a concept, but this new concept did not resolve the issues of combining children and horror. This main challenge was not resolved but eventually dodged, as the horror genre and Hollywood more broadly changed their production models and diminished the market viability of children's horror film.

In the present analysis, however, I demonstrated how a shift in media could quickly change this situation. Even though these new children's horror texts worked from exactly the same assumptions as those in the film cycle, namely that children are legitimate audiences of horror and that the genre can adapt to their needs, they were almost universally read without controversy. What is at stake here is not branding, different attitudes toward pre-adolescence, or even the specificities of this or that medium, though all of these factors are implicated. Rather the viability of children's horror as part of children's culture is the direct result of the cultural struggles and negotiations of the film cycle. This negotiation includes not just the emergence and establishment of pre-adolescence, but also the idea that children and horror should remain separate concepts. Children's horror can work outside of the cinema because television and publishing are able to comply with this segregation.

The *Goosebumps* franchise makes this crystal clear. Its brand was the result of a happy combination of market constraints (children's culture only, not the mainstream) and cultural attitudes (pre-teens as a distinct social group), producing the most successful vision of children's horror to this day. Note its four key elements: the assumption of pre-teens as a separate demographic; the acknowledgment of their specific group-anxieties, particularly puberty; the selection of child-oriented media to allow for these themes to remain central; and the use of separate marketing frameworks (horror for children, not-horror for parents and other adults).

This structure—based equally on a clear view of pre-adolescence and on the separation of child- and adult-oriented culture, specifically horror— is not only the foundation of *Goosebumps* and the vast majority of children's horror titles to this day. It can also be seen, with varying degrees of clarity, in the films of the cycle, from *The Watcher in the Woods* to *Casper* and most notably in *The Gate*, as the culture struggled to articulate a viable combination of childhood and horror.

Thus, in spite of the great changes brought about by pre-adolescence, the children's horror trend brings us right back to the beginning. Everything is just as it has always been: children and adults (and their respective horrors) remain clearly separated. Children's culture can receive horror so long as it emphasizes the cultural associations of childhood, not horror. And horror can likewise accept young audiences so long as each text still emphasizes the cultural associations of the genre, not childhood. In other words, horror and childhood remain antagonistic ideas, incompatible and difficult to reconcile in mainstream popular culture.

This is perhaps the biggest point made through the children's horror trend. The boundaries of childhood can and do change alongside the culture which produces them, and the same happens to the boundaries of horror (albeit, it would seem, with more resistance). In each instance, new configurations can eventually become accepted—but only if and when the new demarcations are clear and able to remain so. Blurred boundaries, especially as they apply to concepts related to identity and cultural power, are simply too uncomfortable to sustain. This status quo continues to apply in relation to new children's horror, most obviously in the cinema where the medium's preference for broad, indistinct audiences continues to dominate. I address this, with special focus on these theatrical echoes, in the book's conclusion.

Conclusion.
Sometimes It Comes Back: Children's Horror Today

As any *Goosebumps* fan could tell you, horror never ends. Last chapters are always twist chapters, meant not to conclude but to transition forward into a new threat, a new obstacle, a new narrative. The same is true for children's horror: the trend, the film cycle, and this study, too. This conclusion means to tie up loose ends and summarize key arguments without intending to close the case on children's horror—on the contrary, my goal is to show the many ways in which it remains open.

This open ending was already suggested in the previous chapter, where I argued that children's horror has in fact continued to exist, and rather inconspicuously too, in children's television and fiction well after the end of the trend. But it is also true that children's horror has sometimes resurfaced in film after the early 1990s in titles like *Monster House* (2006), *Coraline* (2009), *The Hole, Cirque du Freak: The Vampire's Assistant* (2009), *Frankenweenie, ParaNorman, Goosebumps* (2015) and *Goosebumps 2: Haunted Halloween* (2018), plus *The House with a Clock in Its Walls* (2018), to name some of the most notorious. These films have attained some visibility and even critical and popular acclaim, but they are far from embodying a continuation, or even a revival, of the children's horror trend.

Instead, they are echoes—they speak to the legacy of children's horror, certainly, but above all they repeat its difficulties, endlessly rehashing struggles around childhood and maturity, the horror genre, the meaning of film, and the particulars of the Millennial generation. And, as it had been during the trend, it is in the cinema that children's horror becomes the most challenging.

This conclusion begins by reviewing the main arguments in this book, before diving into a discussion of some notorious echo titles and the way they illustrate the on-going (and some emerging) conflicts of children's horror. In the process, I hope to again emphasize the historical significance of the children's horror trend, and to demonstrate its continued usefulness as a cultural artifact providing a window into American attitudes about childhood, horror, and film, both then and now.

Summary: The Insights of Children's Horror

This book chronicled a series of transformations in American culture attached to the concept of pre-adolescence. Throughout, I claimed that the children's horror trend (1980–1998), and particularly its film cycle (1980–1995), offers a good way into the topic because of the way it challenged (and affirmed) the boundaries of childhood and maturity. Virtually all children's horror titles of this period have a direct connection to America's developing understandings of pre-adolescence and the identities of pre-teens and, whether through text or context, all of them explicitly problematize it in relation to other more established cultural concepts, namely family, childhood innocence, American identity, and the meaning of the horror genre. These struggles are moreover linked to a number of tangible industrial shifts, such as the introduction of the PG-13 rating and the developing cultural identities of different media. My goal with this study was to appreciate how and why all of these changes are related, in the process drawing a map of the children's horror trend.

I started with *The Watcher in the Woods*, the first Disney horror film. As I argued in Chapter 1, *The Watcher* demonstrates how America was beginning to negotiate two different views of childhood: the traditional notion of all minors as uniformly vulnerable and the emerging idea that there was a liminal space between the innocence of childhood and the maturity of adolescence. Disney had a name for this in-between audience: pre-teens. But despite their marketing attempts to explain this demographic, there were very few points of reference in the wider culture with which to understand it. Indeed, *The Watcher* was (and remains) a perplexing film because it exists entirely outside of its contemporary frameworks. There was no precedent for it, and even though it borrowed heavily from the tradition of horror and of children's film, the way it then combined these elements was deeply alienating to the audiences of both genres.

An aggravating part of this issue was the absence of an appropriate rating for films like *The Watcher*. It was obviously not an R feature, but the PG rating misled audiences into downplaying Disney's warnings about the film's intensity. This ambiguity is a recurrent feature throughout the children's horror cycle and it is extremely significant because classification systems are a manifestation of cultural agreements about childhood. Even if they have mainly been understood as industrial mechanisms to prevent censorship, it is plain that ratings also serve a practical social purpose by placing media texts into pre-established brackets of suitability. This process is grounded on morality, revealing expectations about what constitutes appropriate knowledge for people in each life stage and about norms of social organization, that is, how a culture has agreed to break up the life cycle in the first place. As classification is almost entirely preoccupied with children, ratings unveil a culture's thinking about childhood and its meanings.

I developed this point in Chapter 2, where I charted the road to the PG-13 rating through controversies around three films connected to the children's horror cycle: *Poltergeist, Indiana Jones and the Temple of Doom*, and *Gremlins*. My key point there was that PG-13 was not a response to increasingly violent content, even if the violence in these films was part of the issue. Instead, I read PG-13 as a reaction to the intensification of the struggles over pre-adolescence and the boundaries of childhood first seen in *The Watcher*. I therefore proposed PG-13 as a cultural acknowledgment that American attitudes toward childhood had changed in significant and permanent ways.

PG-13 clearly announced a segmentation and a restructuring of this concept by recognizing pre-teens as an independent social group, distinct from younger children and from older teenagers, and therefore with different maturity levels and suitability needs. But the discussions around the new rating also clearly signaled that childhood as it had been understood before—as a period of innocence, hope, and family values—was still an important concept in America, one that the culture wished to preserve. As the responses to *Gremlins* and its irreverence showed, the willingness to accept pre-adolescence was peppered with some reluctance to throw the baby out with the bath water.

I took this argument further in Chapter 3 by noting how PG-13 fixed this problem of ambiguity in relation to the identity of the children's film, but while simultaneously creating new issues for that of the horror genre. Because it filtered all challenging films out of the PG bracket, PG-13 was essential to the preservation of the traditional meanings of the PG rating, that is, family, innocence, and wholesome values. Many children's horror films produced after 1984 privileged this connection to the children's film by moderating their tone and intensity in order to achieve a PG rating.

A few, however, took on the new options offered by PG-13, creating a new baby and bath water problem: though audiences were ready for children's horror at a PG-13 intensity level, the most dedicated horror champions were not willing to let go of what they felt was the genre's ultimate defining feature—its separation from mainstream values and mainstream consumption.

As an example of this new conflict, I pointed to *The Gate*, one of the most iconic children's horror titles. There is no mistaking *The Gate* for anything other than a horror film. Its narrative is intense, and not once does it let its characters or its audience laugh way the terror. But though it is much more serious than *Gremlins*, *The Gate* still managed an overall lighter tone because it was equally committed to being a children's film. Where *Gremlins* posed cynical challenges to innocence and family, *The Gate* promoted it all, and where *Gremlins* shied away from a child's perspective *The Gate* wanted nothing else. Effectively, *The Gate* brought the ideology of the children's film into the form and shape of the horror genre.

And, accordingly, its reception was split right down the middle. Those who read *The Gate* first as a children's film tended to notice the film's connection to pre-teen audiences and their specific anxieties and to praise both its use of horror and its happy ending. Those who read it first as a horror film criticized its tone and its perspective and denounced it as a ruin to the genre. This split is a reversal of the ambiguity seen in reactions to *Gremlins* and comes from a similar desire to preserve genre expectations. It also points to the double challenge of PG-13: while it secured the meaning of PG and, through it, of the children's and family film, it simultaneously weakened the maturity boundaries set by the R rating and therefore compromised the foundation of the horror genre's identity.

Since 1968, when the ratings system was first introduced, horror had been almost exclusively rated R and its contents (as well as the culture around the genre) had been shaped by this classification in ways that went beyond content intensity. Because the ratings system imposed audience segregation in a way that the Code never did, it gave horror a space in which to claim counter-cultural legitimacy. To be rated R, therefore, was to make a deliberate cultural statement: if the mainstream is PG, and if this is where children's entertainment exists, then horror could only exist in opposition to it. It is no coincidence that most films of this era share a particularly dark tone attached to clear social commentary, and many were moreover part of an artistic avant-garde for film technique and aesthetics[1]—all things that appealed predominantly to mature audiences.

But this kind of statement was harder to make when the line between the mainstream and the restricted was blurred by an in-between classification like PG-13. The dislike expressed for *The Gate* and other hybrids comes precisely out of this concern. These films could not be considered horror because they accepted, and even targeted, immature audiences—and with them, the dreaded mainstream. This attitude is clearly dominant in the rating trends for horror films as early as 1985 and much more obviously in the 1990s, when in spite of (and because of) its obvious commercial advantages, PG-13 simply did not have a presence in horror.

This was the argument I put forth in Chapter 4, where I began to explain why and how the children's horror cycle faded away in the 1990s. As I suggested, horror actively rejected young audiences after the introduction of PG-13, an effort accomplished in great part by a return of the genre to the now-canonical 1970s, a decade perceived to be serious and mature, unlike the excessive and childish 1980s. As a result of this nostalgia, horror in the 1990s became sophisticated, intellectual, deliberately artistic, and, of course, inseparable from the R rating. Once again, the genre's identity was grounded in all of the things that would mark a film as not meant for children, therefore making it incompatible with the idea of children's horror.

This antagonism is visible in the deep ambiguity of the children's horror films of the early 1990s. My example here was *The Nightmare Before Christmas*, which presented itself as neither horror nor for children despite matching the themes and tone of children's horror. Instead, its marketing framed it as an auteur statement—intellectual, artistic, technologically groundbreaking—a line adopted by critics and audiences, who readily interpreted *Nightmare* as a film meant to be appreciated primarily by discerning adults.

This ploy conveniently avoided the hybridism of the children's horror label, protecting *Nightmare* on both the children's and the horror front. Somewhat paradoxically, this framework also allowed *Nightmare Before Christmas* to target families, who in the 1990s were fast becoming the new most profitable film audience. This was in no small part because of how they dominated the market—in the 1990s, Boomer/Millennial families were numerous and economically powerful, and their courting inevitably led to the tailoring of narratives and messages to the attitudes and expectations of the adults (that is, the parents) in the audience. We see this at work in the way *Nightmare* evaded the challenges posed by children's horror to childhood by emphasizing the idea of innocence instead.

The issues raised by the inclusion of parents in the target audience were my focus in Chapter 5, where I explored the cultural reinforcement of childhood innocence and the extension of these expectations to pre-adolescence. I thus returned to the problems raised in the *Gremlins* reception. Accepting pre-adolescence demanded a redefinition of childhood which questioned fundamental assumptions about children, namely their innocence and vulnerability. These assumptions did not simply affect the kind of entertainment made for young people; they had wider philosophical and political implications in American culture and identity, particularly in the way they complicated ideas (and ideals) about the family, its shape and its dynamics.

To point out these implications, I noted the rise of attachment parenting culture in the late 1980s and, especially, the 1990s. Attachment-style parenting took John Bowlby's scientific theory of attachment—the idea that deep bonds between infant and mother are critical for proper development—and adapted it into a number of practices which opposed both the independent parenting of the 1970s and the authoritarian styles of the 1950s. Though they are initially based on science, attachment parenting guidelines carry with them particular constructions of the roles of mother, child, and family, which in turn enmesh themselves in social and cultural expectations.

Thus, in the 1990s, when attachment became the mainstream parenting doctrine in American culture, the concept of family was also transformed, in great part to accommodate a second reimagining of the figure of the child: after the "creation" of the pre-teen, which was predicated on agency and independence, childhood was again returned to innocence and dependency.

This second shift came out of a direct conflict with attachment culture because, as I argued, the kind of practices and attitudes it promotes actively require an understanding of childhood as a period of vulnerability and innocence. While this is intuitive for babies and very young children, the notion becomes harder to sustain as puberty approaches, and particularly after pre-adolescence is defined in the 1980s as a release from childhood and as a moment of first empowerment and independence from external guidance, including that of parents. The problems of this lifestyle became apparent when attached Boomer parents were first confronted with the new identities of their pop culture-savvy Millennial pre-teens, and realized that the attachment which had guided their family dynamics was suddenly threatened by the child's transition into independence.

The Witches illustrates a first realization of this problem. Both in its text and marketing, *Witches* was an attempt to update the themes of the 1980s to reflect the expectations of the 1990s by focusing on pre-teens who gain some independence, but not too much, and who face some danger, but not too much. Crucially, the main lesson learned by the hero is a mix of self-reliance and the importance of family ties. Despite this message, audiences and critics were not convinced by the ideological hybridism of *The Witches*, and their disapproval foreshadows the eventual victory of attachment values over childhood. Pop culture seeking the favor of family audiences stopped representing pre-teens as young independent adolescents and began presenting them in ways that matched cultural expectations of vulnerability, innocence, and family attachment.

This change is critical for children's horror, as it meant that the cycle became entirely assimilated into family entertainment and conformed to its expectations. This is illustrated in *Casper*, the last children's horror film. Though *Casper* retains a focus on puberty and pre-adolescence, its treatment of the topic is entirely aligned with attachment values: puberty is understood as a moment of transition for child and parent alike, and the process framed in terms of potential for family unity. The result is a narrative which praises dependence on parental love more than self-reliance and which represents pre-teens in ways that echo childhood more so than adolescence. The inclusion of such a targeted parental address was a key change in the film cycle because it took children's horror away from an exclusive young audience. In effect, the shift made it a horror-inspired family film: more profitable and culturally soothing but also not quite children's horror.

The events of the children's horror film cycle support one of my key claims, which is that the "making" of pre-adolescence caused significant cultural disruption. But while disruption tends to be linked to a transformation in previous attitudes, what we in fact see over the course of these two decades is their reinforcement. Pre-adolescence prompted a restructuring of childhood and with it some questioning of its significance, but it did not ultimately change its meaning. On the contrary, those pre-established associations with innocence and family eventually came to define the figure of the pre-teen and the period of pre-adolescence through the dominance of attachment parenting culture.

There is more children's horror after the end of the film cycle. As I argued in Chapter 6, the peak of children's horror cultural presence happened only *after* the cinema was abandoned in favor of more child-oriented media like television and popular fiction. As the film cycle demonstrated, the cultural position of cinema changed substantially in the 1990s. What had once been a medium perfectly suited to unaccompanied young audiences had now become so focused on attracting large audiences it no longer had the flexibility to target niche groups like children. Industrial and commercial pressures to target families (increasingly defined not as parents and children but as groups of all ages), paired with a growing cultural emphasis on the innocence of childhood, effectively made the cinema environment incompatible with children's horror narratives.

That the obstacle to children's horror was specifically cinema is obvious when we confront the sheer number of popular children's horror content in other media during the same time period. I suggested two important differences between film and other media to explain this situation. The first is built-in audience segregation. Unlike children's film, which always inhabits the same consumption space as other releases and often requires adult attendance, children's television and children's fiction exist on completely separate planes to their adult counterparts. They don't share a space, be that channel, broadcasting slot, publisher, or section in a shop, and therefore are very rarely in competition with content for general audiences. As a result, many of the questions latent in the film cycle and its audience address or tone are never even posed—a text placed unambiguously in the context of children's entertainment is evidently meant for children first.

The second difference is built-in suitability agreements. Back when the Hays Code was in place, American audiences were assured that every film would conform to a particular standard of suitability, regardless of its genre or primary address. In removing these constraints, the ratings system transformed the cinema into a place of competing moral narratives and thematic emphases, which the classifications simply ordered in accordance to dominant attitudes. This meant freedom, but it also meant uncertainty. In media which segregate child audiences, like television, there is no such uncertainty. This is in part because children's entertainment is understood to happen within the existing cultural agreements about childhood (that is, within a "Code"-like system), but it is also because the children's label allows these industries to be specific about the sub-divisions of their content, therefore signaling borderline content more easily. In other words, the cultural placement of these industries squashed ambiguity before it even came into existence—a text placed within the context of children's entertainment must obey the dominant cultural norms of suitability.

The *Goosebumps* franchise is the prime example of these differences and of why children's horror only really flourished outside of the cinema. The "formula" of R.L. Stine's books at once recalls the ethos of 1980s children's horror and rejects the compromises of 1990s cinema: it emphasizes the seriousness of horror over comedy; uses a child's perspective exclusively, with rarely a thought for parents and other adult figures; and focuses exclusively on the themes of puberty and empowerment. But because *Goosebumps* existed only within the well-defined boundaries of children's culture, and because this culture was part of a society that already accepted pre-adolescence as a defined life stage, the franchise was never read as a cultural or ideological threat.

Ultimately, this confinement to children's culture in the mid- to late-1990s (and beyond) was as much a defanging as it was a relief for children's horror. Both the horror genre and children's culture are fraught with conflict over their boundaries and their "proper" use and because identity, legitimacy and morality are at stake in these conflicts, all attempts to revisit the frontiers of either genre are bound to meet resistance—as the film cycle thoroughly illustrated. But when the hybridism is removed, when "children's horror" becomes simply "children's culture," as it did after the film cycle, then it gains the freedom to reimagine horror in ways that suit its aims, even if they do not conform to that genre's more widely accepted character.

This liberation from generic expectations and legitimacy contests is also the reason why children's horror has continued to be relevant—and why it will continue to be so. As I said, children's horror never left children's entertainment, not even after the trend ended in the late 1990s. Old titles are still popular and new ones are released and received with as much enthusiasm. The vast majority still follows the "formula" first suggested in *The Gate* and later perfected in *Goosebumps*, so children's horror texts remain for the most part focused on issues around puberty and the changes it brings to a child's sense of self, agency, and independence. This insistence on the topic goes beyond mere acceptance of pre-adolescence as part of growing up; it acknowledges this transition as one of major significance in children's lives, recognizing and validating the anxieties it brings along.

This review of my timeline and arguments already reveals some of the wider implications of this study; nevertheless, the next three sections will expand on the matter.

The (Il)Legitimacy of Children in Horror

One of the most significant things about the children's horror trend was the way it separated the concepts of childhood and otherness in the context of the horror genre. There were practical and ideological consequences to making children "us" and not "them," namely the questioning of one of the biggest motifs in the genre and of horror's claim to countercultural status. I have argued that children's horror had a strong impact on the shape of wider horror and of children's position in it (both as audiences and as protagonists), but it would be naïve to say that horror today fully accepts the legitimacy of children as participants in the genre. The reality is a compromise: while children have transcended narrative otherness and become appropriate protagonists in mainstream horror, this is where their legitimacy ends. The idea of actual children watching horror (or worse, being its target audience) still sits uneasy with horror production and consumption. They are not "us," but "us/them."

M. Night Shyamalan's *The Visit* (2015) illustrates the point. Its story could easily be a *Goosebumps* book: siblings Becca and Tyler become increasingly alarmed by their grandparents's outlandish behavior during a visit, until they realize these are not their grandparents at all but dangerous strangers. The narrative is committed to the children's perspectives, and the intensity is moderate throughout (PG-13), making this a clear children's horror echo. Indeed, it was described more or less as such by some critics, including Manohla Dargis in the *New York Times*, who labeled it "an amusingly grim fairy tale ... a 'Hansel and Gretel' redo [with] Spielbergian family dynamic."[2]

But not all reviews were this accepting—especially when penned by writers with an overt interest in horror. Horror critic Jake Dee, for example, read the Spielberg dynamics as "out of place heartfelt moments," the amusing fairy tale as a "diluted PG-13 attempt at true terror" and the Hansel and Gretel inspiration as merely an "anodyne horror story." His conclusion is telling: "Had this gone the hard R-route [how much] more memorable the overall experience just might be."[3] The parallels with *The Gate*'s reception are hard to miss: while general critics read *The Visit* as intentionally child-friendly film, horror critics understood the same elements not as part of the film's targeted address but as filmmaking flaws.

There is one important difference in the reception of *The Visit*, however, and that is the lack of comment on the age of the protagonists. Even negative reviews like the one above made no suggestion that aging up the characters would have made the film better. The children are simply accepted as a valid protagonist for a horror story, their age so unremarkable it is only mentioned as part of the plot's description. This nonchalance is an important part of the children's horror trend's legacy.

But an equally important part of this legacy is severe tonal discordance. In its effort to avoid connotations to the family film while also retaining a believable young hero, *The Visit* fluctuates wildly in tone, sometimes aggressive and sometimes soothing without ever really combining the two. Which side prevails seems to depend on whether the viewer expected a child-friendly narrative or not. "It's as though Shyamalan reconsidered," mused Peter Martin, "and decided to protect rather than endanger [the child characters]. While that's understandable from a parental standpoint, it ensures that *The Visit* bears only a fleeting resemblance to a funhouse joy ride."[4] For Brad Wheeler, on the other hand, the dissonance comes in only with the last sequence, which is "unlike the look and the feel of the preceding 90 minutes—heavier, scarier, something from something rated R."[5]

As these comments make clear, genre labels and ratings still carry powerful associations today, and these external cues are strong enough to override important narrative elements such as perspective and characterization—and, perhaps, even intent. One might wonder, after all, why Shyamalan was compelled to filming a children's story but not to making it a children's film. That the director has never even addressed the possibility of his film being targeted at pre-teens is in itself evidence of the ambiguity that still surrounds this audience.

This same uncertainty was taken to an extreme conclusion in *Scouts Guide to the Zombie Apocalypse* (2015), a film "originally conceived as a PG-13 zombie film for kids" which eventually became "an R-rated, adult zombie film." The stated reasons behind the change are what the reader of this book will expect: for one producer, the R allowed them "to push the envelope a little bit because we've all seen zombie films at this point"; for another, "it's just so much more fun."[6] Both of these explanations assume that the core audience for a zombie film is an adult with extensive knowledge of the horror genre, an attitude also explicitly stated by Christopher Landon, the film's director and the principal driving force behind the shift in tone. "For me," Landon revealed, "it was just about the gore, because ... they were trying to go PG-13 and it was never going to happen. I'm a big horror fan and when I see a zombie movie I want gore, I want to see guts and all that stuff because it's fun."[7]

It is impossible not to draw a connection here with *The Lost Boys*, another children's horror turned R-rated because of its director's determination to separate horror and children. But where *Lost Boys* maintained some of its pre-teen target and focus, *Scouts* tried to eliminate it completely. This is a curious choice, seeing as Landon cites many child-oriented films as his inspiration, including *Gremlins*. "We're actually making an '80s movie," he has said. "I describe it as a gory R-rated version of *The Goonies*."[8] Except a gory, R-rated, and child-free version of *The Goonies* is nothing at all like *The Goonies*.

Yet, in spite of its paradoxical nature, Landon was not alone in this sentiment. "Amblin! Amblin-esque," the production team repeated in interviews. "I can't tell you how many times we've used the term Amblin-esque with this film, especially back when it was more of a zombie film for kids.... These [children's horror] films did such a beautiful job of making it fun but still really scare the bejeezus out of you."[9] These comments simultaneously acknowledge the extreme influence (emotional as well as industrial) of the children's horror cycle and of other pre-teen-focused films of the same period while also revealing their incompatibility with the present culture. Landon actually spells this out:

> I'm just proud of making a movie that feels like something that I watched when I was a kid. I've missed these movies; I feel like they're not being made anymore and I think everything is either $5 million and small or it's a gigantic tent pole, and we've lost the spirit. I'm really grateful [to be making] a movie that I think that audiences really want to see but they are just not getting.[10]

I find the last part of that quotation especially fascinating, because *Scouts* is, in fact, the result of a concerted effort to avoid the Amblin audience, the Amblin rating, and the tone of the 1980s and of the films Landon watched as a child. Juxtapose, for instance, the above-cited loving comments about films watched in childhood and this comment from Landon: "there's so many tits and there's so much blood and stuff in this movie that there's no chance that we're not a hard R."[11] The contradiction between these two visions is obvious in the end result, a film which only half-addresses the absurdity of starring adults dressed as children and using toy-like weapons and a film whose main reference point is decontextualized nostalgia.

My comments here are not meant as a critique of the film's quality but only as a note on the continued difficulty to reconcile children and horror. The goal of *Scouts* was never to reproduce the 1980s, or specifically the children's horror cycle, but to isolate its superficial features and approximate them in the context of adult-centric horror. Those Amblin-esque details may be initially echoed in *Scouts* but the film ultimately rejects them because they cannot be reconciled with the project's horror affiliation.

Ironically, one of the things Landon chose to leave behind was the project's most unique selling point. The thing that "hasn't been seen before" in horror is not gore but what the first draft of *Scouts* offered: a zombie film for kids.

The Visit, Scouts, and other nostalgic echoes like *Stranger Things* illustrate the deep schism between the period of children's horror and today's attitudes about the proper place of children in horror. Most importantly, they show how a deeper understanding of the children's horror trend helps to clarify the shape of contemporary horror. The disruption caused by the film cycle in particular may have been punctual, but it was also profound—its principles and motifs were not only influential for a generation of children but have been digested and transformed as those children became adults, particularly adult horror fans. Why has the opposition between children and horror been preserved, even by those who once benefited from its temporary dissolution, even by those who remember it nostalgically? If Landon et al. are significant evidence, it would appear that this memory serves mainly to highlight the fragility of these boundaries. Maturity, and the exclusivity it implies, are central to horror's identity today *because* they were once overthrown.

PG-13 and the End of Children's Cinema?

Horror has been an emphasis of this study, but its conclusions have very clear implications beyond this genre. Indeed, young audiences are a challenge not just in horror but in cinema more generally. As I lamented in a couple of chapters, the impact of PG-13 on the developments of children's cinema has been mostly ignored in the academy, where scholars have preferred to focus on other forms of children's media and other forms of film. Outside of the academy, however, the repercussions of PG-13 are no secret at all, as illustrated by this passage in Scott Mendelson's review of *Goosebumps*:

> I talk quite a bit about the death of the out-and-out kid movie. No, I'm not talking about animated features, I'm talking about live-action, G or PG-rated features that are explicitly pitched to a kid-friendly level. Back in the early 2000s, when the general audience-friendly, PG-13, four-quadrant, global blockbuster fantasy franchise film basically took over the industry, we didn't just lose the adult-skewing movies outside of the awards season, we lost the kid films too.[12]

If the point is not made in the academy, this omission speaks volumes about the little value given to children's film and the extent to which the ratings system has been understood as somehow external to the film industry. But filmmakers and producers, much like the critics, have been explicitly addressing the problem for a while, even if not intentionally: the vast majority of contemporary titles which echo children's horror are deeply nostalgic for the 1980s. This nostalgia is not a desire to return to the moment of the film cycle—it is a longing for a time *before the end of children's film*.

See, for instance, *Monster House*. Though it is set in the present day, its tone and address were read by the vast majority of critics as unmistakably nostalgic. For one critic, the film was a flash back to "films from the early 1980s like *Gremlins, Poltergeist, Raiders of the Lost Ark* and the Joe Dante segment of *Twilight Zone*—films that were aimed at younger audiences but still had a certain intensity to them. This is something that has been largely lost in family films in the last few years."[13] Another reviewer echoed these thoughts, connecting them even more explicitly to the pre-teen perspective of children's horror and other trends of the 1980s:

> There is something decidedly '80s about *Monster House*.... Chock-full of effective PG frights, exuberant innocence [and] an honest, believable look at pre-teen emotions, all hooked into a universally recognisable premise.... *Monster House* is rich enough to transport you instantly back to childhood, '80s or otherwise.[14]

A similar example, though more openly nostalgic, is J.J. Abrams' *Super 8* (2013). Critics described it as "a poetic rendering of preadolescent anguish in a horror-film setting"[15]—a description as good as any of the character of the children's horror trend—and as a film which recalls "not just early Spielberg but '80s favourites *Stand by Me* and *The Monster Squad*,"[16] two titles in the same tradition. As with *Monster House*, the nostalgia identified here is for something deeper than a historical period. As Roger Ebert suggested in his review, *Super 8*'s nostalgia was "not for a time but for a style of filmmaking, when shell-shocked young audiences were told a story and not pounded over the head with aggressive action. Abrams treats early adolescence with tenderness and affection."[17] Ebert's observation is in itself nostalgic for that attitude—back in 1985, the critic wrote how *Goonies*, much like *Gremlins*, was Spielberg's way of "congratulating [children] on their ability to take the heavy-duty stuff."[18]

What has driven these perspectives out of mainstream family film? Why is nostalgia the only way of recalling them today? The dominance of the PG-13 rating is key to these answers, but not simply because of how it has driven industrial practice, as Mendelson implies; it is also because of the sociocultural transformations that prompted its creation in the first place. The way pre-adolescence changed the concept of childhood means that certain narratives and representations are now preferred, namely those which fit the still-dominant attachment discourse of innocence. These preferences constrain the storytelling and representation modes of the 1980s because those features were rooted on different views of childhood and family.

Children's horror echoes, therefore, must be modified in order to fit the contemporary expectations of family entertainment—just as they are also tailored to meet current horror standards. Nostalgia is an important clue to this mandatory adaptation (as it was in the previous section) but it is not the only one. Note also the predominance of animation in today's children's horror. Other than special effects and puppets, animation never had a strong presence in the trend until the film cycle was over, yet it dominates the trend's echoes and is clearly correlated with their success. Of the recent children's horror echoes that have unequivocally targeted themselves at children, over half have been fully animated, rated PG, and fairly successful (e.g., *Coraline*), with the remaining live-action titles rated PG-13 and not as popular with audiences (e.g., *The Hole*). In television, however, the situation is reversed, and most children's horror is live-action.

These choices are not arbitrary; they are ways of explicitly coding these texts as part of children's culture. Animation, television, and the PG rating all serve to signal a text's suitability for children. Champions of animation will find this statement irksome, but even they must be ready to admit that animation generally appeals to children and that this connection is deeply established in popular discourse (indeed, this is a recurring issue in animation studies). The same can be said for television, though less contentiously since television subdivides itself explicitly into adult and children's spaces.

My point here is that cinema—unlike animation, unlike television—tends to be perceived as a medium for adults by default. Any theatrical feature with an interest in child audiences must explicitly signal its difference (through animation or the PG rating), or else find a way to justify its presence in the cinema by amplifying its appeal to adult audiences (often through the use of explicit nostalgia, or a move toward PG-13). There is no middle ground, so the concept of children's cinema is inevitably limited.

Again, the best illustration of these difficulties is the films themselves, and the first *Goosebumps* adaptation provides an excellent example. As I argued in this study, the "formula" of these books is child-oriented and focused on puberty. This has been the case throughout the franchise's life, with no exception—until this film adaptation. Because it must exist as a legitimate theatrical release, the *Goosebumps* film cannot adapt any of the books without reshaping the whole brand to fit the cinema's expectations. As reviewer A.A. Dowd pointed out,

> [The film] rarely recalls the old preteen page-turners for which it's named.... This here is *Goosebumps* for today's kids, meaning that [Stine's stories have] been replaced by the kind of noisy, frenetic amusement-park ride that now passes for all-ages entertainment.... Squint hard enough and it is possible to see the phantom impression of an Amblin entertainment, especially given the Spielbergian dead-daddy backstory Zach's provided. But drawing that parallel only underlines how sanitized, how danger-free, family films have gotten in the two decades since Stine's bestselling heyday.[19]

Dowd's comments are framed as a critique of contemporary Hollywood but it is clear that the problem was with the removal of the "formula" at the heart of "the old preteen page-turners" which were a part of Dowd's childhood. As his conclusion implies, the kind of storytelling found in family films today is quite incompatible with that found in the *Goosebumps* series.[20]

See Hannah's narrative arc for the most explicit example. This character originates in the *Goosebumps* novel *The Ghost Next Door*, in which Hannah discovers that she has died and stayed on earth (after spending much of the book's adventure believing her new neighbor, Danny, to be the ghost in question). In the book's final act, Hannah saves Danny's life, an action which allows her to finally accept her own death and pass over. Hannah's final request before leaving for the afterlife to be reunited with her parents is that Danny never forget her. In this story, the monster is clearly "within": Hannah's ghostliness is a direct reference to the death of her childhood self, and her reluctance to accept it a direct parallel to the worries of pre-adolescence. Ultimately, the way Hannah beats her "monster" is through the nuanced recognition that the things of childhood should be preserved (through Danny, who still exists in that world) but that they have a proper time and place, which she has now outgrown. With this reassurance in place, Hannah is ready to begin her adolescent (after)life. Her last request that Danny never forget her is meaningful as a reassurance to Danny—and the young reader—for when his time comes to leave the world of childhood behind.

This message is nowhere to be found in the film, in no small part because Hannah's perspective never drives the story. In the adaptation, her ghostliness also serves as the twist but the impact of this realization is all on the other characters, namely Zach, who now understands he will need to give up his girlfriend if he wants to save the town. Hannah herself seems resigned to her fate, though she requests that Zach never forget her after she is gone. The film eventually reunites the young couple in its closing sequence, in which Stine brings Hannah back to life by writing a new book for her—a scene which serves only Zach's character arc, with no interest on what the consequences of becoming a real girl might be for Hannah.

This erasure of her perspective has other important consequences. One of the most obvious is the separation between hero and monster, a fundamental dynamic not just in *The Ghost Next Door* but in *Goosebumps* more generally. Because Hannah is not the hero of the film nor is she the villain, her liminality as both "real girl" and "creation" has no narrative impact. Neither is this question transposed to the other main characters, not even Stine, who is the film's main protagonist, since the darker side of his personality is externalized in Slappy and the other monsters. Though this could suggest deeper meaning to the monsters in the film there is no narrative weight to it because the film's emphasis is placed not on identity or self-acceptance but on relationships: primarily Zach and Hannah, but also, on a very secondary level, the family bonds between Zach and his mother, and Hannah and her "father," Stine.

All of this is the result of following the template not of a children's story but of family entertainment. As had been the case with *Scouts*, nostalgia seems to have been considered as an avenue to fix this problem: the goal, according to the producer, had been to "make a movie that harkened to the past. Amblin movies, things like *Goonies* or *Gremlins* or even movies like *Stand by Me*, where there's a great dynamic between kids."[21] And, as in *Scouts*, this inspiration could not be actualized in a contemporary feature film. Just as *Scouts* was not really meant to be a children's horror film, *Goosebumps* was also not written to be a children's film nor was it adapted in order to transpose the books' philosophy to the cinema. To expect these things, as Dowd did, is to invite disappointment. Children's film—at least when understood as a parallel to the kind of children's fiction illustrated by the *Goosebumps* series—cannot sustain itself in the film industry today; only family entertainment remains viable.[22]

The Millennial Twist (or, the Generation Who Came of Age Twice)

While charting the emergence of pre-adolescence, I framed this as a uniquely Millennial event. My point was not that there have never been pre-teens before the 1980s and 1990s but that the way pre-adolescence is understood culturally and socially underwent a drastic transformation in this period. And while this transformation is now over, the consequences of its emergence are still being felt today. One does not simply add a whole new stage to the life cycle—transforming childhood requires a transformation of adolescence and, significantly, of adulthood too.

This is very much suggested in the kind of cultural tensions which currently surround the Millennial generation and their experience of adulthood. An apt summary of the issue can be found in the much-debated *New York Times Magazine* article "What Is It About 20-Somethings?" in which author Robin Marantz Henig asked the question that "pops up everywhere": "why are so many people in their 20s taking so long to grow up?"[23]

Current pop culture trends also navigate these concerns, most notably the contemporary wave of nostalgia for the 1980s, and the newly conflicted understandings of coming of age narratives. The two points are linked, of course, because the 1980s were notoriously full of coming of age stories, including those in the children's horror trend. The recent echo titles, therefore, begin to suggest that there could be something interesting in Millennial transitions into adulthood.

Take *Scouts* as an example again. It was described as "a coming of age movie" by its producers: "It's these three boys who are making that transition from childhood to adulthood." This interpretation of the term coming of age is curious because the characters are certainly not children, and given the sexual emphases in the script they have clearly already left childhood behind. The use of the term, then, seems to be dictated more by what the characters are becoming (and by the struggle of that transition) than by what precisely they are leaving behind. In this sense, the concept of childhood is used somewhat loosely, encompassing adolescence and serving as a general symbol for immaturity.

But in the child-oriented films of the 1980s that inspired *Scouts*, childhood was far from symbolic. As I argued here, the use of child characters in child-specific situations grounds the coming of age narratives into an actual psychological, biological, and social transition away from childhood and into adolescence. Coming of age was not understood as a journey toward an end point, like it is portrayed in *Scouts*, but as a journey away from a starting position, childhood. The reversal of this definition is important—and it is critical that it happens just as most Millennials left their twenties. To put it clearly: if coming of age narratives as described in the children's horror trend are directly tied to Millennial transitions into adolescence, their revival and reversal just as Millennials began their thirties might also be tied to this generation's transition into adulthood.

This notion of "coming of age" narratives being tied to the Millennial life cycle has also been nicely illustrated, if unintentionally, by Scott Mendelson (himself a Millennial) in his review of *The Visit*: "If my life is a succession of director fandoms, I came of age on Tim Burton, spent my college years worshipping M. Night Shyamalan, and became an actual adult during Christopher Nolan's blockbuster years."[24] Note how Mendelson distinctly separates "coming of age" and "becoming an actual adult," suggesting that the two are not in fact the same thing. He associates here "coming of age" with a transition out of childhood, but not into adulthood; instead, this transition leads into a period of education (the college years), and only then to a final transition toward "actual" adulthood.

At this point, the consequences of an established pre-adolescence period become very clear. If these brief years are now a culturally and socially established transition point, then adolescence can no longer be the default transitional period of life, where coming of age narratives take place, as it had been since the concept first emerged.[25] Instead, adolescence must be understood as a legitimate life stage in and of itself, requiring a transition at the start (pre-adolescence), and another at the end. The specifics of this second coming of age moment are still uncertain. It is often simply referred to as young adulthood, or emerging adulthood if a current scholarly term is preferred,[26] or even in journalistic terms simply as the moment of the "twixter"[27] and the "20-something."[28] But however this second transition is or comes to be understood, the notion of a strict childhood/adulthood life progression no longer matches our social and cultural expectations.

As in Mendelson's autobiographical comment above, pop culture provides a very useful way to understand these new questions, as it seems to have tied the 1980s–1990s to the 2000s–2010s in very specific ways. Besides *Goosebumps*, recent years have seen the nostalgic revivals of many other classics of Millennial childhood: *Indiana Jones and the Kingdom of the Crystal Skull* (2008), *The Mummy: Tomb of the Dragon Emperor* (2008), *The Karate Kid* (2010), *Teenage Mutant Ninja Turtles* (2014), the *Transformers* series, plus *Jurassic World: The Fallen Kingdom* (2018), *Ghostbusters* (2016), and the new *Star Wars* trilogy, not to mention Nickelodeon's latest revival channel, The Splat, dedicated exclusively to reruns of 1990s hits.

In addition to these, Millennials have revived a number of other franchises which were not originally aimed at children but found a young (and devoted) audience through television, VHS, toys and video games in the 1990s: *Predators* (2010) and *The Predator* (2018), the *Alien* series (2012, 2017), *RoboCop* (2014), *Mad Max: Fury Road* (2015), *Terminator Genisys* (2015), and *The X-Files* (2016). These and other titles like *The Goonies* or

The Fresh Prince of Bel-Air emblazon t-shirts and all sorts of prestige and collector's merchandise aimed at adults, including highly detailed action figures, made not for play but display.

There is a certain irony in these trends, which suggest contemporary mainstream film as repackaged children's film even as the existence of children's film remains uncertain. But what this wave of nostalgia and revival also underlines is the strength of the link between the period of Millennial pre-adolescence (1980s and 1990s) and that of Millennial young adulthood (2000s and 2010s)—two moments of important transition in life, maturity, and identity, made tangible through the pop culture themes and motifs that were meaningful to the children of the 1990s.

In their study of this generation, Howe and Strauss wondered, "How will Millennials rebel against the elder-built world? One often hears it said that every generation rebels [but] the Millennials won't."[29] The emergence of the pre-teen and its triggering of a "discovery" of young adulthood provides at least some food for thought on how the Millennial generation might have impacted the shape of pop culture, and the media. This is how they have changed—though maybe not rebelled against—some of some of the most fundamental elder-built concepts of western culture: childhood, adulthood, and everything in between.

Appendix. A Selection of Children's Horror

A. Before the Trend: Early Wave

Children's horror doesn't properly start until 1980 but we can find some exciting precursors in the 1970s. All of these examples contain at least one element of what would become the children's horror film cycle, though not all fit the description set in the introduction.

- The *Scooby Doo* franchise (1969–present)
- *Escape to Witch Mountain* (John Hough, 1975, G)
- *Return to Boggy Creek* (Tom Moore, 1977, PG)
- *Child of Glass* (John Erman, 1978, TV). The most significant precursor. It was adapted from Richard Peck's children's horror novel *The Ghost Belonged to Me*, and produced for television by Ron Miller. It aired as part of the anthology series *The Magical World of Disney*.
- *Phantasm* (Don Coscarelli, 1979, R)

B. The Children's Horror Film Cycle, 1980–1995

The films below comprise all of the most interesting and noteworthy theatrical releases in the cycle. All fit the definition of children's horror I presented in the introduction and therefore vary in their classifications

170 Appendix. A Selection of Children's Horror

and modes of audience address, as well as tone. For significant theatrical releases after 1995 see Appendix D: After the Trend. Television features have been included in Appendix C.

- *The Watcher in the Woods* (John Hough, 1980, PG)
- *The Dark Crystal* (Jim Henson & Frank Oz, 1982, PG)
- *Poltergeist* (Tobe Hooper, 1982, PG)
- *Something Wicked This Way Comes* (Jack Clayton, 1983, PG)
- *Firestarter* (Mark L. Lester, 1984, R)
- *Ghostbusters* (Ivan Reitman, 1984, PG)
- *Indiana Jones and the Temple of Doom* (Steven Spielberg, 1984, PG)
- *Gremlins* (Joe Dante, 1984, PG)
- *The Black Cauldron* (Ted Berman & Richard Rich, 1985, PG)
- *Silver Bullet* (Daniel Attias, 1985, R)
- *Return to Oz* (Walter Murch, 1985, PG)
- *Invaders from Mars* (Tobe Hooper, 1986, PG)
- *The Quest* (Brian Trenchard-Smith, 1986, PG)
- *Critters* (Stephen Herek, 1986, PG-13)
- *The Gate* (Tibor Takács, 1987, PG-13)
- *The Monster Squad* (Fred Dekker, 1987, PG-13)
- *The Lost Boys* (Joel Schumacher, 1987, R)
- *Lady in White* (Frank LaLoggia, 1988, PG-13)
- *Critters 2: The Main Course* (1988, PG-13)
- *Return of the Living Dead: Part II* (Ken Wiederhorn, 1988, R)
- *Little Monsters* (Richard Greenberg, 1989, PG)
- *Gate II: Trespassers* (Tibor Takács, 1990, R)
- *Gremlins 2* (Joe Dante, 1990, PG-13)
- *The Willies* (Brian Peck, 1990, PG-13)
- *The Witches* (Nicolas Roeg, 1990, PG)
- *Arachnophobia* (Frank Marshall, 1990, PG-13)
- *Troll 2* (Drake Floyd, 1990, PG-13)
- *Ernest Scared Stupid* (John Cherry, 1991, PG)
- *The Addams Family* (Barry Sonnenfeld, 1991, PG-13)
- *The People Under the Stairs* (Wes Craven, 1991, R)

- *Pet Sematary II* (Mary Lambert, 1992, R)
- *Hocus Pocus* (Kenny Ortega, 1993, PG)
- *Jurassic Park* (Steven Spielberg, 1993, PG-13)
- *Addams Family Values* (Barry Sonnenfeld, 1993, PG-13)
- *The Nightmare Before Christmas* (Henry Selick, 1993, PG)
- *Jumanji* (Joe Johnston, 1995, PG)
- *Casper* (Brad Silberling, 1995, PG)

C. The Children's Horror Trend, 1980–1997

While the film cycle was fairly concise, the rest of the trend was simply too broad and prolific to attempt anything resembling full documentation here. I will therefore only present my selection of noteworthy texts, to which the interested (or nostalgic) reader will certainly be able to add.

Some of these titles, particularly in the medium of television, rely more heavily than others on dual address so, as in the case of the film cycle, there is unavoidable ambiguity in the lists that follow. Not every title had a rating but I have included those that could be ascertained, particularly for the video releases.

C1: Television and Video

- *Tales from the Crypt* (HBO, 1989–1996)
- *It* (Tommy Lee Wallace, 1990, TV-14)
- *Are You Afraid of the Dark?* (Nickelodeon, 1990–1996)
- *Eerie, Indiana* (NBC, 1991–1992)
- *Stepmonster* (Jeremy Stanford, 1993, PG-13)
- *Tales from the Cryptkeeper* (ABC, 1993–1994)
- *Aaahh!!! Real Monsters* (Nickelodeon, 1994–1997)
- *Goosebumps* (Fox Kids, 1995–1998)
- *Frankenstein and Me* (Robert Tinnell, 1996, PG)
- *Shadow Zone: The Undead Express* (Stephen Williams, 1996, PG-13)
- *Shadow Zone: My Teacher Ate My Homework* (Stephen Williams, 1997, PG)

- *Tower of Terror* (D.J. MacHale, aired in 1997 as part of *The Magical World of Disney*)
- *New Tales from the Cryptkeeper* (CBS, 1997)
- *Nightmare Ned* (ABC, 1997)
- *Eerie, Indiana: The Other Dimension* (Fox Kids, 1998)
- *The Werewolf Reborn!* (Jeff Burr, 1998, PG)
- *Frankenstein Reborn!* (Julian Breen, 1998, PG)
- *Don't Look Under the Bed* (Kenneth Johnson, 1999, TV-PG)

C2: Children's Fiction

Children's horror fiction was very prolific during this period, so I present only a small selection here. This list has no stand-alone novels because children's horror fiction is almost always presented as part of a series—a publishing strategy to clearly separate horror and signal the tone of these narratives to parents and young readers.

- *Scary Stories to Tell in the Dark*, a series of three books by Alvin Schartz (Harper & Row, 1981, 1984, 1991)
- *Short & Shivery*, an anthology series by Robert D. San Souci (Yearling Books, 1987–1998)
- *Point Horror*, a series by various authors including Diane Hoh, Christopher Pike and Caroline B. Cooney (Scholastic, 1988–2014). Not all titles in this series are child-oriented; some have a clear teen focus.
- *Goosebumps*, a series by R.L. Stine (Scholastic, 1992–1997)
- *Deadtime Stories*, a series by Annette and Gina Cascone (Starscape, 1996–1997)
- *Ghosts of Fear Street*, a series by R.L. Stine, although possibly ghostwritten (Simon & Schuster, 1996–1998)

D. After the Trend: Children's Horror Today

D1: Contemporary Children's Horror (Children's Fiction, Television and Video)

As explained in Chapter 6, children's horror has a firm presence in contemporary children's culture and as such its titles are too extensive to list exhaustively here. I present a brief selection only, meant to point the reader to examples of children's horror understood as a genre within children's culture (rather than a trend from the past). Theatrical titles, which tend to be more openly nostalgic and conflicted (see the conclusion), are listed in D2: Children's Horror Echoes.

- *Courage the Cowardly Dog* (Cartoon Network, 1999–2002)
- The numerous *Goosebumps* spin-off book series, including *Goosebumps 2000* (Scholastic, 1998–2000), *Goosebumps HorrorLand* (Scholastic, 2008–2012), *Goosebumps: Most Wanted* (Scholastic, 2012–2016) and *Goosebumps: SlappyWorld* (Scholastic, 2017–present)
- *Believe* (Robert Tinnell, 2000, PG)
- *Cry Baby Lane* (Peter Lauer, 2000, TV-Y7),
- *Mom's Got a Date with a Vampire* (Stephen Boyum, 2000, TV-PG),
- *The Nightmare Room* (Kids' WB, 2001–2002)
- *When Good Ghouls Go Bad* (Patrick Read Johnson, 2001, PG)
- *The Scream Team* (Stuart Gillard, 2002, TV-PG)
- *The Haunting Hour: Don't Think About It* (Alex Zamm, 2007, PG),
- *Mostly Ghostly* (Richard Correll, 2008, PG)
- *The Boy Who Cried Werewolf* (Eric Bross, 2010, TV-PG),
- *My Babysitter's a Vampire* (Bruce McDonald, 2010, TV-PG),
- *R.L. Stine's The Haunting Hour* (Hub Network, 2010–2014)
- *Girl vs. Monster* (Stuart Gillard, 2012, TV-PG),
- *Deadtime Stories* (Nickelodeon, 2012–2013)
- *Spooksville* (Hub Network, 2013–2014).
- *Mostly Ghostly: Have You Met My Ghoulfriend?* (Peter Hewitt, 2014, PG),
- *Mostly Ghostly: One Night in Doom House* (Ron Oliver, 2016, PG)

D2: Children's Horror Echoes (Film)

Despite its diminutive size, this is a fairly extensive list of children's horror echo films since the trend's end. See the conclusion for a full explanation of these films's context and how it differs from that of the texts listed in D1.

- *The Little Vampire* (Uli Edel, 2000, PG)
- *The Haunted Mansion* (Rob Minkoff, 2003, PG)

- *A Series of Unfortunate Events* (Brad Silberling, 2004, PG)
- *Monster House* (Gil Kenan, 2006, PG)
- *Coraline* (Henry Selick, 2009, PG)
- *The Hole* (Joe Dante, 2009, PG-13)
- *Cirque du Freak: The Vampire's Assistant* (Paul Weitz, 2009, PG-13)
- *Super 8* (J.J. Abrams, 2011, PG-13)
- *Frankenweenie* (Tim Burton, 2012, PG)
- *ParaNorman* (Chris Butler & Sam Fell, 2012, PG)
- *Scouts' Guide to the Zombie Apocalypse* (Christopher Landon, 2015, R)
- *Goosebumps* (Rob Letterman, 2015, PG)
- *The Visit* (M. Night Shyamalan, 2015, PG-13)
- *Krampus* (Michael Dougherty, 2015, PG-13)
- *Stranger Things* (Netflix, 2016–present)
- *It* (Andy Muschietti, 2017, R)
- *Goosebumps 2: Haunted Halloween* (Ari Sandel, 2018, PG)
- *The House with a Clock in Its Walls* (Eli Roth, 2018, PG)

Chapter Notes

Introduction

1. My use of the word trend (and, later on, film cycle) is meant to highlight the fundamental link between children's horror and this particular historical moment, as opposed to terms like genre or subgenre, which suggest continuity and stability.

2. Philippe Ariès, *Centuries of Childhood: A Social History of Family Life* (London: Jonathan Cape Ltd, 1965), 411–12.

3. Adolescence and the teenager, too, have been "discovered" in this way. See, for instance, Grace Palladino, *Teenagers: An American History* (New York: BasicBooks, 1996).

4. Neil Postman, *The Disappearance of Childhood* (London: W.H. Allen, 1983), 85.

5. *Ibid.*, 77.

6. *Ibid.*, 80.

7. Bill Strauss Neil Howe, *Millennials Rising: The Next Great Generation* (New York: Vintage, 2000).

8. Bill Clinton, "Speech in Memphis," PresidentialRhetoric.com, http://www.presidentialrhetoric.com/historicspeeches/clinton/memphis.html.

9. Hillary Clinton, "It Takes a Village—DNC Address," AmericanRhetoric.com, https://www.americanrhetoric.com/speeches/hillaryclintontakesavillage.htm.

10. Some important contributions of this period include: Ellen Seiter, *Sold Separately: Children and Parents in Consumer Culture* (New Brunswick, N.J.: Rutgers University Press, 1993); David Buckingham, *Children Talking Television: The Making of Television Literacy* (London: Falmer Press, 1993); *The Children's Culture Reader*, (New York: New York University Press, 1998); *Kids' Media Culture*, (Durham: Duke University Press, 1999); *Childhood in America*, (New York: New York University Press, 2000).

11. Kevin S. Sandler, *The Naked Truth Why Hollywood Doesn't Make X-Rated Movies* (New Brunswick, N.J.: Rutgers University Press, 2007), 43.

12. Kim Newman, *Nightmare Movies: Horror on Screen Since the 1960s* (London: Bloomsbury, 2011), 6.

13. *Ibid.*, 214.

14. *Ibid.*, 204.

15. *The BFI Companion to Horror* (London: Cassell, 1996), 310.

16. Mark Jancovich, "Genre and the Audience: Genre Classifications and Cultural Distinctions in the Mediation of the Silence of the Lambs," in *Horror, the Film Reader*, ed. Mark Jancovich (London: Routledge, 2002), 152.

17. James B. Twitchell, *Dreadful Pleasures: An Anatomy of Modern Horror* (Oxford: Oxford University Press, 1985), 7.

18. Jancovich, 159.

19. Robin Wood, *Hollywood from Viet-*

nam to Reagan—And Beyond (New York: Columbia University Press, 2003), 145.

20. Jacqueline Rose, *The Case of Peter Pan; or the Impossibility of Children's Fiction* (Philadelphia: University of Pennsylvania Press, 1993).

21. Jack Zipes, *Sticks and Stones: The Troublesome Success of Children's Literature from Slovenly Peter to Harry Potter* (New York: Routledge, 2001), 155.

22. Kimberley Reynolds, "Introduction," in *Frightening Fiction*, ed. Kimberley Reynolds, Geraldine Brennan, Kevin McCarron (London: Continuum, 2001), 1.

23. Ibid.

24. Kate Ferguson Ellis, *The Contested Castle: Gothic Novels and the Subversion of the Domestic Ideology* (Urbana: University of Illinois Press, 1989), x.

25. See for example, Laurie Barowski Ron Leone, "MPAA Ratings Creep: A Longitudinal Analysis of the PG-13 Rating Category in US Movies," *Journal of Children and Media* 5, no. 1 (2011).

26. Michael Medved, "New Films Show PG-13 Is Hollywood's Trojan Horse," in *Jewish World Review* (2001).

27. Different policy suggestions can be found, for instance, in Joanne Cantor Brad J. Bushman, "Media Ratings for Violence and Sex: Implications for Policymakers and Parents," *American Psychologist* 58, no. 2 (2003).

28. The most thorough and authoritative account of the history of the ratings system is found in Stephen Vaughn, *Freedom and Entertainment: Rating the Movies in an Age of New Media* (Cambridge: Cambridge University Press, 2006). Other important studies of the ratings include Jon Lewis, *Hollywood v. Hard Core: How the Struggle Over Censorship Saved the Modern Film Industry* (New York: New York University Press, 2000); Kevin S. Sandler, *The Naked Truth: Why Hollywood Doesn't Make X-Rated Movies* (New Brunswick, NJ: Rutgers University Press, 2007).

29. *Reading in the Dark: Horror in Children's Literature and Culture*, ed. Jessica McCort (Jackson: University Press of Mississippi, 2016); K. Shyrock Hood, *Once Upon a Time in a Dark and Scary Book: The Messages of Horror Literature for Children* (Jefferson: McFarland, 2018); Anna Jackson; Roderick McGillis; Karen Coats, *The Gothic in Children's Literature: Haunting the Borders*, Children's Literature and Culture (London: Routledge, 2007).

30. Timothy Morris, *You're Only Young Twice: Children's Literature and Film* (Urbana: University of Illinois Press, 2000), 85.

31. Jessica R. McCort, editor, *Reading in the Dark: Horror in Children's Literature and Culture*, 5.

32. Catherine Lester, "The Children's Horror Film: Characterizing an 'Impossible' Subgenre," *Velvet Light Trap*, no. 78 (2016): 23.

33. This relationship has been thoroughly explored in academic studies of genre. See, for example, Rick Altman, *Film/Genre* (London: British Film Institute, 1999); Barbara Klinger, *Melodrama & Meaning: History, Culture, and the Films of Douglas Sirk* (Bloomington: Indiana University Press, 1994); Mark Jancovich and Lincoln Geraghty, eds. *Shifting Definitions of Genre: Essays on Labeling Films, Television Shows and Media* (Jefferson: McFarland, 2008).

34. Lester, 22.

35. The other peak period in children's horror film, the 2010s, is a consequence of the first one. See the book's conclusion for a thorough discussion of the ways in which films of the 2010s echo the issues of the 1980s.

36. See the book's conclusion for a discussion of this, and the appendix for a selection of titles.

Chapter 1

1. Janet Wasko, *Understanding Disney: The Manufacture of Fantasy* (Cambridge: Polity, 2001), 31.

2. Scott Michael Bosco, "The Watcher in the Woods: The Mystery Behind the Mystery," in *Digital Cinema*.

3. Ibid.

4. Douglas Gomery, "Disney's Business History: A Reinterpretation," in *Disney Discourse: Producing the Magic Kingdom*, ed. Eric Smoodin (London: Routledge, 1994), 78.

5. J.P. Telotte, *The Mouse Machine: Disney and Technology* (Urbana: University of Illinois Press, 2008), 44.

6. Ron Grover, *The Disney Touch: Disney, Abc & the Quest for the World's Greatest Media Empire* (New York: McGraw-Hill, 1997), 8; *ibid*.
7. Bart Mills, "Disney Looks for a Happy Ending to Its Grim Fairy Tale," *American Film*, July-August 1982, 1.
8. Ed Blank, "Bette Davis Superb; 'Watcher' Average," *The Pittsburgh Press*, February 1 1982.
9. Sally Ogle Davis, "Walt Disney Productions' Falling Star—Disney Can't Seem to Make Successful Movies Any More," *Lakeland Ledger*, November 28 1980.
10. *Ibid*.
11. *Ibid*.
12. Mills, 53.
13. Aljean Harmetz, "Another Disney Break with Tradition: Independent Producer to Film for Studio," *The Miami News*, March 1980.
14. Joseph Stannard, "Out of the Woods," *Sight and Sound*, March 2011.
15. Bosco.
16. John Hough, "Commentary on Alternate Ending 2," in *The Watcher in the Woods* (Starz/Anchor Bay, 2002).
17. Aljean Harmetz, "'Watcher in Woods,' Revised $1 Million Worth, Tries Again," in *New York Times* (1981).
18. Mills, 53.
19. Stannard.
20. Skip Sheffield, "Market for 'Watcher' a Mystery," *Boca Raton News*, November 26 1981.
21. *Ibid*.
22. Anon, "Disney's 'Watcher in the Woods' Rescued," *Lakeland Ledger*, November 27 1981.
23. Terry Pace, "In Review: Disney Staying in Woods with 'Watcher,'" *Times Daily*, November 27 1981.
24. Terry Hazlett, "'Watcher in Woods:' Tricks Are for Kids," *Observer-Reporter*, February 3 1982.
25. George Hatza, "Don't Be a Watcher of Disney's Barren 'Woods,'" *Reading Eagle*, November 8 1981.
26. Blank.
27. John Hough, Film Commentary (Starz/Anchor Bay, 2002).
28. Sheffield.
29. Hatza.
30. See Chapter 4 for an extended explanation of why this association was especially strong in the 1970s.
31. Hatza.
32. Wood, 65.
33. As Chapter 3 details, the motif of the evil child was soon parodied in children's horror.
34. Quoted in Stannard.
35. Bosco.
36. Hough, *Film Commentary*.
37. Scott Michael Bosco, *The Watcher in the Woods—The Mystery Disclosed Booklet* (Anchor Bay Entertainment, Inc., 2002).
38. *Ibid*.
39. *Ibid*.
40. Hough, *Film Commentary*.
41. Pace.
42. Edward Jones, "'Watcher in the Woods' Doesn't Measure Up," *The Free Lance-Star*, October 15 1981.
43. Blank.
44. Scott Michael Bosco, "Interview with Harrison Ellenshaw," in *Digital Cinema*.
45. Scott Michael Bosco, *The Watcher in the Woods—The Mystery Disclosed* Booklet (Anchor Bay Entertainment, Inc., 2002).
46. *Ibid*.
47. John Hough, "Commentary on Alternate Ending 1," in *The Watcher in the Woods* (Starz/Anchor Bay, 2002).
48. Gomery, 78.
49. Cited in Mills, 56.
50. Dan Kois, "The Black Cauldron—Is the Movie That Almost Killed Disney Animation Really That Bad?," in *Slate*.
51. Michael Peraza, "Cauldron of Chaos," http://michaelperaza.blogspot.com/search/label/Black%20Cauldron.
52. See Chapters 3 and 4.

Chapter 2

1. See, for instance, Sandler, *The Naked Truth Why Hollywood Doesn't Make X-Rated Movies*; Lewis.
2. See for example Brad J. Bushman.
3. This argument is expressed in the books cited above, but also in the documentary *This Film Is Not Yet Rated* (Kirby Dick, 2006).
4. This view is explicitly argued in Medved.
5. For example, Ron Leone.

6. The Classification and Rating Administration, "History of the Ratings," https://filmratings.com/history.
7. Vaughn, 117.
8. Jim Windolf, "Q&A Steven Spielberg," Vanity Fair, https://www.vanityfair.com/news/2008/02/spielberg_qanda200802.
9. Stephen Prince, *A New Pot of Gold: Hollywood Under the Electronic Rainbow, 1980–1989* (New York: Scribner, 2000), 367.
10. Dave Kehr, "Poltergeist," *Chicago Reader*, Https://www.chicagoreader.com/chicago/poltergeist/Film?oid=11118037.
11. Newman, *Nightmare Movies: Horror on Screen Since the 1960s*, 231.
12. Vincent Canby, "Film: 'Poltergeist' from Spielberg," *New York Times*, http://movies2.nytimes.com/books/97/06/15/reviews/spielberg-poltergeist.html.
13. Ibid.
14. "Disney Movie Needs Ghost Writer," *The Day*, April 17, 1980.
15. Lester Friedman, *Citizen Spielberg* (Urbana: University of Illinois, 2006), 103.
16. Prince, 367.
17. See his *Gremlins* review later in this chapter, or his views on *The Good Son*, in Chapter 4.
18. Todd McCarthy, "Indiana Jones and the Temple of Doom," *Variety*, https://variety.com/1984/film/reviews/indiana-jones-and-the-temple-of-doom-1200426218/.
19. Vincent Canby, "Screen: 'Indiana Jones,' Directed by Spielberg," *New York Times*, https://www.nytimes.com/1984/05/23/movies/screen-indiana-jones-directed-by-spielberg.html.
20. "Film: 'Poltergeist' from Spielberg."
21. A similar comparison was made by Pauline Kael: "there are sequences that are like what children dream up when they're having a gross-out and trying to top each other" (178).
22. Aljean Harmetz, "'Indiana Jones' May Spell Doom for Current Movie Rating System," *The Palm Beach Post*, May 23 1984.
23. Ellen Goodman, "Change the Films, Not the Ratings," *Los Angeles Times* 1984.
24. Anthony Breznican, "PG-13 Remade Hollywood Ratings System," *Seattle Pi* (2004).
25. James White, "The Story Behind Gremlins," *Total Film* (2009).
26. David Chute, *Film Comment*, May-June 1984.
27. Breznican.
28. Pauline Kael, *State of the Art: Film Writings 1983–1985* (London: Marion Boyars, 2009), 188.
29. White.
30. This tactic was later reused with *Nightmare Before Christmas* (see Chapter 4).
31. Anon, "Gremlins! Will You Let Your Children See Them?" *Daily Express*, October 2 1984.
32. Vincent Canby, "Screen: 'Gremlins,' Kiddie Gore," *New York Times* (1984).
33. Alexander Walker, *Evening Standard*, July 12 1984.
34. Ibid.
35. David Edelstein, *Voice*, July 24 1984.
36. Michael Wood, "Little Devils," *New Society*, December 13 1984.
37. Kael, 189.
38. Gene Siskel and Roger Ebert, "Gremlins," in *At the Movies* (Buena Vista Television, 1984).
39. Kael, 188.
40. Ibid., 189.
41. Canby, "Screen: 'Gremlins,' Kiddie Gore."
42. Kael, 185.
43. Edelstein.
44. Walker.
45. Roger Ebert, "The Goonies," Roger Ebert.com (1985).
46. Ibid.

Chapter 3

1. See, for example, the popularity of pre-teen-targeted non-horror titles such as *Explorers* (1985), *The Goonies* (1985), *Flight of the Navigator* (1986), *The Wizard* (1989), or *Home Alone* (1990).
2. Hal Hinson, "'Indiana Jones and the Last Crusade," *The Washington Post*, https://www.washingtonpost.com/wp-srv/style/longterm/movies/videos/indianajonesandthelastcrusadepg13hinson_a0a93b.htm??noredirect=on.
3. Joseph McBride, "Indiana Jones and the Last Crusade," *Variety*, https://variety.com/1989/film/reviews/indiana-jones-and-the-last-crusade-1200428090/.

4. Caryn James, "Review/Film; Indiana Jones in Pursuit of Dad and the Grail," *New York Times*, https://www.nytimes.com/1989/05/24/movies/review-film-indiana-jones-in-pursuit-of-dad-and-the-grail.html.

5. Roger Ebert, "Indiana Jones and the Last Crusade," RogerEbert.com, https://www.rogerebert.com/reviews/indiana-jones-and-the-last-crusade-1989.

6. "Gremlins 2: The New Batch," Roger Ebert.com, https://www.rogerebert.com/reviews/gremlins-2-the-new-batch-1990.

7. Hal Hinson, "Gremlins 2: The New Batch," *The Washington Post*, http://www.washingtonpost.com/wp-srv/style/longterm/movies/videos/gremlins2thenewbatchpg13hinson_a0a978.htm.

8. *Johnny Dangerously* (1984), *The Woman in Red* (1984), *Micki & Maude* (1984), *The Flamingo Kid* (1984), *Night of the Comet* (1984), *Young Sherlock Holmes* (1985), *Once Bitten* (1985), *Weird Science* (1985), *National Lampoon's European Vacation* (1985), *Little Shop of Horrors* (1986), *Big Trouble in Little China* (1986), *Crocodile Dundee* (1986), *Ferris Bueller's Day Off* (1986), *Pretty in Pink* (1986), *Dirty Dancing* (1987), *Can't Buy Me Love* (1987), *Some Kind of Wonderful* (1987), *Adventures in Babysitting* (1987), *The Naked Gun* (1988), *High Spirits* (1988), *Scrooged* (1988), *She's Having a Baby* (1988), *National Lampoon's Christmas Vacation* (1989), *Look Who's Talking* (1989), *Weekend at Bernie's* (1989) and *Say Anything...* (1989).

9. *Dune* (1984), *Runaway* (1984), *Dreamscape* (1984), *Cocoon* (1985), *Red Sonja* (1985) and *Solarbabies* (1986).

10. *Red Dawn* (1984), *Mrs. Soffel* (1984), *Garbo Talks* (1984), *The Razor's Edge* (1984), *The River* (1984), *The Color Purple* (1985), *Raising Arizona* (1987), *License to Kill* (1989) and *The Abyss* (1989).

11. Sheila Benson, "Batman," *Los Angeles Times*, http://articles.latimes.com/1989-06-23/entertainment/ca-2570_1_bruce-wayne-kim-basinger-s-vicki-vale-jack-nicholson-s-joker/2.

12. Jay Boyar, "Batman Review," *Orlando Sentinel*, http://articles.orlandosentinel.com/1989-07-30/entertainment/8907272738_1_michael-keaton-batman-kim-basinger.

13. Roger Ebert, "Batman," RogerEbert.com, http://www.rogerebert.com/reviews/batman-1989.

14. *House II: The Second Story*, *Howling III* (1987), *Killer Klowns from Outer Space*, *Elvira: Mistress of the Dead* (1988), *Stuff Stephanie in the Incinerator* (1989), *The Return of Swamp Thing*, and *Transylvania Twist* (1989).

15. Anon, "The Story Behind the Lost Boys," http://www.gamesradar.com/the-story-behind-the-lost-boys/.

16. *Ibid.*

17. *Ibid.*

18. *Ibid.*

19. Kim Newman, *Nightmare Movies: A Critical History of the Horror Film, 1968–88* (London: Bloomsbury, 1988), 204.

20. This is also related to the critical enshrining of the 1970s as the golden age of horror, something I address in greater detail in Chapter 4.

21. Andrew Dowler, "The Gate," *Cinema Canada*, July/August 1987.

22. Twitchell.

23. Heather Wixson, "Class of 1987: Director Tibor Takács Reflects on His Coming-of-Age Horror Fairy Tale the Gate," Daily Dead, https://dailydead.com/class-of-1987-director-tibor-takacs-reflects-on-his-coming-of-age-horror-fairy-tale-the-gate.

24. Kevin Thomas, "Allegory for Teens Lurks Amid Scary Fun of Sequel to 'the Gate,'" *L.A. Times-The Washington Post* 1992.

25. B. Alan Orange, "Exclusive: Tibor Takacs Takes Us Back Through 'the Gate: Monstrous Special Edition,'" http://movieweb.com/exclusive-tibor-takacs-takes-us-back-through-the-gate-monstrous-special-edition/.

26. Charles Webb, "Mtv Geek's Frightful Faves: Reopening 'the Gate' (1987)," http://geek-news.mtv.com/2012/10/10/mtv-geeks-frightfulfaves-reopening-the-gate-1987.

27. Michael Nankin and Randall William Cook Tibor Takács, "Audio Commentary," in *The Gate* (Lionsgate, 2009).

28. *Ibid.*

29. William Paul, *Laughing, Screaming: Modern Hollywood Horror and Comedy* (New York: Columbia University Press, 1994). Pag 282–283.

30. Tibor Takács.
31. *Ibid.*
32. *Ibid.*
33. Wixson.
34. *Ibid.*
35. Tibor Takács.
36. Robert Saucedo, "Badass Interview: The Gate's Tibor Takacs," http://birthmoviesdeath.com/2012/02/09/badass-interview-the-gates-tibor-takacs.
37. *Ibid.*
38. Frank N. Magill, *Magill's Cinema Annual 1988* (Pasadena, CA: Salem Press, 1988).
39. Johanna Steinmetz, "Terror Swings with Humor in 'The Gate,'" *Chicago Tribune*, May 18, 1987.
40. Saucedo.
41. Orange.
42. Saucedo.
43. Edward Jones, "Special Effects Make 'Gate' a Cut Above Average Thriller," *The Free Lance-Star*, June 10, 1987.
44. Christopher Hicks, "Too Many Other Shows Swing on 'The Gate,'" *The Deseret News*, May 21, 1987.
45. Orange.
46. Eventually, these conflicts affected the film's sequel, *The Trespassers* (1990), which received an R for drug use despite remaining close in spirit to its predecessor.
47. Tibor Takács.
48. Frank N. Magill, *Magill's Cinema Annual, 1988* (Pasadena, CA: Salem Press, 1988).
49. Hicks.
50. *Ibid.*
51. Michael Wilmington, "Movie Review: Bevy of Beasties Run Wild in 'Gate,'" *Los Angeles Times*, May 19, 1987.
52. Dave Kehr, "'The Lost Boys' a Vampire Film Thirsting for a Good Story," *Chicago Tribune*, July 31, 1987.
53. Rita Kempley, "'The Lost Boys' (R)," in *The Washington Post* (1987).
54. Vincent Canby, "Film: 'Monster Squad,'" *New York Times*, https://www.nytimes.com/1987/08/14/movies/film-monster-squad.html.
55. Anon, "Movie Review: 'Monster Squad' Is Fun for the Kid in All of Us," http://articles.latimes.com/1987-08-14/entertainment/ca-755_1_monster-squad.
56. Ken W. Hanley, "Tales from the Video Store: Meeting "the Monster Squad," Fangoria, Http://www.fangotv.com/tales-from-the-video-store-meeting-the-monster-squad/.
57. Newman, *Nightmare Movies: Horror on Screen Since the 1960s*, 35–36.
58. "The Monster Squad Review," *Empire*, https://www.empireonline.com/movies/monster-squad/review/.

Chapter 4

1. David Sanjek, "Same as It Ever Was: Innovation and Exhaustion in the Horror and Science Fiction Films of the 1990s," in *Film Genre 2000: New Critical Essays*, ed. Wheeler W. Dixon (New York: State University of New York Press), 114.
2. *Ibid.*, 116.
3. *Ibid.*
4. Steffen Hantke, ed. *American Horror Film: The Genre at the Turn of the Millennium* (Jackson: University Press of Mississippi, 2010), xxi.
5. Jancovich.
6. Vincent Canby, "Review/Film; Methods of Madness in 'Silence of the Lambs,'" *New York Times*, https://www.nytimes.com/1991/02/14/movies/review-film-methods-of-madness-in-silence-of-the-lambs.html.
7. *Ibid.*
8. Hal Hinson, "'Mary Shelley's Frankenstein' (R)," http://www.washingtonpost.com/wp-srv/style/longterm/movies/videos/maryshelleysfrankensteinrhinson_a01af8.htm.
9. Todd McCarthy, "Review: 'Bram Stoker's Dracula,'" http://variety.com/1992/film/reviews/bram-stokers-dracula-1200431014/.
10. Vincent Canby, "Coppola's Dizzying Vision of Dracula," *New York Times*, http://www.nytimes.com/movie/review?res=9E0CE2D61539F930A25752C1A964958260.
11. Todd McCarthy, "Review: 'Wolf,'" http://variety.com/1994/film/reviews/wolf-1200437584/.
12. Roger Ebert, "Wolf," http://www.rogerebert.com/reviews/wolf-1994.
13. Todd McCarthy, "Review: 'Interview with the Vampire,'" *Variety*, http://variety.com/1994/film/reviews/interview-with-the-vampire-1200439504/.

14. *Ibid.*

15. Roger Ebert, "Candyman," Roger Ebert.com, http://www.rogerebert.com/reviews/candyman-1992.

16. In the case of remakes this return was quite literal, as in Scorsese's acclaimed *Cape Fear* (1991), a remake of a 1960s feature.

17. James Berardinelli, "Wes Craven's New Nightmare (United States, 1994)," ReelViews, http://www.reelviews.net/reelviews/wes-craven-s-new-nightmare.

18. Leonard Klady, "Review: 'Scream,'" *Variety*, http://variety.com/1996/film/reviews/scream-1117436711/.

19. Derek Elley, "Review: 'I Know What You Did Last Summer,'" *Variety*, http://variety.com/1997/film/reviews/i-know-what-you-did-last-summer-111731125/.

20. Owen Gleiberman, "Movie Review: 'I Know What You Did Last Summer,'" *Entertainment Weekly*, https://ew.com/article/1997/10/24/movie-review-i-know-what-you-did-last-summer-2/.

21. *Ibid.*

22. Lawrence van Gelder, "Film Review; Creepy Guys, Ghost Stories, Teen-Age Sex: Uh-Oh.," *New York Times*, https://www.nytimes.com/1997/10/17/movies/film-review-creepy-guys-ghost-stories-teen-age-sex-uh-oh.html.

23. Mick LaSalle, "'Summer' Isn't Quite a Scream/Story Eventually Turns Formulaic," *San Francisco Gate*, https://www.sfgate.com/movies/article/Summer-Isnt-Quite-a-Scream-Story-eventually-3010531.php.

24. Roger Ebert, RogerEbert.com, https://www.rogerebert.com/reviews/wes-cravens-new-nightmare-1994.

25. Michael Sauter, "The Island of Dr. Moreau," *Entertainment Weekly*, https://ew.com/article/1997/01/10/island-dr-moreau-2/.

26. Peter Stack, "Film Review—Brando's Beastly 'Island of Dr. Moreau'/Opportunities Wasted in Tired Sci-Fi Remake," *San Francisco Gate*, https://www.sfgate.com/movies/article/FILM-REVIEW-Brandos-Beastly-Island-of-Dr-2969817.php.

27. Roger Ebert, "The Haunting," Roger Ebert.com, http://www.rogerebert.com/reviews/the-haunting-1999.

28. Mick LaSalle, "'the Haunting' Is Pretty Stupid," *San Francisco Gate*, https://www.sfgate.com/movies/article/The-Haunting-Is-Pretty-Stupid-2918680.php.

29. "'Anaconda' Something to Hiss at/Big Snake Slithers Through Lame Action," *San Francisco Gate*, https://www.sfgate.com/movies/article/Anaconda-Something-to-Hiss-At-Big-snake-2825947.php.

30. Lisa Schwarzbaum, "Anaconda," *Entertainment Weekly*, https://ew.com/article/1997/04/18/anaconda/.

31. Todd McCarthy, "Review: 'The Sixth Sense,'" *Variety*, http://variety.com/1999/film/reviews/the-sixth-sense-1200458827/.

32. Stephen Holden, "A Satanic Cult Caper in the Bible Belt," *New York Times*, http://www.nytimes.com/movie/review?res=9F0CE6DE1F3BF933A05752C0A965958260&partner=Rotten%2520Tomatoes.

33. Peter Stack, "Carpenter's 'Village of the Damned' a Dreary Place," *San Francisco Chronicle*, http://www.sfgate.com/movies/article/Carpenters-Village-of-the-Damned-a-Dreary-Place-3034711.php.

34. Richard Harrington, "'Village of the Damned' (R)," *The Washington Post*, http://www.washingtonpost.com/wp-srv/style/longterm/movies/videos/villageofthedamnedrharrington_c01363.htm.

35. Hal Hinson, "'The Good Son' (R)," *The Washington Post*, http://www.washingtonpost.com/wp-srv/style/longterm/movies/videos/thegoodsonrhinson_a0a843.htm.

36. Roger Ebert, "The Good Son," Roger Ebert.com, http://www.rogerebert.com/reviews/the-good-son-1993.

37. *Ibid.*

38. Janet Maslin, "Demons' Eye Problems Compound Creepiness," *New York Times*, http://www.nytimes.com/movie/review?res=990CE7D71238F93BA15757C0A963958260.

39. See Medved's criticisms in Chapter 2 or Joanne Cantor, *Mommy, I'm Scared: How Tv and Movies Frighten Children and What We Can Do to Protect Them* (San Diego, California: Harcourt, Brace & Co., 1998).

40. John Hartl, "'The Nightmare Before Christmas' Returns," *The Seattle Times*, October 22, 2000.

41. Tim Burton, *Burton on Burton*, ed. Mark Salisbury (London: Faber, 2000), 9.
42. *Ibid.*, 24–25.
43. *Ibid.*, 39.
44. Anon, "The Nightmare Before Christmas 3-D: 13 Years and Three Dimensions Later," http://uk.ign.com/articles/2006/10/20/the-nightmare-before-christmas-3-d-13-years-and-three-dimensions-later?page=1.
45. *Ibid.*
46. Marlow Stern, "Henry Selick on Directing 'the Nightmare Before Christmas,'" http://www.thedailybeast.com/articles/2013/10/29/henry-selick-on-directing-the-nightmare-before-christmas.html.
47. Jeff Strickler, "Merry Scary Christmas," *The Star Tribune*, October 22, 1993.
48. Stern.
49. Betsy Sharkley, "Tim Burton's 'Nightmare' Comes True," *New York Times*, October 10, 1993.
50. Scott Mendelson, "'Nightmare Before Christmas' Turns 20: From Shameful Spawn to Disney's Pride," *Forbes*, http://www.forbes.com/sites/scottmendelson/2013/10/15/how-the-nightmare-before-christmas-went-in-20-years-from-shameful-offspring-to-disneys-favorite-son/.
51. Paul Sherman, "Disney Has Dreams of Profits from 'Nightmare,'" *The Boston Herald*, October 28, 2000.
52. This unproblematic embracing of *Nightmare Before Christmas* as a film suitable for young viewers is in line with what had previously happened with *The Gate* (see Chapter 3), and reflects a growing socio-cultural agreement over the boundaries of the pre-teen category. This point is developed further in the next chapter.
53. Janet Maslin, "Infiltrating the Land of Sugar Plums," *New York Times*, October 9, 1993.
54. *Ibid.*
55. Desson Howe, "'The Nightmare Before Christmas' (PG)," *The Washington Post*, October 22, 1993.
56. Maslin, "Infiltrating the Land of Sugar Plums."
57. Betsy Sharkley, "Tim Burton's 'Nightmare' Comes True," *ibid.*, October 10.
58. Stern.
59. Burton, 32.
60. *Ibid.*, 4–5.
61. Joe Morgenstem, "Tim Burton, Batman and the Joker," *New York Times*, April 9, 1989.
62. Burton, 36.
63. *Ibid.*, 19.
64. Howe.
65. Maslin, "Infiltrating the Land of Sugar Plums."
66. Quentin Curtis, "Amazing What You Can Do in a Fortnight," *The Independent*, November 27, 1994.
67. Maslin, "Infiltrating the Land of Sugar Plums."
68. Kenneth Turan, "Movie Reviews: Burton Dreams Up a Delightful 'Nightmare,'" *Los Angeles Times* 1993.
69. Howe.
70. Todd McCarthy, "Review: 'The Nightmare Before Christmas,'" *Variety*, http://variety.com/1993/film/reviews/the-nightmare-before-christmas-1200433742/.
71. David Ansen, "Movies: Tim Burton Looks at Holiday Hell," *Newsweek*, November 1, 1993.
72. Turan.
73. Roger Ebert, "Burton's Dreamy 'Nightmare,'" *Chicago Sun-Times*, October 27, 2000.
74. Maslin, "Infiltrating the Land of Sugar Plums."
75. Turan.
76. Bill Jones, "He Kept His Nightmare Alive," *The Phoenix Gazette*, October 22, 1993.
77. Hartl.
78. Curtis.
79. Turan.
80. Jones.
81. McCarthy, "Review: 'The Nightmare Before Christmas.'"
82. Turan.
83. Sharkley.
84. *Ibid.*
85. Jones.
86. Elisabeth Perrin, "Tim Burton Guides to the Screen Another Tale from the Dark Side," *The Chicago Sun-Times*, October 17, 1993.
87. *Ibid.*
88. Jones.

Chapter 5

1. Robert C. Allen, "Home Alone Together: Hollywood and the 'Family Film,'" in *Identifying Hollywood's Audiences: Cultural Identity and the Movies*, ed. Melvyn Stokes and Richard Maltby (London: British Film Institute, 1999), 110.
2. *Ibid.*, 116.
3. *Ibid.*, 111.
4. See, for instance, Sharon Hays, *The Cultural Contradictions of Motherhood* (New Haven, CT: Yale University Press, 1996); Judith Warner, *Perfect Madness: Motherhood in the Age of Anxiety* (London: Vermillon, 2006).
5. Filipa Antunes, "Attachment Anxiety: Parenting Culture, Adolescence and the Family Film in the Us," *Journal of Children and Media* 11, no. 2 (2017).
6. The likelihood of this common ideological ground between diverse demographics can be seen in the political strategies used during this period: both Democrat and Republican electoral campaigns used the symbolism of childhood and children to advance their cause, often in indistinguishable ways. See Henry Jenkins, *The Children's Culture Reader* (New York: New York University Press, 1998).
7. William Sears; Martha Sears; Robert Sears; James Sears, *The Baby Book: Everything You Need to Know About Your Baby—from Birth to Age Two*, Second Edition ed. (Boston: Little, Brown and Company, 2003), 11.
8. Kate Pickert, "The Man Who Remade Motherhood," Time, http://time.com/606/the-man-who-remade-motherhood/.
9. Sears, 17.
10. Neil MacFarquhar, "What's a Soccer Mom Anyway?," *New York Times* 1996.
11. *Ibid.*
12. Peter Kramer, "Would You Take Your Child to See This Film? The Cultural and Social Work of the Family-Adventure Movie," in *Contemporary Hollywood Cinema*, ed. Murray Smith Steve Neale (London: Routledge, 1998), 294.
13. Donald Sturrock, *Storyteller: The Life of Roald Dahl* (London: William Collins, 2016), 535.
14. Caryn James, *Review/Film; When the Ladies Take Off Their Wigs, Head for Home. Fast.* (New York Times, 1990).
15. Desson Howe, "'The Witches' (PG)," *The Washington Post* 1990.
16. Dave Kehr, "A Little Bit of Magic," *Chicago Tribune*, August 28, 1990.
17. Rita Kempley, "'The Witches' (PG)," *The Washington Post*, http://www.washingtonpost.com/wp-srv/style/long term/movies/videos/thewitchespgkempley_a0a14e.htm.
18. Michael Wilmington, "Movie Review: 'Witches': Adult Children's Fantasy," *Los Angeles Times*, August 24, 1990.
19. James, *Review/Film; When the Ladies Take Off Their Wigs, Head for Home. Fast.*
20. Roger Ebert, "The Witches," Roger Ebert.com, https://www.rogerebert.com/reviews/the-witches-1990.
21. James, *Review/Film; When the Ladies Take Off Their Wigs, Head for Home. Fast.*
22. Kehr, "A Little Bit of Magic."
23. Anon, "Movies," *Boca Raton News*, October 12, 1990.
24. Wilmington, "Movie Review: 'Witches': Adult Children's Fantasy."
25. James, *Review/Film; When the Ladies Take Off Their Wigs, Head for Home. Fast.*
26. Ebert, "The Witches."
27. Box Office Mojo, "The Witches Weekly Gross," https://www.boxofficemojo.com/movies/?page=weekly&id=witches.htm.
28. Anon, "Home Court Advantage," *Los Angeles Times*, http://articles.latimes.com/1996-04-15/entertainment/ca-58749_1_felicity-dahl.
29. Sturrock, 536.
30. Anon, "Home Court Advantage."
31. American Library Association, "100 Most Frequently Challenged Books: 1990–1999," ALA.org, http://www.ala.org/advocacy/bbooks/100-most-frequently-challenged-books-1990%E2%80%931999.
32. Caryn James, "Friendly and Translucent? He's Back," *New York Times*, May 26, 1995.
33. Brad Silberling, 2008.
34. James, "Friendly and Translucent? He's Back."
35. Rita Kempley, "'Casper,'" *The Washington Post*, May 26, 1995.
36. Barbara Shulgasser, "'Casper' the

Sappy Spook," *The San Francisco Examiner*, May 26, 1995.

37. Owen Gleiberman, "Casper," in *Entertainment Weekly* (1995).

38. Silberling.

39. "Behind the Scenes," in *Casper*, ed. Brad Silberling (Universal Pictures UK, 2008).

40. Mick LaSalle, "'Casper' Raises Spirits and Tugs Heartstrings," *The San Francisco Chronicle*, May 26, 1995.

41. Gleiberman, "Casper."

42. James, "Friendly and Translucent? He's Back."

43. *Ibid.*

44. Gleiberman, "Casper."

45. LaSalle, "'Casper' Raises Spirits and Tugs Heartstrings."

46. *Ibid.*

47. Roger Ebert, "Casper," RogerEbert.com, http://www.rogerebert.com/reviews/casper-1995.

48. Gleiberman, "Casper."

49. James Berardinelli, "Casper (1995)," http://www.imdb.com/reviews/36/3658.html.

50. James, "Friendly and Translucent? He's Back."

51. LaSalle, "'Casper' Raises Spirits and Tugs Heartstrings."

52. James, "Friendly and Translucent? He's Back."

53. Ebert, "Casper."

54. Berardinelli, "Casper (1995)."

55. Silberling.

56. *Ibid.*

57. Kat's puberty transformation can also be read as the move to a new place and a new house. The house, particularly in the context of Gothic horror, is often a symbol of personal identity and agency so it is meaningful that this new house is where Kat finds Casper and is confronted with the challenges of puberty/death.

58. Though death functions as a metaphor for puberty in *Casper*, the mother's death, which takes place before the film starts, has a different symbolic function, namely to single out Kat and Dr. Harvey's relationship as the focus of the story. This way, *Casper* clearly addresses the way preadolescence affects parents and children specifically, as opposed to the dynamics of the couple, or of the couple in relation to the rest of the family unit.

59. Silberling.

60. Rita Kempley, "'Beethoven,'" *The Washington Post*, April 3, 1992.

61. Jeanne Cooper, "'Home Alone,'" *ibid.*, November 16, 1990.

62. For a more detailed examination of how this particular question was negotiated, see Antunes.

63. As I argued in Chapter 4, horror responded to this situation by using the rating system to carve out a restricted niche which opposed this model, but even this strategy proved unsustainable as the genre noticeably leaked into the mainstream template in the form of PG-13 titles in the 2000s.

Chapter 6

1. This includes choose-your-own-adventure stories, as well as storybooks with a gameplay element, often involving the use of dice, pen and paper (e.g., the *Fighting Fantasy* series).

2. David Hill, "Who's Afraid of R.L. Stine," Education Week, http://www.edweek.org/tm/articles/1996/03/01/06stine.h07.html.

3. Select examples are listed in the Appendix.

4. Sheila Wilensky, "The Heyday of Children's Bookselling," *Publishers Weekly*, https://www.publishersweekly.com/pw/by-topic/childrens/childrens-industry-news/article/48020-the-heyday-of-childrens-bookselling.html.

5. Heather Hendershot, *Nickelodeon Nation: The History, Politics, and Economics of America's Only TV Channel for Kids* (New York: New York University Press, 2004), 135–36.

6. *Ibid.*, 137.

7. Jen Doll, "R.L. Stine Has Been Giving Us Goosebumps for 20 Years," The Wire, http://www.thewire.com/entertainment/2012/07/rl-stine-has-been-giving-us-goosebumps-20-years/54789/.

8. Marlow Stern, "'Goosebumops' Creator R.L. Stine on 20th-Anniversary Series," *Newsweek*, http://www.newsweek.com/goosebumps-creator-rl-stine-20th-anniversary-series-65631.

Notes—Chapter 6

9. Doll.
10. Horrornews.net, "Rl Stine Receives Honors in Guinness World Records," HNN, http://horrornews.net/35191/rl-stine-receives-honors-in-guinness-world-records/.
11. A. Billen, "Little Shocks for Horrors," *The Observer*, February 25, 1996.
12. Joyce M. Rosenberg, "Goosebumps: So Successful They're Scary," *Lawrence Journal-World*, October 27, 1996.
13. Mary B.W. Tabor, "Hints of Horror, Shouts of Protest," *New York Times*, April 2, 1997.
14. *Ibid.*
15. Diane Brady, "R.L. Stine on Writing Horror for Grown-Ups," http://www.bloomberg.com/bw/articles/2012-11-01/r-dot-l-dot-stine-on-writing-horror-for-grown-ups.
16. Linda Hall, "Interview with R.L Stine," *Hamilton News*, http://www.nzherald.co.nz/hamilton-news/lifestyle/news/article.cfm?c_id=1503360&objectid=11078381.
17. *Ibid.*
18. *Ibid.*
19. Lawrie Mifflin, "Spotlight; Something Creepy This Way Comes," *New York Times*, October 22, 1995.
20. "The Media Business; Fox to Morph 'Power Rangers' Into 'Goosebumps' Every Friday," *New York Times*, May 8, 1995.
21. Mary B.W. Tabor, "Hints of Horror, Shouts of Protest," *ibid.*, April 2, 1997.
22. Mary W. Tabor, "At Home With: R.L. Stine; Grown-Ups Deserve Some Terror, Too," *ibid.*, September 7, 1995.
23. W. Devon; Vicky S., "Author, R.L. Stine," Teen Ink, http://www.teenink.com/nonfiction/interviews/article/5422/Author-R-L-Stine/.
24. Matthew Peterson, "Interview with R.L. Stine," The Author Hour, http://theauthorhour.com/r-l-stine/.
25. Jacque Wilson, "R.L. Stine Aims to Give Adults 'Goosebumps,'" CNN, http://edition.cnn.com/2012/10/09/living/stine-red-rain-adult-novel.
26. I. Jeanne Dugan, "Goosebumps:The Things That Ate the Kids' Market," *Bloomberg Business*, http://www.bloomberg.com/bw/stories/1996-11-03/goosebumps-the-thing-that-ate-the-kids-market.
27. James Parker, "Horror for Kids—How Goosebumps Outlasted Harry Potter by Terrifying Fourth-Graders and Mocking Their Parents," *The Atlantic*, http://www.theatlantic.com/magazine/archive/2012/03/horror-for-kids/308885/.
28. *Ibid.*
29. Morris, 58.
30. Reynolds, 1.
31. *Ibid.*, 3.
32. Scholastic, "Parent Guide to Goosebumps."
33. Jen Doll, "R.L. Stine: The Lost Interview," *The Village Voice*, http://www.villagevoice.com/news/rl-stine-the-lost-interview-6714409.
34. *Ibid.*
35. *Ibid.*
36. Peter Gutierrez, "The R.L. Stine Interview, Part 3: Kids and Horror," *School Library Journal*, http://blogs.slj.com/connect-the-pop/2012/07/transliteracy/the-r-l-stine-interview-part-3-kids-and-horror/.
37. American Library Association;, "100 Most Frequently Challenged Books: 1990–1999," http://www.ala.org/bbooks/100-most-frequently-challenged-books-1990%E2%80%931999.
38. Tabor.
39. *Ibid.*
40. Rosenberg.
41. For a discussion of the broader question of horror fiction and children's reading see Kirsten Kowalewski, "Where Are the Scary Books? the Place of Scary Books for Children in School and Children's Libraries," in *Reading in the Dark: Horror in Children's Literature and Culture*, ed. Jessica R. McCort (Jackson: University Press of Mississipi, 2016).
42. Tabor.
43. Peter Gutierrez, "The R.L. Stine Interview, Part 2: The Value of Series Fiction," *School Library Journal*, http://blogs.slj.com/connect-the-pop/2012/07/english/the-r-l-stine-interview-part-2-the-value-of-series-fiction/.
44. Doll, "R.L. Stine Has Been Giving Us Goosebumps for 20 Years."
45. "R.L. Stine: The Lost Interview."
46. "R.L. Stine Has Been Giving Us Goosebumps for 20 Years."
47. *Ibid.*

48. "R.L. Stine: The Lost Interview."
49. The next chapter addresses the change in circumstances with the recent film adaptations (2015, 2017).
50. Meredith Woerner, "Goosebumps Filmmakers Reveal How Rl Stine Became the Star of Their Movie," io9, http://io9.com/goosebumps-filmmakers-reveal-how-rl-stine-became-the-st-1700671432.
51. This is, incidentally, what happened with the two recent film adaptations, justified by a wave of Millennial nostalgia. See the Conclusion, where I position both titles as echoes of children's horror.
52. Hall.
53. R.L. Stine, *It Came from Ohio! My Life as a Writer* (New York: Scholastic, 1997), 118.
54. Hall.
55. Stine.
56. Morris, 68.
57. *Ibid.*, 84.
58. *Ibid.*, 85.
59. *Ibid.*, 77.
60. Doll, "R.L. Stine Has Been Giving Us Goosebumps for 20 Years."
61. Parker.
62. R.L. Stine, *Live Chat* (The Hub, 2010).
63. Tabor.

Conclusion

1. Well-known examples include *Night of the Living Dead* (1968), *Rosemary's Baby* (1968), *The Exorcist*, *The Texas Chainsaw Massacre* (1974), *Carrie* (1976), *The Omen*, and *The Brood* (1979).
2. Manohla Dargis, "Review: 'The Visit' Is 'Hansel and Gretel' with Less Candy and More Camcorders," *New York Times*, http://www.nytimes.com/2015/09/11/movies/review-the-visit-is-hansel-and-gretel-with-less-candy-and-more-camcorders.html?_r=0.
3. Jake Dee, "The Visit (Movie Review)," Arrow in the Head, http://www.joblo.com/horror-movies/news/the-visit-movie-review-226.
4. Peter Martin, "Review: The Visit, a Fleeting Resemblance to a Funhouse Joy Ride," twitch, http://twitchfilm.com/2015/09/review-the-visit-a-fleeting-resemblance-to-a-funhouse-joy-ride.html.
5. Brad Wheeler, "The Visit: Pastoral Horror Comedy Is a Genuinely Fun Affair," *The Globe and Mail*, http://www.theglobeandmail.com/arts/film/film-reviews/the-visit-pastoral-horror-comedy-is-a-genuinely-fun-affair/article26315289/.
6. Jake Dee, "Set Visit: Scouts Guide to the Zombie Apocalypse (Part 2)," Arrow in the Head, http://www.joblo.com/horror-movies/news/set-visit-scouts-guide-to-the-zombie-apocalypse-part-2-183.
7. Staci Layne Wilson, "Scout's Guide to the Zombie Apocalypse—Exclusive Set Visit Interview: Christopher Landon," Dread Central, http://www.dreadcentral.com/news/122173/scouts-guide-to-the-zombie-apocalypse-exclusive-set-visit-interview-christopher-landon/.
8. *Ibid.*
9. Dee, "Set Visit: Scouts Guide to the Zombie Apocalypse (Part 2)."
10. Wilson.
11. *Ibid.*
12. Scott Mendelson, "Review: 'Goosebumps' Is a Scary Good, Kid-Friendly Lovecraftian Horror Comedy," *Forbes*, http://www.forbes.com/sites/scottmendelson/2015/10/05/review-goosebumps-is-a-scary-good-kid-friendly-lovecraftian-horror-comedy/.
13. Peter Sobcynski, "Interview: Gil Kenan—Landlord of the "Monster House," efilmcritic.com, http://www.efilmcritic.com/feature.php?feature=1895&printer=1.
14. Ian Freer, "Monster House," Empire Online, http://www.empireonline.com/reviews/ReviewComplete.asp?FID=10518.
15. Richard Corliss, "Super 8: Just as Great as You Hoped It Would Be," *Time*, http://entertainment.time.com/2011/06/02/super-8-movie-review/2/.
16. Jamie Graham, "Super 8 Review," *GamesRadar*, http://www.gamesradar.com/super-8-review/.
17. Roger Ebert, "Super 8," RogerEbert.com, http://www.rogerebert.com/reviews/super-8-2011.
18. Roger Ebert, "The Goonies," Roger Ebert.com, http://www.rogerebert.com/reviews/the-goonies-1985.
19. A.A. Dowd, "Goosebumps Bears Little Resemblance to the Kid-Lit Horror Books It Pillages," A.V. Club, http://www.

avclub.com/review/goosebumps-bears-little-resemblance-kid-lit-horror-226738.

20. Even small adaptation decisions give evidence of this. Instead of pitching a boy/girl team of children against one threat, as in the books, the film loosely pairs two male teens with R.L. Stine and his "daughter," Hannah, against an ensemble of all the *Goosebumps* monsters. This choice was likely motivated by a desire to make the film as commercially appealing as possible: having all the monsters means no favourites are excluded; presenting Stine as a character adds an extra layer of fan interest; and aging the characters up allows for romantic relationships, bringing the story more in line with expectations of teen-focused entertainment. These are profitable decisions, but they are also obstacles to the fulfilment of the *Goosebumps* "formula."

21. Donna Dickens, "'Goosebumps' Producer Neal Moritz Almost Gave Up on the Whole Idea," HitFix, http://www.hitfix.com/harpy/goosebumps-producer-neal-moritz-almost-gave-up-on-the-whole-idea.

22. *Goosebumps 2* provides further evidence of this. While the film corrects some of the issues I raise here by focusing on younger protagonists and addressing some of their anxieties, the plot is still dominated by the action created by a parade of monsters and concerned with the older sister's romantic storyline.

23. Robin Marantz Henig, "What Is It About 20-Somethings?," *New York Times*, http://www.nytimes.com/2010/08/22/magazine/22Adulthood-t.html?pagewanted=all.

24. Scott Mendelson, "Review: M. Night Shyamalan's 'the Visit' Is A Glorious Return to Form," *Forbes*, http://www.forbes.com/sites/scottmendelson/2015/09/09/review-m-night-shyamalans-the-visit-is-a-glorious-return-to-form/.

25. Palladino.

26. Jeffrey Jensen Arnett, *Emerging Adulthood: The Winding Road from the Late Teens Through the Twenties* (Oxford: Oxford University Press, 2004).

27. Lev Grossman, "Grow Up? Not So Fast," *Time*, http://content.time.com/time/magazine/article/0,9171,1018089,00.html.

28. Henig.

29. Neil Howe and William Strauss, *Millennials Rising: The Next Great Generation* (New York: Vintage, 2000), 58.

Works Cited

Allen, Robert C. "Home Alone Together: Hollywood and the 'Family Film.'" In *Identifying Hollywood's Audiences: Cultural Identity and the Movies,* edited by Melvyn Stokes and Richard Maltby. London: British Film Institute, 1999.
Altman, Rick. *Film/Genre.* London: British Film Institute, 1999.
American Library Association. "100 Most Frequently Challenged Books: 1990–1999." ALA.org, http://www.ala.org/advocacy/bbooks/100-most-frequently-challenged-books-1990%E2%80%931999.
Ansen, David. "Movies: Tim Burton Looks at Holiday Hell." *Newsweek,* November 1, 1993.
Antunes, Filipa. "Attachment Anxiety: Parenting Culture, Adolescence and the Family Film in the Us." *Journal of Children and Media* 11, no. 2 (2017): 214–28.
Ariès, Philippe. *Centuries of Childhood: A Social History of Family Life.* London: Jonathan Cape Ltd, 1965.
Arnett, Jeffrey Jensen. *Emerging Adulthood: The Winding Road from the Late Teens Through the Twenties.* Oxford: Oxford University Press, 2004.
"Behind the Scenes." In *Casper,* edited by Brad Silberling: Universal Pictures UK, 2008.
Benson, Sheila. "Batman." *The Los Angeles Times,* http://articles.latimes.com/1989-06-23/entertainment/ca-2570_1_bruce-wayne-kim-basingers-vicki-vale-jack-nicholsons-joker/2.
Berardinelli, James. "Casper (1995)." http://www.imdb.com/reviews/36/3658.html.
———. "Wes Craven's New Nightmare (United States, 1994)." ReelViews, n.d., http://www.reelviews.net/reelviews/wes-cravens-new-nightmare.
Billen, A. "Little Shocks for Horrors." *The Observer,* February 25, 1996.
Blank, Ed. "Bette Davis Superb; 'Watcher' Average." *The Pittsburgh Press,* February 1, 1982, 7.
Bosco, Scott Michael. "Interview with Harrison Ellenshaw." *Digital Cinema,* March 27, 2002.
———. "The Watcher in the Woods: The Mystery Behind the Mystery." *Digital Cinema,* May 5, 2002.
———. *The Watcher in the Woods—The Mystery Disclosed Booklet.* Anchor Bay Entertainment, Inc., 2002.
Boyar, Jay. "Batman Review." *Orlando Sentinel,* July 30, 1989, http://articles.orlandosentinel.com/1989-07-30/entertainment/8907272738_1_michael-keaton-batman-kim-basinger.
Brady, Diane. "R.L. Stine on Writing Horror for Grown-Ups." November 1, 2012, http://

www.bloomberg.com/bw/articles/2012-11-01/r-dot-l-dot-stine-on-writing-horror-for-grown-ups.

Breznican, Anthony. "PG-13 Remade Hollywood Ratings System." *Seattle Pi*, August 23, 2004, https://www.seattlepi.com/ae/movies/article/PG-13-remade-Hollywood-ratings-system-1152332.php.

Buckingham, David. *Children Talking Television: The Making of Television Literacy*. London: Falmer Press, 1993.

Burton, Tim. *Burton on Burton*. Edited by Mark Salisbury London: Faber, 2000.

Bushman, Brad J., and Joanne Cantor. "Media Ratings for Violence and Sex: Implications for Policymakers and Parents." *American Psychologist* 58, no. 2 (2003).

Canby, Vincent. "Coppola's Dizzying Vision of Dracula." *New York Times*, November 13, 1992, http://www.nytimes.com/movie/review?res=9E0CE2D61539F930A25752C1A 964958260.

———. "Disney Movie Needs Ghost Writer." *The Day*, April 17, 1980, 41.

———. "Film: 'Monster Squad.'" *New York Times*, August 14, 1987, https://www.nytimes.com/1987/08/14/movies/film-monster-squad.html.

———. "Film": Poltergeist" from Spielberg." *New York Times*, June 4, 1982, http://movies2.nytimes.com/books/97/06/15/reviews/spielberg-poltergeist.html.

———. "Review/Film; Methods of Madness in 'Silence of the Lambs.'" *New York Times*, February 14, 1991, https://www.nytimes.com/1991/02/14/movies/review-film-methods-of-madness-in-silence-of-the-lambs.html.

———. "Screen: 'Gremlins,' Kiddie Gore." *New York Times*, June 8, 1984, C:10.

———. "Screen: 'Indiana Jones,' Directed by Spielberg." *New York Times*, May 23, 1984, https://www.nytimes.com/1984/05/23/movies/screen-indiana-jones-directed-by-spielberg.html.

Cantor, Joanne. *Mommy, I'm Scared: How TV and Movies Frighten Children and What We Can Do to Protect Them*. San Diego, California: Harcourt, Brace & Co., 1998.

Chute, David. *Film Comment*, May-June 1984, n.p.

The Classification and Rating Administration. "History of the Ratings." https://filmratings.com/history.

Clinton, Bill. "Speech in Memphis." November 13, 1993, PresidentialRhetoric.com, http://www.presidentialrhetoric.com/historicspeeches/clinton/memphis.html.

Clinton, Hillary. "It Takes a Village—DNC Address." August 27, 1996, AmericanRhetoric.com, https://www.americanrhetoric.com/speeches/hillaryclintontakesavillage.htm.

Cooper, Jeanne. "'Home Alone.'" *Washington Post*, November 16, 1990.

Corliss, Richard. "Super 8: Just as Great as You Hoped It Would Be." *Time*, June 2, 2011, http://entertainment.time.com/2011/06/02/super-8-movie-review/2/.

Curtis, Quentin. "Amazing What You Can Do in a Fortnight." *The Independent*, November 27, 1994.

Dargis, Manohla. "Review: 'The Visit' Is 'Hansel and Gretel' with Less Candy and More Camcorders." *New York Times*, September 10, 2015, http://www.nytimes.com/2015/09/11/movies/review-the-visit-is-hansel-and-gretel-with-less-candy-and-more-camcorders.html?_r=0.

Davis, Sally Ogle. "Walt Disney Productions' Falling Star—Disney Can't Seem to Make Successful Movies Any More." *Lakeland Ledger*, November 28, 1980, 13.

Dee, Jake. "Set Visit: Scouts Guide to the Zombie Apocalypse (Part 2)." *Arrow in the Head*, August 28, 2015, http://www.joblo.com/horror-movies/news/set-visit-scouts-guide-to-the-zombie-apocalypse-part-2-183.

———. "The Visit (Movie Review)." *Arrow in the Head*, September 10, 2015, http://www.joblo.com/horror-movies/news/the-visit-movie-review-226.

Devon, Vicky, S.W. "Author, R.L. Stine." Teen Ink, n.d., http://www.teenink.com/nonfiction/interviews/article/5422/Author-R-L-Stine/.

Dickens, Donna. "'Goosebumps' Producer Neal Moritz Almost Gave Up on the Whole

Idea." HitFix, July 22, 2015, http://www.hitfix.com/harpy/goosebumps-producer-neal-moritz-almost-gave-up-on-the-whole-idea.
"Disney's 'Watcher in the Woods' Rescued." *Lakeland Ledger*, November 27, 1981, 35.
Doll, Jen. "R.L. Stine Has Been Giving Us Goosebumps for 20 Years." *The Wire*, July 19, 2012, http://www.thewire.com/entertainment/2012/07/rl-stine-has-been-giving-us-goosebumps-20-years/54789/.
_____. "R.L. Stine: The Lost Interview." *The Village Voice*, January 24, 2012, http://www.villagevoice.com/news/rl-stine-the-lost-interview-6714409.
Dowd, A.A. "Goosebumps Bears Little Resemblance to the Kid-Lit Horror Books It Pillages." A.V. Club, October 15, 2015, http://www.avclub.com/review/goosebumps-bears-little-resemblance-kid-lit-horror-226738.
Dowler, Andrew. "The Gate." *Cinema Canada*, July/August 1987, 25–26.
Dugan, I. Jeanne. "Goosebumps: The Things That Ate the Kids' Market." *Bloomberg Business*, November 3, 1996, http://www.bloomberg.com/bw/stories/1996-11-03/goosebumps-the-thing-that-ate-the-kids-market.
Ebert, Roger. "Batman." Rogerebert.com, June 23, 1989, http://www.rogerebert.com/reviews/batman-1989.
_____. "Burton's Dreamy 'Nightmare.'" *Chicago Sun-Times*, October 27, 2000.
_____. "Candyman." Rogerebert.com, October 16, 1992, http://www.rogerebert.com/reviews/candyman-1992.
_____. "Casper." Rogerebert.com, May 26, 1995, http://www.rogerebert.com/reviews/casper-1995.
_____. "The Good Son." Rogerebert.com, September 24, 1993, http://www.rogerebert.com/reviews/the-good-son-1993.
_____. "The Goonies." Rogerebert.com, January 1, 1085, https://www.rogerebert.com/reviews/the-goonies-1985.
_____. "Gremlins 2: The New Batch." Rogerebert.com, June 15, 1990, https://www.rogerebert.com/reviews/gremlins-2-the-new-batch-1990.
_____. "The Haunting." Rogerebert.com, July 1, 1999, http://www.rogerebert.com/reviews/the-haunting-1999.
_____. "Indiana Jones and the Last Crusade." Rogerebert.com, May 24, 1989, https://www.rogerebert.com/reviews/indiana-jones-and-the-last-crusade-1989.
_____. "Super 8." Rogerebert.com, June 8, 2011, http://www.rogerebert.com/reviews/super-8-2011.
_____. "Wes Craven's New Nightmare." Rogerebert.com, October 14, 1994, https://www.rogerebert.com/reviews/wes-cravens-new-nightmare-1994.
_____. "The Witches." Rogerebert.com, August 24, 1990, https://www.rogerebert.com/reviews/the-witches-1990.
_____. "Wolf." Rogerebert.com, June 17, 1994, http://www.rogerebert.com/reviews/wolf-1994.
Ebert, Roger, and Gene Siskel. "Gremlins." In *At the Movies*: Buena Vista Television, 1984.
Edelstein, David. *Voice*, July 24, 1984.
Elley, Derek. "Review: 'I Know What You Did Last Summer.'" *Variety*, October 13, 1997, http://variety.com/1997/film/reviews/i-know-what-you-did-last-summer-11173 1125/.
Ellis, Kate Ferguson. *The Contested Castle: Gothic Novels and the Subversion of the Domestic Ideology*. Urbana: University of Illinois Press, 1989.
Fass, Paula S., and Mary Ann Mason, eds. *Childhood in America*. New York: New York University Press, 2000.
Freer, Ian. "Monster House." Empire Online, July 28, 2006, http://www.empireonline.com/reviews/ReviewComplete.asp?FID=10518.
Friedman, Lester. *Citizen Spielberg*. Urbana: University of Illinois, 2006.
Gelder, Lawrence van. "Film Review; Creepy Guys, Ghost Stories, Teen-Age Sex: Uh-Oh." *New York Times*, October 17, 1997, https://www.nytimes.com/1997/10/17/movies/film-review-creepy-guys-ghost-stories-teen-age-sex-uh-oh.html.

Geraghty, Lincoln, and Mark Jancovich, eds. *Shifting Definitions of Genre: Essays on Labeling Films, Television Shows and Media*. Jefferson: McFarland, 2008.

Gleiberman, Owen. "Casper." *Entertainment Weekly*, June 2, 1995, https://ew.com/article/1995/06/02/casper/.

_____. "Movie Review: 'I Know What You Did Last Summer.'" *Entertainment Weekly*, October 24, 1997, https://ew.com/article/1997/10/24/movie-review-i-know-what-you-did-last-summer-2/.

Gomery, Douglas. "Disney's Business History: A Reinterpretation." In *Disney Discourse: Producing the Magic Kingdom*, edited by Eric Smoodin, 71–86. London: Routledge, 1994.

Goodman, Ellen. "Change the Films, Not the Ratings." *Los Angeles Times*, 1984, C5.

Graham, Jamie. "Super 8 Review." GamesRadar, June 1, 2011, http://www.gamesradar.com/super-8-review/.

"Gremlins! Will You Let Your Children See Them?" *Daily Express*, October 2, 1984, n.p.

Grossman, Lev. "Grow Up? Not So Fast." *Time Magazine*, January 16, 2005, http://content.time.com/time/magazine/article/0,9171,1018089,00.html.

Grover, Ron. *The Disney Touch: Disney, ABC & the Quest for the World's Greatest Media Empire*. New York: McGraw-Hill, 1997.

Gutierrez, Peter. "The R.L. Stine Interview, Part 2: The Value of Series Fiction." *School Library Journal*, July 4, 2012, http://blogs.slj.com/connect-the-pop/2012/07/english/the-r-l-stine-interview-part-2-the-value-of-series-fiction/.

_____. "The R.L. Stine Interview, Part 3: Kids and Horror." *School Library Journal*, July 11, 2012, http://blogs.slj.com/connect-the-pop/2012/07/transliteracy/the-r-l-stine-interview-part-3-kids-and-horror/.

Hall, Linda. "Interview with R.L Stine." *Hamilton News*, October 15, 2012, http://www.nzherald.co.nz/hamilton-news/lifestyle/news/article.cfm?c_id=1503360&objectid=11078381.

Hanley, Ken W. "Tales from the Video Store: Meeting "the Monster Squad."" *Fangoria*, August 14, 2014, http://www.fangotv.com/tales-from-the-video-store-meeting-the-monster-squad/.

Hantke, Steffen, ed. *American Horror Film: The Genre at the Turn of the Millennium*. Jackson: University Press of Mississippi, 2010.

Harmetz, Aljean. "Another Disney Break with Tradition: Independent Producer to Film for Studio." *The Miami News*, March 1980, 48.

_____. "'Indiana Jones' May Spell Doom for Current Movie Rating System." *The Palm Beach Post*, May 23, 1984, 48.

_____. "'Watcher in Woods,' Revised $1 Million Worth, Tries Again." *New York Times*, October 20, 1981, https://www.nytimes.com/1981/10/20/movies/watcher-in-woods-revised-1-million-worth-tries-again.html.

Harrington, Richard. "'Village of the Damned' (R)." *The Washington Post*, April 28, 1995, http://www.washingtonpost.com/wp-srv/style/longterm/movies/videos/villageofthedamnedrharrington_c01363.htm.

Hartl, John. "'The Nightmare Before Christmas' Returns." *The Seattle Times*, October 22, 2000.

Hatza, George. "Don't Be a Watcher of Disney's Barren 'Woods.'" *Reading Eagle*, November 8, 1981, 49.

Hays, Sharon. *The Cultural Contradictions of Motherhood*. New Haven, CT: Yale University Press, 1996.

Hazlett, Terry. "'Watcher in Woods': Tricks Are for Kids." *Observer-Reporter*, February 3, 1982, 16.

Hendershot, Heather. *Nickelodeon Nation: The History, Politics, and Economics of America's Only TV Channel for Kids*. New York: New York University Press, 2004.

Henig, Robin Marantz. "What Is It About 20-Somethings?" *New York Times*, August 22, 2010, http://www.nytimes.com/2010/08/22/magazine/22Adulthood-t.html?pagewanted=all.

Hicks, Christopher. "Too Many Other Shows Swing on 'the Gate.'" *The Deseret News,* May 21, 1987, 29.
Hill, David. "Who's Afraid of R.L. Stine." *Education Week,* March 1, 1996, http://www.edweek.org/tm/articles/1996/03/01/06stine.h07.html.
Hinson, Hal. "'The Good Son' (R)." *The Washington Post,* September 24, 1993, http://www.washingtonpost.com/wp-srv/style/longterm/movies/videos/thegoodsonrhinson_a0a843.htm.
____. "Gremlins 2: The New Batch." *The Washington Post,* June 15, 1990, http://www.washingtonpost.com/wp-srv/style/longterm/movies/videos/gremlins2thenewbatch-pg13hinson_a0a978.htm.
____. "'Indiana Jones and the Last Crusade.'" *The Washington Post,* May 24, 1989, https://www.washingtonpost.com/wp-srv/style/longterm/movies/videos/indianajonesandthelastcrusadepg13hinson_a0a93b.htm??noredirect=on.
____. "'Mary Shelley's Frankenstein' (R)." *The Washington Post,* November 4, 1994, http://www.washingtonpost.com/wp-srv/style/longterm/movies/videos/maryshelleysfrankensteinrhinson_a01af8.htm.
Holden, Stephen. "A Satanic Cult Caper in the Bible Belt." *New York Times,* January 3, 1993, https://www.nytimes.com/1993/01/30/movies/review-film-a-satanic-cult-caper-in-the-bible-belt.html.
"Home Court Advantage." *Los Angeles Times,* April 15, 1994, http://articles.latimes.com/1996-04-15/entertainment/ca-58749_1_felicity-dahl.
Hood, K. Shyrock. *Once Upon a Time in a Dark and Scary Book: The Messages of Horror Literature for Children.* Jefferson: McFarland, 2018.
Horrornews.net. "RL Stine Receives Honors in Guinness World Records." HNN, May 31, 2011, http://horrornews.net/35191/rl-stine-receives-honors-in-guinness-world-records/.
Hough, John. "Commentary on Alternate Ending 1." In *The Watcher in the Woods*: Starz/Anchor Bay, 2002.
____. "Commentary on Alternate Ending 2." In *The Watcher in the Woods*: Starz/Anchor Bay, 2002.
____. *Film Commentary.* Starz/Anchor Bay, 2002.
Howe, Desson. "'The Nightmare Before Christmas' (PG)." *The Washington Post,* October 22, 1993, https://www.washingtonpost.com/wp-srv/style/longterm/movies/videos/thenightmarebeforechristmaspghowe_a0b003.htm.
____. "'The Witches' (PG)." *The Washington Post,* August 31, 1990, http://www.washingtonpost.com/wp-srv/style/longterm/movies/videos/thewitchespghowe_a0b298.htm.
Howe, Neil, and William Strauss. *Millennials Rising: The Next Great Generation.* New York: Vintage, 2000.
Jackson, Anna, Roderick McGillis and Karen Coats. *The Gothic in Children's Literature: Haunting the Borders.* Children's Literature and Culture. London: Routledge, 2007.
James, Caryn. "Friendly and Translucent? He's Back." *New York Times,* May 26, 1995.
____. "Review/Film; Indiana Jones in Pursuit of Dad and the Grail." *New York Times,* May 24, 1989, https://www.nytimes.com/1989/05/24/movies/review-film-indiana-jones-in-pursuit-of-dad-and-the-grail.html.
____. "Review/Film; When the Ladies Take Off Their Wigs, Head for Home. Fast." *New York Times,* August 24, 1990, https://www.nytimes.com/1990/08/24/movies/review-film-when-the-ladies-take-off-their-wigs-head-for-home-fast.html.
Jancovich, Mark. "Genre and the Audience: Genre Classifications and Cultural Distinctions in the Mediation of the Silence of the Lambs." In *Horror, the Film Reader,* edited by Mark Jancovich. London: Routledge, 2002.
Jenkins, Henry, ed. *The Children's Culture Reader.* New York: New York University Press, 1998.
Jones, Bill. "He Kept His Nightmare Alive." *The Phoenix Gazette,* October 22, 1993.
Jones, Edward. "Special Effects Make 'Gate' a Cut Above Average Thriller." *The Free Lance-Star,* June 10, 1987, 21.

___. "'Watcher in the Woods' Doesn't Measure Up." *The Free Lance-Star*, October 15, 1981, 22.
Kael, Pauline. *State of the Art: Film Writings 1983–1985*. London: Marion Boyars, 2009.
Kehr, Dave. "A Little Bit of Magic." *Chicago Tribune*, August 28, 1990.
___. "'The Lost Boys' a Vampire Film Thirsting for a Good Story." *Chicago Tribune*, July 31, 1987.
___. "Poltergeist" *Chicago Reader*, N.d., Https://www.chicagoreader.com/chicago/poltergeist/Film?oid=11118037.
Kempley, Rita. "'Beethoven.'" *The Washington Post*, April 3, 1992.
___. "Casper.'" *The Washington Post*, May 26, 1995.
___. "'The Lost Boys' (R)." *The Washington Post*, July 31, 1987, https://www.washingtonpost.com/wp-srv/style/longterm/movies/videos/thelostboysrkempley_a0ca6c.htm.
___. "'The Witches' (PG)." *The Washington Post*, August 24, 1990, http://www.washingtonpost.com/wp-srv/style/longterm/movies/videos/thewitchespgkempley_a0a14e.htm.
Kids' Media Culture, edited by Marsha Kinder. Durham: Duke University Press, 1999.
Klady, Leonard. "Review: 'Scream.'" *Variety*, December 21, 1996, http://variety.com/1996/film/reviews/scream-1117436711/.
Klinger, Barbara. *Melodrama & Meaning: History, Culture, and the Films of Douglas Sirk*. Bloomington: Indiana University Press, 1994.
Kois, Dan. "The Black Cauldron—Is the Movie That Almost Killed Disney Animation Really That Bad?" *Slate*, October 19, 2010, http://www.slate.com/articles/arts/dvdextras/2010/10/the_black_cauldron.html.
Kowalewski, Kirsten. "Where Are the Scary Books? the Place of Scary Books for Children in School and Children's Libraries." In *Reading in the Dark: Horror in Children's Literature and Culture*, edited by Jessica R. McCort. Jackson: University Press of Mississippi, 2016.
Kramer, Peter. "Would You Take Your Child to See This Film? The Cultural and Social Work of the Family-Adventure Movie." In *Contemporary Hollywood Cinema*, edited by Murray Smith Steve Neale, 294–307. London: Routledge, 1998.
LaSalle, Mick. "'Anaconda' Something to Hiss At/Big Snake Slithers Through Lame Action." *San Francisco Gate*, October 10, 1997, https://www.sfgate.com/movies/article/Anaconda-Something-to-Hiss-At-Big-snake-2825947.php.
___. "'Casper' Raises Spirits and Tugs Heartstrings." *The San Francisco Chronicle*, May 26, 1995.
___. "'The Haunting' Is Pretty Stupid." *San Francisco Gate*, July 23, 1999, https://www.sfgate.com/movies/article/The-Haunting-Is-Pretty-Stupid-2918680.php.
___. "'Summer' Isn't Quite a Scream/Story Eventually Turns Formulaic." *San Francisco Gate*, March 27, 1998, https://www.sfgate.com/movies/article/Summer-Isnt-Quite-a-Scream-Story-eventually-3010531.php.
Leone, Ron and Laurie Barowski. "MPAA Ratings Creep: A Longitudinal Analysis of the PG-13 Rating Category in US Movies." *Journal of Children and Media* 5, no. 1 (2011).
Lester, Catherine. "The Children's Horror Film: Characterizing an 'Impossible' Subgenre." *Velvet Light Trap*, no. 78 (2016): 22–38.
Lewis, Jon. *Hollywood V. Hard Core: How the Struggle Over Censorship Saved the Modern Film Industry*. New York: New York University Press, 2000.
MacFarquhar, Neil. "What's a Soccer Mom Anyway?" *New York Times*, October 20, 1996, https://www.nytimes.com/1996/10/20/weekinreview/what-s-a-soccer-mom-anyway.html.
Magill, Frank N. *Magill's Cinema Annual, 1988: A Survey of the Films of 1987*. Pasadena, CA: Salem Press, 1988.
Martin, Peter. "Review: The Visit, a Fleeting Resemblance to a Funhouse Joy Ride." twitch, n.d., http://twitchfilm.com/2015/09/review-the-visit-a-fleeting-resemblance-to-a-funhouse-joy-ride.html.

Maslin, Janet. "Demons' Eye Problems Compound Creepiness." *New York Times*, April 28, 1995, http://www.nytimes.com/movie/review?res=990CE7D71238F93BA15757 C0A963958260.
____. "Infiltrating the Land of Sugar Plums." *New York Times*, October 9, 1993.
McBride, Joseph. "Indiana Jones and the Last Crusade." *Variety*, May 24, 1989, https:// variety.com/1989/film/reviews/indiana-jones-and-the-last-crusade-1200428090/.
McCarthy, Todd. "Indiana Jones and the Temple of Doom." *Variety*, May 16, 1984, https:// variety.com/1984/film/reviews/indiana-jones-and-the-temple-of-doom-1200426218/.
____. "Review: 'Bram Stoker's Dracula.'" *Variety*, November 8, 1992, http://variety.com/ 1992/film/reviews/bram-stokers-dracula-1200431014/.
____. "Review: 'Interview with the Vampire.'" *Variety*, November 6, 1994, http://variety. com/1994/film/reviews/interview-with-the-vampire-1200439504/.
____. "Review: 'The Nightmare Before Christmas.'" *Variety*, October 8, 1993, http:// variety.com/1993/film/reviews/the-nightmare-before-christmas-1200433742/.
____. "Review: 'The Sixth Sense.'" *Variety*, August 2, 1999, http://variety.com/1999/film/ reviews/the-sixth-sense-1200458827/.
____. "Review: 'Wolf.'" *Variety*, June 13, 1994, http://variety.com/1994/film/reviews/ wolf-1200437584/.
Medved, Michael. "New Films Show PG-13 Is Hollywood's Trojan Horse." In *Jewish World Review*, July 6, 2001, http://www.jewishworldreview.com/cols/medved070601.asp.
Mendelson, Scott. "'Nightmare Before Christmas' Turns 20: From Shameful Spawn to Disney's Pride." *Forbes*, October 15, 2013, http://www.forbes.com/sites/scott mendelson/2013/10/15/how-the-nightmare-before-christmas-went-in-20-years-from-shameful-offspring-to-disneys-favorite-son/.
____. "Review: 'Goosebumps' Is a Scary Good, Kid-Friendly Lovecraftian Horror Comedy." *Forbes*, October 5, 2015, http://www.forbes.com/sites/scottmendelson/2015/10/05/ review-goosebumps-is-a-scary-good-kid-friendly-lovecraftian-horror-comedy/.
____. "Review: M. Night Shyamalan's 'the Visit' Is a Glorious Return to Form." *Forbes*, September 9, 2015, http://www.forbes.com/sites/scottmendelson/2015/09/09/ review-m-night-shyamalans-the-visit-is-a-glorious-return-to-form/.
Mifflin, Lawrie. "The Media Business; Fox to Morph 'Power Rangers' Into 'Goosebumps' Every Friday." *New York Times*, May 8, 1995, https://www.nytimes.com/1995/05/08/ business/the-media-business-fox-to-morph-power-rangers-into-goosebumps-every-friday.html.
____. "Spotlight; Something Creepy This Way Comes." *New York Times*, October 22, 1995.
Mills, Bart. "Disney Looks for a Happy Ending to Its Grim Fairy Tale." *American Film*, July-August 1982, 52–56.
Morgenstem, Joe. "Tim Burton, Batman and the Joker." *New York Times*, April 9, 1989, https://www.nytimes.com/1989/04/09/magazine/tim-burton-batman-and-the-joker.html.
Morris, Timothy. *You're Only Young Twice: Children's Literature and Film*. Urbana: University of Illinois Press, 2000.
"Movie Review: 'Monster Squad' Is Fun for the Kid in All of Us." *Los Angeles Times*, August 14, 1987, http://articles.latimes.com/1987-08-14/entertainment/ca-755_1_ monstersquad.
"Movies." *Boca Raton News*, October 12, 1990, 25.
Newman, Kim. *The BFI Companion to Horror*. London: Cassell, 1996.
____. "The Monster Squad Review." Empire, January 1, 2000, https://www.empireonline. com/movies/monstersquad/review/.
____. *Nightmare Movies: A Critical History of the Horror Film, 1968–88*. London: Bloomsbury, 1988.
____. *Nightmare Movies: Horror on Screen Since the 1960s*. London: Bloomsbury, 2011.
"The Nightmare Before Christmas 3-D: 13 Years and Three Dimensions Later." IGN, Oc-

tober 20, 2006, http://uk.ign.com/articles/2006/10/20/the-nightmare-before-christmas-3-d-13-years-and-three-dimensions-later?page=1.

Orange, B. Alan. "Exclusive: Tibor Takacs Takes Us Back Through 'the Gate: Monstrous Special Edition.'" Movieweb, October 20, 2009, http://movieweb.com/exclusive-tibor-takacs-takes-us-back-through-the-gate-monstrous-special-edition/.

Pace, Terry. "In Review: Disney Staying in Woods with 'Watcher.'" *Times Daily*, November 27, 1981, 49.

Palladino, Grace. *Teenagers: An American History.* New York: BasicBooks, 1996.

Parker, James. "Horror for Kids—How Goosebumps Outlasted Harry Potter by Terrifying Fourth-Graders and Mocking Their Parents." *The Atlantic*, March 2012, http://www.theatlantic.com/magazine/archive/2012/03/horror-for-kids/308885/.

Paul, William. *Laughing, Screaming: Modern Hollywood Horror and Comedy.* New York: Columbia University Press, 1994.

Peraza, Michael. "Cauldron of Chaos." September 9, 2010, http://michaelperaza.blogspot.com/search/label/Black%20Cauldron.

Perrin, Elisabeth. "Tim Burton Guides to the Screen Another Tale from the Dark Side." *The Chicago Sun-Times*, October 17, 1993.

Peterson, Matthew. "Interview with R.L. Stine." The Author Hour, January 21, 2010, http://theauthorhour.com/r-l-stine/.

Pickert, Kate. "The Man Who Remade Motherhood." *Time*, May 21, 1012, http://time.com/606/the-man-who-remade-motherhood/.

Postman, Neil. *The Disappearance of Childhood.* London: W.H. Allen, 1983.

Prince, Stephen. *A New Pot of Gold: Hollywood Under the Electronic Rainbow, 1980–1989.* New York: Scribner's, 2000.

Reading in the Dark: Horror in Children's Literature and Culture. Edited by Jessica McCort Jackson: University Press of Mississippi, 2016.

Reynolds, Kimberley. "Introduction." In *Frightening Fiction*, edited by Kimberley Reynolds; Geraldine Brennan; Kevin McCarron, 1–18. London: Continuum, 2001.

Rose, Jacqueline. *The Case of Peter Pan; or the Impossibility of Children's Fiction.* Philadelphia: University of Pennsylvania Press, 1993.

Rosenberg, Joyce M. "Goosebumps: So Successful They're Scary." *Lawrence Journal-World*, October 27, 1996, 22.

Sandler, Kevin S. *The Naked Truth: Why Hollywood Doesn't Make X-Rated Movies.* New Brunswick, NJ: Rutgers University Press, 2007.

Sanjek, David. "Same as It Ever Was: Innovation and Exhaustion in the Horror and Science Fiction Films of the 1990s." In *Film Genre 2000: New Critical Essays*, edited by Wheeler W. Dixon. New York: State University of New York Press.

Saucedo, Robert. "Badass Interview: The Gate's Tibor Takacs." Birth. Movies. Death., February 9, 2012, http://birthmoviesdeath.com/2012/02/09/badass-interview-the-gates-tibor-takacs.

Sauter, Michael. "The Island of Dr. Moreau." *Entertainment Weekly*, January 10, 1997, https://ew.com/article/1997/01/10/island-dr-moreau-2/.

Scholastic. "Parent Guide to Goosebumps." https://www.scholastic.com/parents/books-and-reading/books-and-reading-guides/parent-guide-to-goosebumps.html.

Schwarzbaum, Lisa. "Anaconda." *Entertainment Weekly*, April 18, 1997, https://ew.com/article/1997/04/18/anaconda/.

Sears, William, Martha Sears, Robert Sears, and James Sears. *The Baby Book: Everything You Need to Know About Your Baby—from Birth to Age Two.* 2d ed. Boston: Little, Brown and Company, 2003.

Seiter, Ellen. *Sold Separately: Children and Parents in Consumer Culture.* New Brunswick, NJ: Rutgers University Press, 1993.

Sharkley, Betsy. "Tim Burton's 'Nightmare' Comes True." *New York Times*, October 10, 1993.

Sheffield, Skip. "Market for 'Watcher' a Mystery." *Boca Raton News*, November 26, 1981, 14.

Sherman, Paul. "Disney Has Dreams of Profits from 'Nightmare.'" *The Boston Herald*, October 28, 2000.
Shulgasser, Barbara. "'Casper' the Sappy Spook." *The San Francisco Examiner*, May 26, 1995.
Silberling, Brad. "Casper DVD Commentary." (2008).
Sobcynski, Peter. "Interview: Gil Kenan—Landlord of the 'Monster House.'" July 24, 2006, efilmcritic.com, http://www.efilmcritic.com/feature.php?feature=1895&printer=1.
Stack, Peter. "Carpenter's 'Village of the Damned' a Dreary Place." *San Francisco Chronicle*, April 28, 1995, http://www.sfgate.com/movies/article/Carpenters-Village-of-the-Damned-a-Dreary-Place-3034711.php.
———. "Film Review—Brando's Beastly 'Island of Dr. Moreau' / Opportunities Wasted in Tired Sci-Fi Remake." *San Francisco Gate*, April 23, 1996, https://www.sfgate.com/movies/article/FILM-REVIEW-Brandos-Beastly-Island-of-Dr-2969817.php.
Stannard, Joseph. "Out of the Woods." *Sight and Sound*, March 2011, 11.
Steinmetz, Johanna. "Terror Swings with Humor in 'the Gate.'" *Chicago Tribune*, May 18, 1987.
Stern, Marlow. "'Goosebumps' Creator R.L. Stine on 20th-Anniversary Series." *Newsweek*, July 30, 2012, http://www.newsweek.com/goosebumps-creator-rl-stine-20th-anniversary-series-65631.
———. "Henry Selick on Directing 'the Nightmare Before Christmas.'" *The Daily Beast*, October 29, 2013, http://www.thedailybeast.com/articles/2013/10/29/henry-selick-on-directing-the-nightmare-before-christmas.html.
Stine, R.L. *It Came from Ohio! My Life as a Writer*. New York: Scholastic, 1997.
———. *Live Chat*. The Hub, 2010.
"The Story Behind the Lost Boys." GamesRadar, March 11, 2010, http://www.gamesradar.com/the-story-behind-the-lost-boys/.
Strickler, Jeff. "Merry Scary Christmas." *The Star Tribune*, October 22, 1993.
Sturrock, Donald. *Storyteller: The Life of Roald Dahl*. London: William Collins, 2016.
Tabor, Mary. "At Home With: R.L. Stine; Grown-Ups Deserve Some Terror, Too." *New York Times*, September 7, 1995.
———. "Hints of Horror, Shouts of Protest." *New York Times*, April 2, 1997.
Telotte, J.P. *The Mouse Machine: Disney and Technology*. Urbana: University of Illinois Press, 2008.
Thomas, Kevin. "Allegory for Teens Lurks Amid Scary Fun of Sequel to 'The Gate.'" *L.A. Times/Washington Post*, March 19, 1992.
Tibor Takács, Michael Nankin, and Randall William Cook. "Audio Commentary." In *The Gate* Lionsgate, 2009.
Turan, Kenneth. "Movie Reviews: Burton Dreams Up a Delightful 'Nightmare.'" *Los Angeles Times*, Opctober 15, 1993.
Twitchell, James B. *Dreadful Pleasures: An Anatomy of Modern Horror*. Oxford: Oxford University Press, 1985.
Vaughn, Stephen. *Freedom and Entertainment: Rating the Movies in an Age of New Media*. Cambridge: Cambridge University Press, 2006.
Walker, Alexander. Review of *Gremlins*. *London Evening Standard*, July 12, 1984.
Warner, Judith. *Perfect Madness: Motherhood in the Age of Anxiety*. London: Vermillon, 2006.
Webb, Charles. "MTV Geek's Frightful Faves: Reopening 'The Gate' (1987)." MTV News, October 10, 2012, http://geek-news.mtv.com/2012/10/10/mtv-geeks-frightfulfaves-reopening-the-gate-1987.
Wheeler, Brad. "The Visit: Pastoral Horror Comedy Is a Genuinely Fun Affair." *The Globe and Mail*, September 11, 2015, http://www.theglobeandmail.com/arts/film/film-reviews/the-visit-pastoral-horror-comedy-is-a-genuinely-fun-affair/article 26315289/.
White, James. "The Story Behind Gremlins." *Total Film* (2009).

Wilensky, Sheila. "The Heyday of Children's Bookselling." *Publishers Weekly*, July 15, 2011, https://www.publishersweekly.com/pw/by-topic/childrens/childrens-industry-news/article/48020-the-heyday-of-childrens-bookselling.html.

Wilmington, Michael. "Movie Review: Bevy of Beasties Run Wild in 'Gate.'" *Los Angeles Times*, May 19, 1987.

———. "Movie Review: 'Witches': Adult Children's Fantasy." *Los Angeles Times*, August 24, 1990.

Wilson, Jacque. "R.L. Stine Aims to Give Adults 'Goosebumps.'" CNN, October 9, 2012, http://edition.cnn.com/2012/10/09/living/stine-red-rain-adult-novel.

Wilson, Staci Layne. "Scout's Guide to the Zombie Apocalypse—Exclusive Set Visit Interview: Christopher Landon." Dread Central, August 28, 2015, http://www.dreadcentral.com/news/122173/scouts-guide-to-the-zombie-apocalypse-exclusive-set-visit-interview-christopher-landon/.

Windolf, Jim. "Q&A Steven Spielberg." *Vanity Fair*, January 2, 2008, https://www.vanityfair.com/news/2008/02/spielberg_qanda200802.

"The Witches Weekly Gross." https://www.boxofficemojo.com/movies/?page=weekly&id=witches.htm.

Wixson, Heather. "Class of 1987: Director Tibor Takács Reflects on His Coming-of-Age Horror Fairy Tale the Gate." Daily Dead, July 11, 2017, https://dailydead.com/class-of-1987-director-tibor-takacs-reflects-on-his-coming-of-age-horror-fairy-tale-the-gate.

Woerner, Meredith. "Goosebumps Filmmakers Reveal How RL Stine Became the Star of Their Movie." io9, April 28, 2015, http://io9.com/goosebumps-filmmakers-reveal-how-rl-stine-became-the-st-1700671432.

Wood, Michael. "Little Devils." *New Society*, December 13, 1984, n.p.

Wood, Robin. *Hollywood from Vietnam to Reagan—And Beyond*. New York: Columbia University Press, 2003.

Zipes, Jack. *Sticks and Stones: The Troublesome Success of Children's Literature from Slovenly Peter to Harry Potter*. New York: Routledge, 2001.

Index

Aaahh!!! Real Monsters (1994–1997) 133, 171
Abrams, J.J. 162
The Abyss (1989) 179*n*10
The Addams Family (1991) 109, 170
Addams Family Values (1993) 171
Adventures in Babysitting (1987) 179*n*8
The Adventures of the Wilderness Family (1975) 35
Aladdin (1992) 106, 122
Alien (film series) 167
Allen, Robert C. 111–112
Amblin 160, 164, 165
Anaconda (1997) 96
Anchor Bay 33
animation 15, 42, 99, 102, 105–106, 163; *see also* stop-motion
Arachnophobia (1990) 170
Are You Afraid of the Dark? (1990–1996) 2, 107, 128, 133, 145, 171
Ariès, Philippe 3–4
Army of Darkness (1992) 94
Atmosfear 128
attachment parenting 22, 98, 111, 112, 113–114, 154–155; and pre-adolescence 114, 124–126
attachment theory 6, 113
audience segregation 88–98, 111–114, 129–133, 135–136, 146–147, 152–156

Barker, Clive 89
Batman (1989) 69, 100, 101
Beauty and the Beast (1991) 43, 100, 106

Beethoven (1992) 126
Believe (2000) 173
Benji (1974) 35
Benson, Sheila 69
Berardinelli, James 92
Big Trouble in Little China (1986) 179*n*8
The Black Cauldron (1985) 26, 42–43, 100, 170; test audience response 42–43
The Black Hole (1979) 31, 41
Blade (1998) 94
Blair Witch Project (1999) 94
Blank, Ed 29–30, 40–41
Boglins 128
Bone Chillers (1996) 108, 128
Bosco, Scott Michael 32–34, 39–40
Bowlby, John 113, 154
The Boy Who Cried Werewolf (2010) 173
Boyar, Jay 69
Brain Dead (1990) 94
Bram Stoker's Dracula (1992) 91, 95
Brazelton, T. Berry 13
The Bride of Frankenstein (1935) 104
The Brood (1979) 36, 186*n*1
Burton, Tim 88, 100–106 137, 167, 174; branding 103–104

The Cabinet of Dr. Caligari (1920) 104, 105
Canby, Vincent 32, 51–52, 53–54, 59–60, 62, 63, 90–91, 105
Candyman (1992) 92
Can't Buy Me Love (1987) 179*n*8

Cape Fear (1991) 181*n*16
Carpenter, John 97
Carrie (1976) 186*n*1
Cascone, Annette 172
Cascone, Gina 172
Casper (1995) 20, 99, 109, 111, 114, 121–127, 141, 144, 147, 155, 171; and childhood innocence 120–123; family and parenting 124; representations 124–126
Cat's Eye (1985) 69
censorship 4, 8, 12, 28, 45–47, 151
Child of Glass (1978) 169
Children of the Corn II: The Final Sacrifice (1992) 97
children's bookstores 131
children's horror: definition 17–21; distinction between film cycle and trend 17–18; problems with this label 14–17, 146–147
children's publishing 129–131, 134, 139–140
children's television 131–133, 135
Child's Play (1988) 15
Chiller (1985) 69, 108
Christmas film 58, 88, 102
cinema 16–17, 20–21, 22, 28, 85–86, 94–96, 102, 106–108, 110, 126–127, 128–129, 146–147, 156–157, 161–165
Cirque du Freak: The Vampire's Assistant (2009) 149, 174
Clemens, Brian 39
Clinton, Bill 5–6
Clinton, Hillary 5
Close Encounters of the Third Kind (1977) 34, 63
Cocoon (1985) 179*n*9
The Color Purple (1985) 179*n*10
coming of age 166–167
Cooney, Caroline B. 172
Coppola, Francis Ford 91
Copycat (1995) 94
Coraline (2009) 149, 163, 174
Courage, the Cowardly Dog (1999–2002) 133, 173
Creepers (book series) 108, 128
Critters (1986) 69, 72, 170
Critters 2: The Main Course (1988) 69, 170
Crocodile Dundee (1986) 179*n*8
Cry Baby Lane (2000) 173
Culkin, Macaulay 97–98
Curtis, Quentin 105

Dahl, Felicity 127
Dahl, Roald 115–121; *see also The Witches* (1990
Dante, Joe 43, 55–58, 61–62, 68, 73, 162, 170, 174; and Spielberg 55–62
Dargis, Manohla 158
The Dark Crystal (1982) 44, 170
Davis, Bette 31
Deadtime Stories (book series) 172
Deadtime Stories (2012–2013) 173
Dee, Jake 158
Deep Blue Sea (1999) 94
Dirty Dancing (1987) 179*n*8
Disney 2, 21, 23, 25–44, 51, 54, 60, 63, 78, 99–108, 122, 131, 135, 150–151; and the G rating 30, 34–35; and the PG rating 30–31, 34–35, 42; and the R rating 43; and technology 29, 31
Disney, Walt 25, 27–30, 60
Disneyland 102
Donner, Richard 70
Don't Look Under the Bed (1999) 107, 172
Double Dare (1986–1993) 132
Dowd, A.A. 164–165
Dowler, Andrew 71, 79
Dreamscape (1984) 179*n*9
Dune (1984) 179*n*9

Ebert, Roger 53, 61, 63–64, 68, 69, 91–92, 93, 96, 98, 117, 119, 120, 162
echo boom 5, 111, 112, 130, 131; *see also* millennial generation
Ed Wood (1994) 100
Eerie, Indiana (1991–1992) 108, 128, 133, 171
Eerie, Indiana: The Other Dimension (1998) 133, 172
Eisner, Michael 25, 27–29, 43, 102
Ellenshaw, Harrison 41
Ellis, Kate 11
Elvira: Mistress of the Dead (1988) 179*n*14
End of Days (1999) 94
Ernest Scared Stupid (1991) 170
Escape to Witch Mountain (1975) 169
E.T.: The Extra-Terrestrial (1982) 50, 56–57, 63, 105, 123
Evil Dead II (1987) 71
The Exorcist (1973) 25, 31, 36, 38, 186*n*1
Explorers (1985) 178*n*1

The Faculty (1998) 94
family entertainment 111–113

Ferris Bueller's Day Off (1986) 179*n*8
film ratings system: and censorship 45–47; and child protection 45–47; introduction of (1968) 27–28; minor changes to 48; *see also* Hays Code
Final Destination (2000) 94
Firestarter (1984) 170
The 5,000 Fingers of Dr. T (1953) 118
The Flamingo Kid (1984) 179*n*8
Flight of the Navigator (1986) 178*n*1
Frankenstein (1931) 104
Frankenstein and Me (1996) 171
Frankenstein Reborn! (1998) 172
Frankenweenie (1984) 100, 104
Frankenweenie (2012) 149, 174
Freaky Stories (1997) 108
The Fresh Prince of Bel-Air (1990–1996) 168
Friday the 13th (1980) 79
From Dusk Till Dawn (1996) 94

G rating: association with family 34–35; and the PG rating 34–35
Garbo Talks (1984) 179*n*10
The Gate (1987) 2, 8, 15, 17, 20, 65–66, 69, 70–83, 103, 110, 116, 141, 147, 152–153, 157, 158, 170; as horror film 79–81; production 74, 78–79; promotion 79; representations 73–77
Gate 2: The Trespassers (1990) 170, 180*n*46
Ghost (1990) 91
Ghostbusters (1984) 170
Ghostbusters (2016) 167
Ghosts of Fear Street 172
Girl vs. Monster (2012) 173
Gleiberman, Owen 92–93
Godzilla (1998) 96
Gomery, Douglas 27–29
The Good Son (1993) 97–98, 120
The Goonies (1985) 63, 70, 80, 160, 162, 165, 167
Goosebumps (2015) 163–165
Goosebumps (franchise) 2, 10–11, 14–15, 19, 21, 108, 128–149, 157, 158, 161, 163–165, 167, 171–174; banned books controversy 138–139; branding 135–141; merchandise 135; representations 141–145
Goosebumps Horrorland 137, 144, 173
Goosebumps: Most Wanted 173
Goosebumps: Slappy World 173
Goosebumps 2: Haunted Halloween (2018) 149, 174, 187*n*22

Goosebumps 2000 (book series) 140, 145
Graveyard School 108
Gremlins (1984) 2, 13, 15, 17, 19–20, 44–45, 49, 55–63, 68, 72, 78, 82–83, 102, 116, 122, 151–152, 154, 160, 162, 165, 170; and family 60–61; merchandise 19, 57–58; and nostalgia 19; production 55–56; promotion 56; and violence 59–60
Gremlins 2: The New Batch (1990) 67–68, 170
Grover, Ron 29
Guts (1992–1996) 132

Hahn, Mary Downing 130
Halloween 58
Halloweentown (1998) 107
Halloweentown High (2004) 107
Halloweentown II: Kalabar's Revenge (2001) 107
Hantke, Steffen 88–89
Harrington, Richard 97
Harry Potter (Series) 139–140
The Haunted Mansion (2003) 107, 173
The Haunting (1963) 31
The Haunting (1999) 95–96
The Haunting Hour: Don't Think About It (2007) 173
Hays Code 7–8, 28, 45, 89, 127, 152, 156
Henig, Marantz Robin 166
Henson, Jim 44, 120
High Spirits (1988) 179*n*8
Hinson, Hal 67, 97
Hocus Pocus (1993) 107, 171
Hoh, Diane 172
The Hole (2009) 73, 149, 163, 174
Home Alone (1990) 97–98, 126
Hooper, Tobe 50–51, 170; and Spielberg 51
horror genre canon (1970s) 89–96
horror genre identity crisis 7–12, 69–72, 89–94
Hough, John 31–33, 35, 39–40, 169–170
House (1985) 70
House II: The Second Story (1987) 70
The House with a Clock in Its Walls (2018) 149, 174
Howe, Desson 104, 117
Howe, Neil 5, 168
Howling III (1987) 179*n*14

I Know What You Did Last Summer (1997) 89, 92–93

In the Mouth of Madness (1995) 94
Indiana Jones and the Kingdom of the Crystal Skull (2008) 167
Indiana Jones and the Last Crusade (1989) 67–68
Indiana Jones and the Temple of Doom (1984) 13, 44–45, 49, 52–55, 59, 61–62, 67–68, 105, 151, 170; and family 61; and violence 52–55
The Innocents (1961) 1, 36
Interview with the Vampire (1994) 91
Invaders from Mars (1953) 118
Invaders from Mars (1986) 65, 118, 170
The Island of Dr. Moreau (1996) 95–96
It (1990) 171
It (2017) 1

Jacob's Ladder (1990) 94
James, Caryn 116–117
Jancovich, Mark 9, 90
Jaws (1975) 34, 49
Jaws: The Revenge (1987) 69
Johnny Dangerously (1984) 179n8
Johnson, Lynn-Holly 32
Jones, Bill 105
Jumanji (1995) 99, 109, 171
Jurassic Park (1993) 96, 99, 109, 171
Jurassic World: The Fallen Kingdom (2018) 167

Kael, Pauline 54, 57, 61
The Karate Kid (2010) 167
Katzenberg, Jeffrey 101
Kehr, Dave 50, 80, 118
Kempley, Rita 80, 117
Killer Klowns from Outer Space (1988) 69, 179n14
King, Stephen 80, 134, 138
Kramer, Peter 114
Krampus (2015) 174

Lady in White (1988) 65, 69, 170
Landon, Christopher 159–161, 174
LaSalle, Mick 93, 96
Laybourne, Geraldine 132
Leetch, Tom 25, 31, 33, 36, 38–41
Lester, Catherine 16–17
License to Kill (1989) 179n10
life cycle 6, 151, 166, 167
The Little Mermaid (1989) 43
Little Monsters (1989) 65, 170
Little Shop of Horrors (1986) 179n8
The Little Vampire (2000) 173
Look Who's Talking (1989) 179n8

The Lost Boys (1987) 8, 70, 72, 80, 83, 91, 94–95, 159–160, 170; production 70; reception 80
Lucas, George 52

Mad Max: Fury Road (2015) 167
The Magical World of Disney (1954–1991) 169
Martin, Peter 159
Mary Shelley's Frankenstein (1994) 91
Maslin, Janet 98, 104
McBride, Joseph 68
McCallum, David 31
McCarthy, Todd 53–54, 91, 106
McCort, Jessica 15–16
Medved, Michael 13
Mendelson, Scott 161–162, 167
Mickey (1992) 97
Micki & Maude (1984) 179n8
millennial generation 2, 3, 5, 7, 131, 134, 150, 155, 165–168; and the Boomer/Millennial family 112, 153; *see also* attachment parenting; echo boom
Miller, Ron 23, 25–43; and Disney's leadership 27–30, 42–43; and the PG-13 rating 30
Mills, Bart 29
Mom's Got a Date with a Vampire (2000) 107, 173
Monster House (2006) 149, 162, 174
The Monster Squad (1987) 20, 65, 69, 81–83, 162, 170
Mostly Ghostly (2008) 173
Mostly Ghostly: Have You Met My Ghoulfriend? (2014) 173
Mostly Ghostly: One Night in Doom House (2016) 173
Motion Picture Association of America (MPAA) 27, 45–46, 49, 54, 66; *see also* Hays Code
Mrs. Soffel (1984) 179n10
The Mummy (1999) 96
The Mummy: Tomb of the Dragon Emperor (2008) 167
The Muppet Movie (1979) 35
My Babysitter's a Vampire (2010) 173

The Naked Gun (1988) 179n8
Nankin, Michael 73–77, 78
National Lampoon's Christmas Vacation (1989) 179n8
National Lampoon's European Vacation (1985) 179n8
Natural Born Killers (1994) 94

NC-17 Rating 28, 45–48, 94
The Neverending Story (1984) 44
New Tales from the Cryptkeeper (1997) 108, 133, 172
Newman, Kim 8–12, 14–16, 50, 62, 70–71, 79, 81–82, 95
Nickelodeon 6, 132–133, 167, 171, 173
The Night Flier (1997) 94
Night of the Comet (1984) 179n8
Night of the Living Dead (1968) 36, 143, 186n1
Night of the Living Dead (1990) 94
The Nightmare Before Christmas (1993) 2, 15, 20, 88, 99–106, 109, 118, 141, 153–154, 171; branding 102–106; production 99–101; promotion 101; release strategy 101
Nightmare Ned (1997) 108, 128, 172
Nightmare on Elm Street (film series) 79, 89
A Nightmare on Elm Street (1984) 78–79
The Nightmare Room (2001–2002) 173
nostalgia 2, 17, 19, 77, 81–82, 93, 134, 160–168, 173–174

The Omen (1976) 1, 36, 186n1
Once Bitten (1985) 179n8

ParaNorman (2012) 16, 17, 149, 174
Peck, Richard 169
Pee-wee's Big Adventure (1985) 100
The People Under the Stairs (1991) 170
Peraza, Michael 42
Pet Sematary II (1992) 171
PG rating: and animation 100, 101; and Disney 30–31, 34–35, 42, 100–101; as industry standard (1970s) 34–35
PG-13 rating: and horror (1980s) 69–72; and horror (1990s); as industry standard 67–69; and Steven Spielberg 49
Phantasm (1979) 33, 169
Pike, Christopher 130, 172
Pinwheel 132; *see also* Nickelodeon
Point Horror (book series) 172
Poltergeist (1980) 13, 45, 50–52, 53–54, 55, 56, 61–62, 72, 80, 151, 162, 170; classification appeal 50; and family 61
Poltergeist II: The Other Side (1986) 67
Poltergeist III (1988) 67
The Poseidon Adventure (1972) 34
Postman, Neil 4, 6, 11
The Predator (2018) 167
Predators (2010) 167

Pretty in Pink (1986) 179n8
Psycho (1960) 40

The Quest (1986) 170

R rating: as cultural symbol 45–48; as horror standard 70–72, 94–96, 159–161, 180n46
Raiders of the Living Dead (1986) 69
Raising Arizona (1987) 179n9
"ratings creep" hypothesis 12–13, 15, 47
Ravenous (1999) 94
The Razor's Edge (1984) 179n10
Reagan, Ronald 5–6
Red Dawn (1984) 179n10
Red Sonja (1985) 179n9
Ren & Stimpy (1991–1995) 132
The Return of Swamp Thing (1989) 69, 179n14
Return of the Living Dead: Part II (1988) 170
Return to Boggy Creek (1977) 169
Return to Halloweentown (2006) 107
Return to Oz (1985) 170
Reynolds, Kimberley 10–11, 14, 16, 136
Ricci, Christina 126
Richards, Kyle 31, 35, 39
The River (1984) 179n10
R.L. Stine's The Haunting Hour (2010–2014) 135, 173
RoboCop (2014) 167
Romero, George 89
Rose, Jacqueline 10
Rosemary's Baby (1968) 186n1
Round the Twist (1989, 1993, 2000, 2001) 107
Rowling, J.K. 139
Runaway (1984) 179n9
Ruthless People (1986) 43

Salute Your Shorts (1991–1992) 132
Sanjek, David 89–90
San Souci, Robert D. 172
Say Anything… (1989) 179n8
Scary Stories to Tell in the Dark (book series) 130, 133, 172
Schartz, Alvin 130, 172
Scholastic 134, 137, 172–173; *see also* children's publishing
Schumacher, Joel 70–71, 80, 94, 170
Schwarzbaum, Lisa 96
Scooby Doo (franchise) 8, 70, 169
Scouts Guide to the Zombie Apocalypse (2015) 2, 159–161, 165, 166

Index

Scream (1996) 9, 89, 92, 93, 95
The Scream Team (2002) 107, 173
Scrooged (1988) 179n8
Sears, William 6, 113; *see also* attachment parenting
Selick, Henry 99–101, 103, 106, 171, 174
A Series of Unfortunate Events (2004) 108, 174
Se7en (1995) 92
Shadow Zone: My Teacher Ate My Homework (1997) 171
Shadow Zone: The Undead Express (1996) 171
Sharkey, Betsy 106
Sherman, Paul 101
She's Having a Baby (1988) 179 (8
Shivers 108
Short & Shivery 130
Shyamalan, M. Night 159, 167, 174
Silence of the Lambs (1991) 90, 92
Silver Bullet (1985) 170
Sisson, Rosemary Anne 39
The Sixth Sense (1999) 91, 96
slashers 92–94
Sleeping Beauty (1959) 15, 42
Sleepy Hollow (1999) 94
Smith, Will 6
Snow White and the Seven Dwarves (1937) 15, 59–60, 122
Solarbabies (1986) 179n9
Solter, Aletha 113
Some Kind of Wonderful (1987) 179n8
Something Wicked This Way Comes (1983) 26, 33, 42, 170
Sphere (1999) 96
Spielberg, Steven 43, 44, 48–58, 61–63, 67–68, 80, 158, 162, 164, 170, 171; and the introduction of PG-13, 49; and Joe Dante 55–62; and Tobe Hooper 51; *see also* Amblin
The Splat 167; *see also* Nickelodeon
Spooksville (2013–2014) 173
Stack, Peter 95, 97
Stamper, J.B. 130
Star Wars (film series) 167
Star Wars (1977) 34, 51
Steinmetz, Johanna 77
Stepmonster (1993) 171
Stine, R.L. 19, 133–146, 157, 164–165, 17, 173, 187n20; branding 134–141; and the publishing industry 134, 139–140
Stir of Echoes (1999) 94
stop-motion 105–106; *see also* animation

Stranger Things (2016–) 2, 73, 161, 174
Strauss, Bill 5, 168
Strickler, Jeff 100–101
Struwwelpeter, Der 10
Stuff Stephanie in the Incinerator (1989) 179n14
Super 8 (2013) 162, 174
Superman (1978) 34
Superman II (1980) 34

Takács, Tibor 72–81, 170
Tales from the Crypt (1989–1990) 171
Tales from the Cryptkeeper (1993–1999) 133, 171
teenage audiences (1990s) 89–95
Teenage Exorcist (1990) 9
Teenage Mutant Ninja Turtles (2014) 167
Terminator Genisys (2015) 167
Terrible Child motif 20, 56, 73–75, 82, 97
The Texas Chainsaw Massacre (1974) 50, 51, 186n1
The Three Musketeers (1993) 101
Tim Burton's The Nightmare Before Christmas (1993) see *The Nightmare Before Christmas* (1993)
Touchstone Pictures 43, 100–102
Tower of Terror (1997) 107, 128, 172
Transformers (film series) 167
Transylvania Twist (1989) 179n14
Troll 2 (1990) 170
Tron (1982) 31
Turan, Kenneth 104–106
Twitchell, James B. 9–10, 71

The Unborn (1991) 97
Under Wraps (1997) 107
Urban Legend (1998) 94
Ury, Allen B. 131

The Vagrant (1992) 94
Valenti, Jack 8, 49
Van Gelder, Lawrence 93
Vaughn, Stephen
Village of the Damned (1960) 36
Village of the Damned (1995) 97–98
Vincent (1982) 100, 104
violence 12–13, 19, 28, 44, 49, 52–55, 59–60, 62–63, 69, 72, 115, 138, 151; *see also* "ratings creep" hypothesis
The Visit (2015) 158–159, 161, 167, 174

Walker, Alexander 60, 62
Walker, Gordon 77
Wasko, Janet 25

The Watcher in the Woods (1980) 25–43, 50, 51, 52, 54, 60, 62, 73–75, 82, 83, 99, 101, 147, 150–151, 170; home media 32–33; production trouble 31–33, 39–41; promotion 34; representations 36–38
Weekend at Bernie's (1989) 179*n*8
Weird Science (1985) 179*n*8
Welch, R.C. 130
The Werewolf Reborn! (1998) 172
Wes Craven's New Nightmare (1994) 92–94
What Ever Happened to Baby Jane? (1962) 40
Wheeler, Brad 159
When Good Ghouls Go Bad (2001) 173
Wilhite, Tom 30
The Willies (1990) 170
The Witches (1990) 20, 109, 111, 114, 115–121, 123, 127, 155, 170; adaptation 115–117, 127; Dahl's boycott 116, 120; and family entertainment 117–121; intensity 118–120
The Wizard (1989) 178*n*1
Wolf (1994) 10, 91, 95
The Woman in Red (1984) 179*n*8
Wood, Robin 9, 37; *see also* Terrible Child motif
The Wraith (1986) 69
Wright, Betty Ren 130

The X-Files (2016) 167
X rating 28, 45–46, 48, 71, 94

Young Frankenstein (1974) 34
Young Sherlock Holmes (1985) 179*n*8

Zipes, Jack 10

www.ingramcontent.com/pod-product-compliance
Lightning Source LLC
Chambersburg PA
CBHW032044300426
44117CB00009B/1183